fP

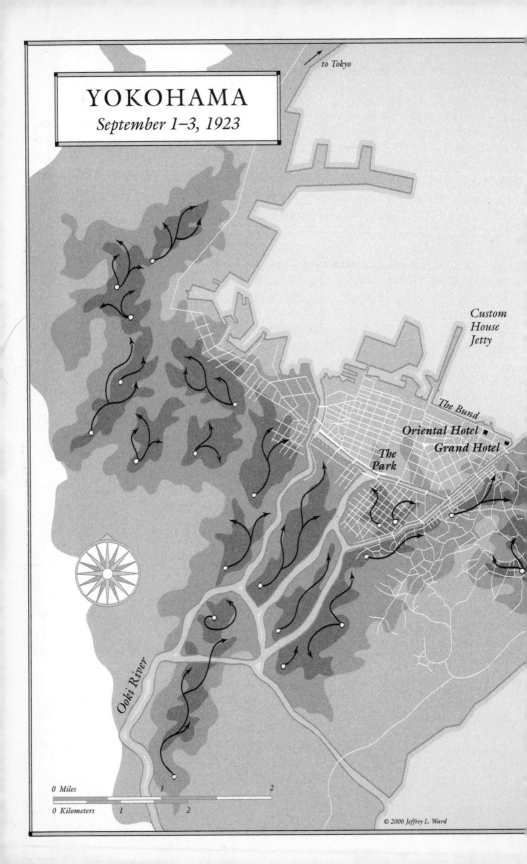

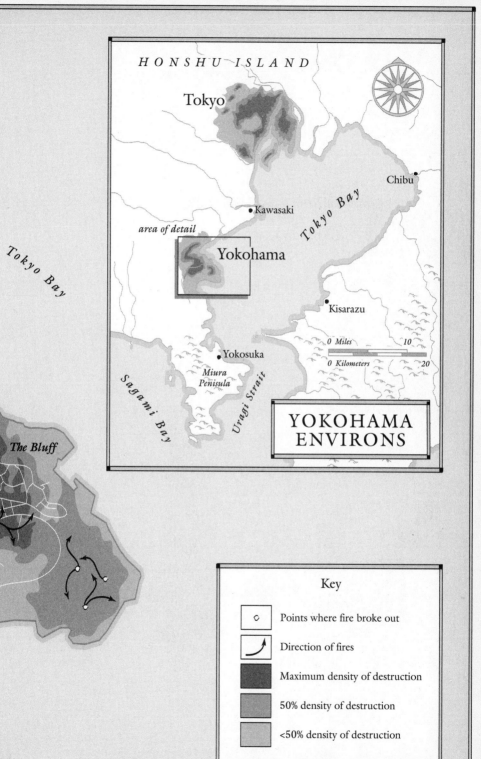

HONSHU ISLAND

Tokyo

Chibu

area of detail

Kawasaki

Tokyo Bay

Yokohama

Tokyo Bay

Kisarazu

0 Miles 10

0 Kilometers 20

Yokosuka

Miura
Penisula

Sagami Bay

Uragi Strait

YOKOHAMA
ENVIRONS

The Bluff

Key

○   Points where fire broke out

↗   Direction of fires

   Maximum density of destruction

   50% density of destruction

   <50% density of destruction

ALSO BY JOSHUA HAMMER

A Season in Bethlehem: Unholy War in a Sacred Place

Chosen by God: A Brother's Journey

Yokohama Burning

The Deadly 1923 Earthquake and
Fire That Helped Forge the Path
to World War II

Joshua Hammer

Free Press
New York London Toronto Sydney

FREE PRESS
A Division of Simon & Schuster, Inc.
1230 Avenue of the Americas
New York, NY 10020

FREE PRESS and colophon are
trademarks of Simon & Schuster, Inc.

For information about special discounts for bulk purchases,
please contact Simon & Schuster Special Sales:
1-800-456-6798 or business@simonandschuster.com

Map © 2006 Jeff L. Ward

Book design by Ellen R. Sasahara

Manufactured in the United States of America

1   3   5   7   9   10   8   6   4   2

Library of Congress Cataloging-in-Publication Data
Hammer, Joshua.
Yokohama burning: the deadly 1923 earthquake and fire
that helped forge the path to World War II / Joshua Hammer
p. cm.
Includes bibliographical references and index.
1. Kanto Earthquake, Japan, 1923. 2. Earthquakes—Japan—Yokohama-shi.
I. Title.
DS888 .H245   2006
952'.1364032—dc22   2006046200

ISBN-13: 978-0-7432-6465-5
ISBN-10:   0-7432-6465-7

For Nadja, Max, and Nick

We lose confidence in the ground we tread on. Whithersoever we may try to escape, we feel ourselves to be in the focus of destruction.

Alexander von Humboldt, *Cosmos* (1845–1847)

CONTENTS

PREFACE

THE HONJO DISTRICT OF EASTERN TOKYO is one of the city's poorer neighborhoods, a nondescript sprawl of low-rent office buildings, noodle bars, and old wooden houses on the east bank of the murky Sumida River. On an asphalt promenade built along the riverbank, an army of the homeless—the forlorn fruit of Japan's long economic recession—have pitched camp, hanging their laundry out to dry and cooking rice in bubbling pots over portable stoves. The district's main landmarks are an old sumo stadium, known as the Kokugikan, a gargantuan municipal museum, and, tucked away in a small park on the grounds of the former Army Clothing Depot, an ugly, reinforced-concrete exhibition hall built in 1930. In gloomy corridors, a thin collection of relics gathers dust on shelves and inside smudged display cases: burned biscuits, metal pipes, a piece of a corrugated iron roof wrapped around a tree trunk. An occasional Boy Scout troop and an errant tourist wander through, but otherwise the place seems forgotten, a neglected backwater in a part of the city that remains as marginalized as it was eighty years ago. The building is the Earthquake Memorial Hall, and it commemorates the most destructive earthquake of them all, the one by which all other seismic events are measured: the Kanto Daishinsai, or Great Kanto Earthquake, that occurred at two minutes before noon on September 1, 1923.

The epic temblor has faded from the national consciousness, shunted aside decades ago in the wake of human-made catastrophes: the annihilation of Hiroshima and Nagasaki, the Allied firebombing of dozens of Japanese cities at the end of World War II. Every ten years an official commemoration takes place, and seismologists are trotted out on television to ponder the question "Can it happen again?" But with only a handful of survivors still alive, nobody speaks much anymore about the earthquake that killed 140,000 people (including hundreds of Americans and Europeans), burned two cities to the ground, unleashed tsunamis, floods, mud slides, and avalanches, and stands as an apocalyptic vision of Japan's eternal instability. "But that's such an old story," I was told by one Japanese friend when I told her I was considering writing a book about the great disaster.

I FIRST HEARD ABOUT the Great Kanto Earthquake a quarter of a century ago, during a year that I lived in Tokyo, teaching English at Sophia University as a Princeton-in-Asia Fellow and writing film reviews for the *Asahi Evening News,* an English-language daily. One winter morning in 1980 I was standing in the kitchen of a friend's home in Kawasaki, a hilly suburb southwest of Tokyo, when an earthquake hit. The violent shaking lasted about twenty seconds: sake cups and tea sets slid off shelves, doors flew open, the house rocked on its foundations so forcefully that I feared it would fly off its hillside perch. After the vibrations subsided, my Japanese hosts picked themselves up and, without a word, swept the porcelain shards from the kitchen floor and carried on as if nothing had happened. Their equanimity was born of experience. The Japanese archipelago is the most active seismic zone on the planet, suffering destructive earthquakes on average once every three years. Fifteen hundred seismic tremors jolt the islands annually. During that afternoon, my friend's stepfather told me that he had been a small boy living in Tokyo at the time of the Kanto Daishinsai, and his dimly remembered tales of fleeing the burning city lodged themselves in my consciousness and remained there.

The earthquake intrigued me. Not only had it been one of the twentieth century's worst natural disasters, but it had struck at a critical moment in Japan's history. In the aftermath of the Great War, the country was booming: Japan had embraced the West, was developing the trappings of a liberal democracy, and was modernizing at a breathless pace. But it was also building a Pacific empire, expanding militarily across Asia. Secret societies of right-wing military officers and proto-fascists, such as the Black Dragons, plotted coups and assassinations in back rooms in Tokyo and dreamed of Asian conquest. These two Japans coexisted in a state of tension. How had the catastrophe affected that balance? Did a link exist between the national trauma and Japan's plunge into World War II? During my year in Japan, I learned about a thriving community of foreigners, mostly Americans and Britons, who had lived in the doomed silk trading port of Yokohama, then one of the most dynamic, heterogeneous cities of the Far East. The portrait that emerged of Yokohama in the 1920s—a nest of spies and sailors, millionaires and riffraff—stayed with me as well.

Years later, when I began to investigate in earnest the earthquake and the era, I searched for firsthand accounts of expatriates living in Japan at the time. At the Wilson Library at the University of North Carolina at Chapel Hill, I found a trove of letters, diaries, and mementos that had belonged to Lyman Cotten, the American naval attaché in Tokyo in 1922 and 1923. From yellowing envelopes, I unfolded brittle copies of the English-language *Japan Times'* "Earthquake Extra," written and produced by an American editor in his suite at Frank Lloyd Wright's Imperial Hotel in the days immediately after the catastrophe. I inspected a Japanese military laissez-passer, with a faded photograph and official red Japanese seal, that Cotten had carried around the stricken capital, which was then under martial law. I sifted through yellowing telegrams dispatched from Nikko, the Japanese Imperial retreat, assuring relatives in America of the Cotten family's safety. These artifacts, combined with Cotten's vivid personal accounts of life in post–Great War Japan and of the disaster, propelled me onward. At the Boston Athenaeum Library across from State House, I uncovered an unpublished manuscript written by an American missionary who had narrowly survived the inferno in Yokohama; her vivid, typewritten narrative had remained on a shelf, unopened, since a fellow missionary donated it to the library in 1924.

I began a search for survivors. I cruised the Internet for clues, sent out a flood of e-mails. I tracked down an octogenarian in San Jose, California, named Jishin Martin; he had been born in Tokyo three days after the disaster, and his missionary parents had named him after the Japanese word for earthquake. Too young to remember the event, he put me in contact with his older brother, James, who had been six years old when the disaster took place. Thrilled to be meeting an eyewitness, I interviewed him at a nursing home in Washington, D.C., only to discover that he and his family had lived on the periphery of the earthquake zone and had survived the catastrophe unscathed. His only memory was bivouacking in a tent at a missionary school for a few days because his house walls had been cracked by the seismic vibrations. I came away disappointed, wondering if I would find any living person who could give the disaster a sense of immediacy.

A few months later, in Japan, I scoured senior citizens' centers, visited the tourism department, met with members of an association of Korean immigrants, and made my way through a succession of municipal ministries and ward offices—without success. Then, just when I was about to give up hope, an official in the Yokohama city government put me in touch with a ninety-three-year-old man who, the official told me, was still living in a house built on the plot of land where he had been born in 1911. One humid morning in July 2004, in the lobby of a shabby municipal building on the port's outskirts, my interpreter and I made the acquaintance of a dapper, wizened pensioner named Shigeo Tsuchiya. I bowed, he bowed, and Tsuchiya's government handler led us into a stuffy conference room. Under fluorescent lights, we sipped green tea and began to talk. "I haven't spoken about this in years," he said. Then he told me his story.

Yokohama Burning

September 1, 1923

We learn geology the morning after the earthquake, on ghastly diagrams of cloven mountains, upheaved plains, and the bed of the sea.

Ralph Waldo Emerson, *The Conduct of Life* (1860)

EIGHT DECADES LATER, when he looked back on that morning, he would remember every detail, every sensation, with preternatural clarity. He would remember the taste of the sticky rice, sour plums, and seaweed that he ate for breakfast, the pungent aroma of his father's morning cigarette. He would remember sliding open the *amado,* the rice-paper door of his house, and rushing to the first day of classes at the Tokubei Elementary School, the excitement and twinge of anxiety familiar to schoolchildren everywhere in early September. He would remember the sultry and clear weather, the gentle salt breeze blowing off the harbor, the old Kangai neighborhood stirring to life again after the suffocatingly humid summer.

The academic year had begun, but in these dying days of the hot season, the weekend would be mostly a time for play: swimming with his friends in the warm waters of Tokyo Bay; exploring the maple and pine forests that ringed the city; walking down to the *hatoba,* the steel and concrete pier that jutted nearly half a mile into Yokohama harbor, to watch sailors and stevedores prepare sleek ocean liners for their two-week Pacific crossings. He might sneak past the doormen at the elegant Grand Hotel on the Bund (the Waterfront boulevard) to observe the Westerners glide through the lobby in a whirl of tuxedos, satin gowns, furs, gold, and diamonds. Yokohama's Foreign Settlement—with its clubs and consulates rising along the seafront, its wealthy silk traders being pulled to their villas on the Bluff by straining rickshaw coolies, its sober Western families walking together to the old stone Christ Church on Main Street on Sunday mornings—was an endless source of entertainment for a Japanese boy in 1923.

He had turned twelve years old that summer, a small, wiry adolescent with large ears, a propensity for mischief, and a fascination for all things Western. His father, an onboard ship mechanic for Nippon Yuusei Kaisha, Japan's largest steamship line, sailed the oceans half the year to Seattle, Marseille, Portsmouth, and other distant ports of call and had instilled in the boy an insatiable curiosity about the wider world. Once every few months, when his father returned to port, European or American acquaintances would come to the house for dinner, and he would sit and study them like museum specimens, examining the texture of their skin, the shapes of their faces, the indecipherable languages that his father had somehow mastered. He had filled his room with postcards and dolls brought back from his father's travels, drank coffee and English "red" tea voraciously, was the first in his class to shun the traditional Japanese kimono in favor of Western dress. At school they called him *baka na gaijin,* the crazy foreigner, and he wore the label proudly, dreaming of the day when he, like his father, could sail around the world on open-ended journeys in search of adventure.

For the moment, there were plenty of adventures in Yokohama. At noon his grandparents were preparing lunch for him and his six-year-old sister, a feast that would start with his favorite late summer treat, a chilled, sweet bean soup called *oshiriko.* Afterward he would walk one mile to Isezaki-cho, Yokohama's gaudy entertainment district, to the Odeon Theater, the only Hollywood movie house in the Japanese part of the city. The Tokubei School principal had forbidden his students from going to the Odeon—the kissing scenes in Hollywood movies would fill their minds with impure thoughts, he said—and often stationed teachers outside the theater to catch transgressors. But his father had told him to ignore the prohibition, even gave him the

5 sen each week for the Saturday matinee. He liked to get to the cinema early for the jazz set played by an eight-piece band led by a popular local conductor, Kyoichi Sunaga. Then the electric lights would dim, the titles would roll, the Japanese narrator would take his place in front, and he would watch, rapt, as forbidden images of Charlie Chaplin, Harold Lloyd, and the Keystone Kops flickered on the screen.

Knapsack filled with textbooks on his back, he darted after the morning recess through unpaved alleys lined with single-story houses with gray-blue tile roofs, dodging horse and buffalo carts, leaping over puddles left from the dawn rainstorm. He sped past his neighborhood *geta* shop, specializing in wooden clogs; the rice cracker store; the umbrella shop; a French-style bakery patronized by a few Japanese connoisseurs. A rickshaw raced by, splashing through a mud puddle and almost knocking him off his feet. From nearly every house came the pleasing aromas of soy sauce, ginger, and fish cooking atop charcoal braziers, *hibachi*. The teeming Kangai neighborhood, built on a drained swamp half a century earlier, had been cited repeatedly by government building inspectors for its susceptibility to earthquake and fire. But people kept building more flimsy wooden dwellings there, packing themselves in ever tighter, lured by the boundless economic opportunities of the Far East's greatest port.

At ten minutes before twelve o'clock, he turned a corner and entered the alley where his grandparents lived. He slid open the door and crossed the threshhold of their house with a cry of "Tadaima" (I've arrived). The scene would remain frozen in his mind for the next eighty years: his grandfather and his sister sat knee-to-knee at a low table, a *kotatsu*, on a tatami mat. Squid and vegetables sizzled over the glowing coals of a hibachi in the corner. Rice simmered on a gas stove. He removed his shoes and slid behind the table as his grandmother ladled oshiriko from a large copper pot into blue porcelain bowls and placed them in front of the family. From a distance of eight decades, he would vividly recall bringing the bowl to his lips just as everything began to shake . . .

I

City of Silk

The freshly arrived foreigner . . . is bound to base his first impressions of Japan on treaty port surroundings, as he naturally lands at one or other of these places, and very often practically gets no farther during his stay . . . [it is] where he finds the greatest number of his countrymen, the greatest selection of Western amusements, the best quarters, and the best food; and where above all, he can make himself understood.

Stafford Ransome, *Japan in Transition* (1899)

A VISITOR ALIGHTING on the hatoba, the main jetty of Yokohama, in 1859, the first year of the Foreign Settlement's existence, stood a good chance of getting his pocket picked or his luggage stolen within minutes of his arrival. Like a Wild West town, Yokohama in its infancy was not a place for the timid. Chinese money exchanges, rum shops, warehouses, and cheap lodges rose along three muddy streets running parallel to Tokyo Bay. Brawls among drunken sailors broke out almost every evening. Crib crackers—the local term for thieves—prowled the alleys, and robberies, knifings, burglaries, swindlings, assaults, and other crimes ran rampant. The Anglican bishop of Hong Kong, who visited the port in 1860, one year after its founding, disparaged Yokohama's population as consisting of "California adventurers, Portuguese desperadoes, and the moral refuse of European nations." The editor of the weekly *Bell's Life in Yokohama* wrote of "dwellers from Mesopotamia . . . strangers of Rome, Jews, and Proselytes, pirates from South America, and 'leavers' from Botany Bay," former prisoners of the first convict colony in Australia. "Nowhere is there a greater influx, unless it be at some gold diggings, of the lawless and dissolute from all countries," wrote Rutherford Alcock, the first British consul in Japan, in 1859.

The few hundred settlers who congregated there lived in constant danger from the elements. Typhoons struck the Japanese coast every September and October, flooding the streets and tearing clapboard houses off their foundations. Fires broke out several times a week, including an 1866 inferno, the Pigpen Fire, that burned down the entire Japanese quarter and one fourth of the Foreign Settlement. (One expatriate attributed the blazes to "carelessness on the part of the natives, the almost universal use of inflammable kerosene, and the utterly inadequate means possessed by both Europeans and native settlers to prevent their spread.") Earth tremors shook the port frequently, rattling nerves, knocking off roof tiles, and causing other minor damage. Disease was a bigger problem.

Human waste and other refuse clogged the drainage canals that emptied into Yokohama harbor. Cholera epidemics swept the population, and the stench of Yokohama summers could be overpowering. "In moving [to Yokohama]," advised the *Japan Times Overland Mail* in March 1869, "carry a vinaigrette with aromatic spirits of vinegar to smell at when exposed to noxious and unpleasant odours. This simple but effective remedy deservedly holds a high place among the preventatives of fever." The paper warned foreigners not to walk around in the early morning or evening with an empty stomach, because at such times "the body is in an unprepared state to throw off miasmatic influences that are concentrated in the air."

On top of all the other hardships, a pervasive sense of isolation hung over Yokohama during those early years. Crowds of news-starved merchants, diplomats, and soldiers gathered at the jetty twice a month for the arrival of schooners from Shanghai bearing sacks of mail. Sporadic telegraph service to Europe via Ceylon provided the only direct communication with the outside world. Cargo arrived from England by sailing ships around the Cape of Good Hope, a 220-day journey. Western women initially refused to come to Yokohama;

to satisfy male desires, representatives of the Tokugawa shogun, the military dictator who ruled Japan from his moated castle in the feudal capital, Edo, in 1860 opened the Gakiro Teahouse, connected to the settlement by a drawbridge thrown over a canal. Designed like a Buddhist temple complex and set amid a grove of cherry trees, it was a "Pleasure Palace," one customer enthused, packed with two hundred government-licensed courtesans. "A deplorable scene of demoralization and profligate life," fumed the bishop of Hong Kong. A visitor in 1862 was more impressed:

> Two officers showed us the building, and pointed out its beauties with as much pride as if they were exhibiting an ancient temple sacred to their dearest gods. This was the courtyard; that was a fishpond with fountains . . . there affixed to the wall was the tariff of charges, which I leave to the imagination; in that house across the court, seated in rows on the verandah, were the "moosemes" [women] themselves. Would we step over, for it was only under male escort that we might enter the main building? My curiosity had, however, been gratified, and I departed.

For close to five hundred years, it had plodded along as a sleepy fishing village, isolated from the busy artery that led to the feudal capital, Edo, by a nearly impassable swamp. But, in the mid-nineteenth century, events far offstage conspired to jolt the derelict backwater into the modern world. In 1842 England defeated China in the First Opium War and forced the emperor to surrender Hong Kong and open five "treaty ports" to British commerce. The victory astonished U.S. officials and fueled their ambitions to establish, by negotiation or by force, a commercial beachhead in the Pacific. At about the same time, the northern Pacific whaling trade reached a peak of activity; hundreds of U.S. ships sailed each year from New England to Japanese coastal waters in pursuit of whale blubber, the source of heating, lamp, and industrial oil before the American Civil War. By the 1840s, a dozen American sailors a year were washing up shipwrecked on Japanese beaches. Captured, tossed into dungeons, and often beaten and tortured, these men obtained their freedom only through the mediation of Dutch traders on the island of Deshima in Nagasaki Bay, the sole foreigners whom the Tokugawa shogunate allowed to live on their archipelago. But the process was cumbersome, and American whalers often languished in captivity for months or even years. Some never made it home at all.

The first official contact between Americans and Japanese was an ignominious failure for the Yankees. In 1846, Commodore James Biddle, a Philadelphia patrician, anchored his vessels, the *Columbus* and the *Vincennes,* off the port of Uraga at the entrance to Tokyo Bay. Biddle allowed curious Japanese soldiers and villagers to swarm over his ships, handed out hundreds of gifts, and personally delivered to a minor official a letter of friendship from President James K. Polk addressed to the Tokugawa shogun. Things turned badly after Biddle agreed to board a Japanese guard boat to fetch the shogun's written reply. As he clambered, in full uniform, aboard the vessel, a hostile Japanese soldier "gave me a blow or push which threw me back into the boat," Biddle recalled. The shogun's officials, interpreting Biddle's behavior as a sign of weakness, told the commodore to leave—and ordered the Americans never to return.

Six years later, in 1852, U.S. President Millard Fillmore planned a second expedition to Japan and asked a legendary figure to lead it: Commodore Matthew Calbraith Perry. The younger brother of War of 1812 hero Oliver Hazard Perry (who had died at thirty-four of yellow fever while on an expedition up the Orinoco River to meet Simón Bolívar, the Latin American revolutionary), the fifty-eight-year-old Perry had already enjoyed a remarkable career as a wartime commander, diplomat, and head of the Brooklyn Navy Yard, where he had overseen the navy's transition from sailing ships to steam-powered vessels. Perry "conformed to the conventional Japanese manner of depicting a warrior: he should look fierce, intense, determined," wrote one biographer, Samuel Eliot Morison. "He was a blunt, yet dignified man, heavy and not graceful, something of a martinet," wrote Henry Coppée, who had served under him in the Mexican War, "a duty man all over, held somewhat in awe by the junior officers, and having little to do with them; seriously courteous to others. The ship seemed to have a sense of importance because he was on board." Perry promised success. "In my former commands upon the coasts of Africa and in the Gulf of Mexico," he wrote to Secretary of State Daniel Webster in 1852, "I found no difficulty in conciliating the good will and confidence of the conquered people, by administering the unrestricted power I held rather to their comfort than to their annoyance. So I believe the people of [Japan], if treated with strict justice and simple kindness, will learn to consider us their friends."

On July 8, 1853, seven and a half months after leaving Norfolk, Virginia, Perry's fleet, two steam-powered men-of-war and two sailing vessels, anchored off Uraga. As one Japanese eyewitness recalled, "People in the town made such a fuss that I asked what was up and was told that off shore there were burning ships. With two or three men I climbed a hill. There we saw a big crowd of people jabbering about the ships. As they drew gradually closer to shore it became clear that they were not Japanese but foreign. What we had mistaken for a

Commodore Matthew Perry, who in 1853–1854 "opened" feudal Japan to the West, as depicted in a contemporary Japanese caricature.

fire was smoke belching forth from these warships and they caused a
great commotion. . . . When we came down the hill the whole town
was astir. Some men rushed to Edo."

Perry told the shogun's men that he would give the dictator six
months to accept an offer of friendship and establish diplomatic relations. The threat of force backed up his courteous words. On February 13, 1854, as he had promised, Perry returned to Japan with a
beefed-up fleet and a more aggressive attitude. Sailing further up Edo
Bay, the Black Ships—three steam frigates and four sailing vessels
this time—anchored in deep water off a ramshackle hamlet hugging
a spit of land at the edge of a marshy peninsula. The Americans
transliterated its name as "Yokuhama," or cross beach. "The dwellings
indicated little thrift, and the village was rendered unsavory by the numerous vats, thatched over to retain urine, compost, and other ma-
nuring substances from evaporating," observed Perry's interpreter,
missionary Samuel Wells Williams. (Williams spoke Dutch, the lingua
franca of the Far East, with his Japanese hosts.) In a hastily built Treaty
House, representatives of the shogun reluctantly agreed to "establish
firm, lasting and sincere friendship between the two nations" and to
create two "ports of reception" at which American ships could be re-
supplied with wood, water, provisions, and coal.

Perry's achievement was, on the surface, a modest one—wary of
pushing the Japanese too fast, he didn't broach the subject of commercial relations—but its significance was enormous. With a nuanced
blend of politesse and threat, the warrior-diplomat had pried open the
secretive feudal state, forced the shogun to engage the world, and set
Japan and the United States on the course of a complex and ever-
changing relationship. The two nations would evolve from trading
partners to jealous rivals, from mutual admirers to implacable enemies. Fittingly, the place where the deal had been struck, Yokohama,
would soon become one of the globe's most dynamic collision points
of East and West—and it would remain so for the next seventy years.

Perry got the American foot through the Japanese door; his suc-
cessors pried the door open further. The Treaty of 1858, signed in
Edo by the shogun and Townsend Harris, the first U.S. consul,
granted the United States the right to trade with the Japanese. The
two sides agreed to set up the first Foreign Settlement in Kanagawa,

fifteen miles south of the capital. This was a "long straggling town," wrote John R. Black in his 1875 book *Young Japan*, "skirting both sides of the famous Tokaido, or Eastern Sea Road, that runs between Yedo, Osaka, and Kyoto." But Kanagawa's harbor, although deep enough to accommodate flat-bottomed native junks, proved too shallow for keeled American schooners and frigates. In the spring of 1859 the Japanese government developed a more remote site on the opposite side of the bay: Yokohama. In its harbor, wrote Joseph Heco, a Japanese fisherman (real name Hamada Hikozo) who had been shipwrecked in America, received U.S. citizenship, and returned to Japan to serve as Harris's interpreter, "the largest ship may ride in perfect safety in all states of the tide or weather."

In a few weeks the port took shape: Japanese authorities threw up bars, warehouses or *godowns* (an adaptation of a Hindi word first adopted by the British in Hong Kong), and bungalows. They built a *hatoba*, or landing place, made up of two granite jetties. Two Far Eastern silk and tea trading firms—Jardine, Matheson & Co. and Walsh, Hall & Co.—moved into large houses on the waterfront. Japanese traders and service providers set up shop in adjacent quarters. In late June, when the British and American consuls arrived in Kanagawa to open their diplomatic residences, they discovered a thriving community in place three miles down the beach. "We turned down the main street, and here witnessed a scene which could hardly have been enacted anywhere except in Russia, where noble [Potemkin] villages appear as if by magic to greet the Empress Catharine," wrote Alcock, the British envoy, on July 1. "Here, out of a marsh by the edge of a deserted bay, a wave of the conjuror's wand had created a bustling settlement. . . . A large wide street was bordered on both sides with . . . houses of timber." On July 4, 1859, in a ceremony near the original Treaty House built for Perry, Yokohama entered history as the first official foreign port established by Harris's commercial treaty.

THE SMATTERING OF American and European traders who came to seek their fortunes in Yokohama had little conception of the society that was hosting them. Cut off from the world for centuries, Japan was feudal, hierarchical, and deeply conservative. About three hundred landholding noblemen, or *daimyos*, backed up by their two-sworded retainers, the samurai, ruled their subjects with often cruel omnipotence. The daimyos, in turn, were forced to swear allegiance to the Tokugawa shogun. Each year the daimyos and their retinues journeyed from their castles across Japan to the Imperial Palace in Edo, to spend six months in the presence of the dictator. The Japanese emperor, who claimed to be a direct descendant of the sun god, Amaterasu, had been reduced to a figurehead and lived in splendid isolation in a palace in the ancient city of Kyoto. He periodically ordered the shogun to close Yokohama and drive the "ugly foreign barbarians" away; the shogun ignored him. But many daimyos, who saw the arrival of the foreigners as a threat to the established order in Japan, took the side of the emperor, formed a secretive cabal called *sonno-joi,* or "Revere the Emperor, Expel the Barbarian," and began plotting to drive them out through terror.

Penetrating the settlement wasn't easy. Natural obstructions surrounded it, including a creek to the south, an estuary to the north, the Pacific Ocean to the east, and a swamp to the west. The shogunate added checkpoints and barriers to control more tightly the movements of foreigners and keep out potential enemies. "A canal [was] cut through the salt water swamp in its rear, uniting the creek and the estuary," wrote Heco. "Each of the bridges [over the canal] . . . was protected by a gate, shut at sunset, and by a guard house, in which yakunin [government guards] were always on duty to watch who entered or left."

The shogunate's precautions weren't enough. In August 1859, two *ronin,* outlaw samurai hired by the daimyos to do their dirty work, bribed or sneaked past guards and, in front of a greengrocer's store on the port's main street, stabbed to death two Russian sailors, Roman Mofet and Ivan Sokolov, who were on shore leave. Three months later samurai murdered the French consul's Chinese servant, apparently mistaking him for a European because he was dressed in Western clothing. Dutch sea captains Nanning Dekker and Wessel de Vos were killed on Yokohama's main street in February of the following year. And on the night of July 5, 1861, fourteen ronin assassins crept into the compound of the British Legation and critically injured two British diplomats.

After the consulate attack, the British and the French garrisoned troops inside the Foreign Settlement, but the samurai killings continued intermittently in the surrounding countryside, and traveling outside of Yokohama required an escort of yakunin, imposing-looking men who wore formal kimono skirts, or *hakama,* and basin-like hats fastened under the chin with double cords. "They were armed with the inevitable two swords in those days, and rode in groups before, behind and on both sides of us," recounted John P. Mollison, a British tea and dynamite trader who had arrived in the settlement in 1867.

YOKOHAMA MIGHT WELL HAVE muddled on like that for decades, grudgingly tolerated by the shogun, its citizens closely watched by his secret police and all but imprisoned within the Foreign Settlement. But the shogun's authority was crumbling. In 1868 a military alliance of daimyos seeking to drive out the Westerners deposed the weakened dictator and brought to power the sixteen-year-old Emperor Meiji. The young ruler moved the imperial capital from Kyoto to Edo, which he renamed Tokyo ("Eastern Capital"). Instead of expelling the barbarians, as his powerless predecessors had tried to do, the new emperor radically changed course: he disarmed the samurai, lifted travel restrictions on foreigners, and encouraged trade with the West. Yokohama became the gateway through which Japan came to the world—and the world came to Japan. A distant calamity hastened the port's rise: a contagious silkworm disease, pebrine, had swept through Europe in the 1860s, killing the larvae or making their cocoons weak and brittle. France's production of cocoons plummeted from 57 million pounds in 1853 to 9 million pounds a decade later, creating an intense hunger for the Japanese product. (Silk production had thrived under imperial protection since a Chinese smuggler brought the first silkworm eggs into the country in A.D. 199.) In 1873, according to the *Japan Gazette,* Yokohama traders exported 11,869 bales of raw silk, worth $7 million, and 1.3 million silkworm eggs, worth $3 million. Tea, introduced to Japan from China in the eleventh century, also brought in millions. Three hundred seventy-five commercial vessels sailed from Yokohama that year; nearly as many arrived.

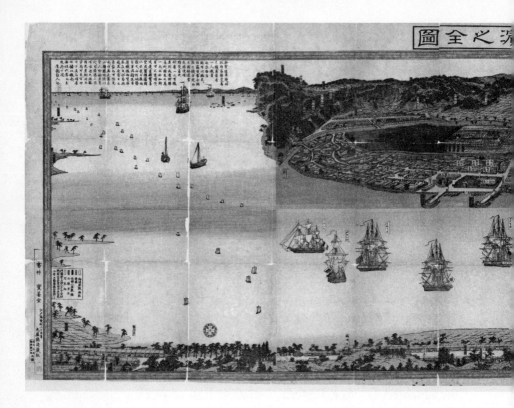

A shopper walking down Main Street in the Foreign Settlement in 1874 could find Manila cigars, bourbon whisky, casks of Allsopp's Pale Ale, canoes, "two-feeder" printing machines, Lea & Perrins Worcestershire sauce, iron safes, balbriggan socks, stick umbrellas, and "fine white flannels for cricketing." Hegt's Brewery sold ale and porter from Britain by the bottle. At Louis Caudrelier's grocery one could pick up wines, spirits, pickles, preserves, and fine glassware. The streets were now paved, the Bund widened, Western women arrived. On the Bluff, the verdant cliffs that rose over the settlement's southern edge, affluent residents threw up gabled, turreted villas with tennis courts and manicured gardens behind white picket fences. The International Hotel on the Bund offered "the best mixed drinks" in town, served by an "experienced barman from America." R. Chiarini's Royal Italian Circus featured "the most colossal combination troupe in the world containing 25 Star performers; and 30 Highly Trained Horses and Ponies." With the samurai gone, Yokohama residents

御開港黄

A panorama of the Yokohama waterfront in the 1800s, depicting an international trading fleet. Tokyo appears in the upper right corner, just in front of Mount Fuji.

organized excursions deep into rural Japan. "It is best to take your own eatables with you, and your cook, if possible," the *Yokohama Guide* advised in 1874. "Little in the way of palatable food, except boiled rice and eggs and broiled fish, can be obtained at the native inns, though foreign drinks are easily obtained." The biggest problem, the guidebook warned, was a serious plague of fleas at country inns. "They may be easily foiled in the following manner: Buy an ichi bu's worth of powdered crude camphor at the native drug shops. At bed-time, sprinkle the camphor abundantly under and upon the bed, and on the floor for a foot or so around the bedding. Sound sleep is warranted as a result."

* * *

YOKOHAMA STILL HAD ROUGH EDGES. In reclaimed swampland behind the Foreign Settlement lay Chinatown, a warren of teetering
two-story brick buildings redolent of sizzling fish, bok choy, and raw
sewage. The crowded quarter was home to eight thousand Chinese,
mostly from Canton, who had first come to Yokohama as small traders
and *shroffs* (accountants) in the 1860s. "Vermilion paper, baggy
clothes, pigtails, harsh voices, and vile odors reign in this Chinatown,"
Eliza Scidmore wrote in *Jinriksha Days in Japan* in 1891. Katherine
Baxter, a travel writer with a particularly sensitive nose, interrupted

The Yokohama business district as it appeared in 1871.

her sampan tour through Yokohama's canals in 1890 because of "evil smells" from open drains and landed at the entrance to Motomachi, a sliver of a Japanese village from which "proceeded the most horrible smell imaginable, that of pickled daikon," a Japanese white radish. On the periphery of the Chinese quarter lay Bloodtown: dingy backstreets lined with gambling dens and grottolike taverns, such as the Rising Sun Saloon, where barkeeps plied sailors with Jackrabbit whisky and knife fights broke out almost every night. When Jack London's sealing ship, *Sophia Sutherland,* called at Yokohama in 1893, London got himself "exciting drunk" in Bloodtown, then dove off a stone jetty and swam back to his vessel in the harbor.

Yokohama in the early twentieth century was an international city packed with adventurers, millionaires, fugitives, and drifters from every corner of the world. The port was "completely free of tradition," rising on the doorsteps of Japan like "a mirage in the desert," wrote one Japanese novelist. Bengali shopkeepers, Lebanese jewelers, Chinese moneychangers, Russian optometrists, French diplomats, Korean laborers, English silk merchants, Spanish missionaries, American tea traders, and citizens and castoffs of two dozen other nations jostled along the Bund, Water Street, and Main Street. When the Russian Revolution broke out in 1917, the port's heterogeneous character grew richer: In sweaty exhibition halls White Russian boxers, refugees from the Bolsheviks who had been welcomed by vehemently anticommunist Japan, fought bloody matches against local jujitsu masters. Japanese men enjoyed seducing Russian baronesses, lonely exotics who had been forced to abandon their fortunes in their hasty flights from Vladivostok or Odessa and who eked out livings as barmaids, dance instructors, or piano teachers. "I have grown tired of fastidious Japanese females," declared one Japanese novelist in 1922. "I have developed a penchant for these truly lascivious, truly erotic Western women; the girls at the Western style hotels . . . thus fill me with great contentment."

At the Gaiety Theater on the Bluff—"a timeworn playhouse on a desolate corner built long ago for foreigners in this open port in the faraway east," the novelist Junichiro Tanizaki called it—touring companies from Europe and America performed *Hamlet,* Oscar Wilde's *Salome,* Bizet's *Carmen,* Puccini's *La Bohème,* and Verdi classics. "I

*Invented by an American missionary in 1868, the rickshaw was a
ubiquitous form of transit in Yokohama. By the early twentieth
century, about 3,500 of them were in use in the city.*

want to breathe in the Western atmosphere that fills the stage," proclaimed Osanai Kaoru, leader of Japan's New Theater movement, an
experimental drama troupe, in 1922. Tanizaki, who spent two years in
Yokohama writing screenplays for a film studio, marveled at the foreign presence, "a riot of loud Western colors and smells—the odor of
cigars, the aroma of chocolate, the fragrance of flowers, the scent of
perfume."

For foreigners, too, Yokohama mesmerized with its sense of Oth-
erness. "To the traveler, standing on the deck of a steamer in Yoko-

hama harbor in the early morning, there may be vouchsafed the lovely view of snow-capped Fuji, rose-tinted by the rays of the rising sun," wrote Frederick Starr, an anthropologist who first came to Japan in 1904. A new arrival from America or Europe would feel an initial shock of recognition, eyeing at the water's edge a neat row of four- and five-story luxury hotels, foreign consulates, and trading houses—wedding cake structures with gabled roofs, balustraded terraces, and columned facades. But the sense of familiarity would vanish moments later. The newcomer would thread through a gauntlet of Japanese women draped in silk kimonos, European and American naval officers in crisp uniforms, black-jacketed chauffeurs standing ramrod straight by their motorcars. Just beyond this throng, barefoot rickshaw coolies jostled for fares, broken English phrases on their lips, the long poles of their two-wheeled carts balanced on their shoulders. Adapted from a seventeenth-century Parisian carriage by an American missionary in Yokohama in 1868, the rickshaw epitomized the port's quirky collision of East and West. Rickshaws "may be found everywhere in the city," advised the guidebook *Yokohama: Past and Present,* compiled by the municipal office in 1908, counting 3,494 two-wheelers in town as of March the previous year. Rudyard Kipling, who made three trips to Yokohama, including a honeymoon that he had to abort when he ran out of cash in the port, celebrated the vehicles. The *Pall Mall Gazette* coined a phrase, "jinrickshawing with the Japanese," in 1890. J. Johnston Abraham's *The Surgeon's Log* describes one memorable 1904 journey from the Bluff to the Bund:

> Hold tight, shouted the chief from the rickshaw in front. Our men had started slowly; but gradually they gained momentum; and soon we were flying down the incline at breakneck pace. . . . It was like bob-sleighing without the snow. A feeling of exhilaration came over us; unconsciously I found myself shouting encouragement. Down we swept past rickshaws painfully crawling up the hill, past brightly lighted shops, past hurrying pedestrians, till at last, panting and exhausted, the men slowed up on the crowded level highway of the Bund.

The silk trade drove the city's energy. Each morning a long convoy of trucks pulled into the Far Eastern entrepôt from rural Japan,

Japanese prostitutes were abundant in Yokohama, to the pleasure of foreign sailors, as depicted in this late-nineteenth-century illustration.

packed with 250-pound bales of the delicate fabric. (By the turn of the twentieth century 1 million farmers, half the total number in Japan, devoted themselves to raising silkworms or to growing mulberry trees, the insects' source of nourishment.) Government inspectors rifled through each bale—checking for the strength of the threads, the symmetry and tightness of the weave—and affixed a blue or red stamp of approval on them. Fifty "factors," or brokers, representatives of the great silk production houses scattered across the archipelago, struck deals with a dozen international exporters, who shipped the silk to their agents in New York and European capitals. A parade of stevedores loaded the bales onto the dozens of steamships that sailed in and out of Yokohama's harbor every week. The United States alone purchased forty thousand bales of silk a month, worth more than $190 million. All told, Japan provided 60 percent of the raw silk demands of the world. "Silkworm-raising peasants have provided Japan with railways, telegraphs, machinery, her splendid army and navy, and the sinews of war," wrote J. Ellis Barker in *The Rural Industries of Japan,* published in Yokohama in 1906. The rest of the world knew Yokohama as the "The City of Raw Silk."

YOKOHAMA ON THE EVE of its moment of destiny, then, was a savory stew of artists and intellectuals, international businessmen, affluent tourists, prostitutes, silk brokers, military operatives, distrustful diplomats, soldiers of fortune, and other colorful characters. Unlike the rest of Japan, it was an open society, cosmopolitan and accessible to the world. Long before the word "globalism" was invented, Yokohama was the most globally oriented city in a xenophobic and claustrophobically closed nation. Footloose foreigners flocked to it for a taste of the exotic Far East; ordinary Japanese came to ogle the *gaijin,* or outsiders, who had established a beachhead eighteen miles from the far more conservative capital. Right-wing Japanese officials and military men regarded the port with deep suspicion, considering it the source of dangerous Western values and ideas.

In April 1922, the Prince of Wales—the future Edward VIII—paid a royal visit to Japan aboard the steamship HMS *Renown* at the invitation of Prince Regent Hirohito. It was Yokohama's crowning moment, the high point of the Anglo-Japanese alliance (a strategic union forged before the Russo-Japanese War) and an opportunity to showcase the Far Eastern entrepôt to the world. The heir to the Japanese throne had spent a month in Great Britain the previous May, hosted by the prince and his father, King George V. He would later admit that the trip—during which he had listened to jazz in smoky nightclubs, toured London in an open motorcar with the king, and watched a procession of captured German warships on a river near Edinburgh—had been the only time in his life when he felt truly free. The Prince of Wales's reciprocal visit culminated with a motor tour around the most English city in the Far East, a visit to the United Club, the city's oldest male-only establishment, and a ball at the Gaiety Theater on the Bluff on Saturday night, April 22, 1922. The *Japan Gazette* reported:

> The Prince motored from the hatoba up Camp Hill through the large Torii of evergreens, erected in his honor under festoons of lighted lanterns, and the swaying flags of Japan and Great Britain, and arrived at the Gaiety at half past nine. The roads on both sides were lined by thousands of Japanese, each carrying a lantern . . . when he left just before midnight, his appearance was the signal for banzais! Ships in the harbor were outlined with white electric light, like phantom craft lighting the way, and new arc lights turned night to day on the hill. . . . Nothing quite like [the ball] was ever experienced here before.

Four days later, at 10:11 in the morning, according to the Central Meteorological Observatory, a sudden movement along a fault beneath Tokyo Bay sent seven shocks ripping through the Kanto Plain, the worst earthquake to strike Yokohama since the Ansei disaster of 1855, when it had been just a fishing village. The first shock, the most severe, lasted for nearly a minute. The Prince of Wales, who had been motoring toward Mount Fuji with his entourage, was nearly thrown from his car and was badly shaken. In Tokyo, the outer walls of the Imperial Palace cracked, bridges fell into canals, and the kitchen of the U.S. Embassy in Akasaka caught fire and suffered severe damage. Across Yokohama, buildings rocked violently; a chimney at the United Club collapsed, and the Gaiety was so structurally weakened that it was forced to suspend film performances for three weeks. People rushed into the streets, crouched under tables, and huddled in doorways. At the Moseikan Restaurant in Chinatown, the roof caved in and killed the eighteen-year-old daughter of the proprietor, the earthquake's only recorded fatality. "Everyone is congratulating themselves for the fate which stayed the earthquake shock until His Royal High-ness had left Yokohama," wrote the social notes columnist of the *Japan Gazette* the next morning. "All say: 'What if it had occurred the night of the Royal Ball?' "

For the residents of Yokohama, the earthquake was a frightening reminder of the fragile foundations on which their city had been built. Coming so soon after the royal ball, it seemed a mocking counter-point to the port's growing self-confidence—some would say arro-gance. At least one expatriate, an American seismologist who lived on the Bluff, departed Japan for good shortly after the earthquake, fear-ing that a far bigger cataclysm was imminent. Most preferred not to dwell on the near-disaster. "Those who have lived for years in some earthquake belt, grow callous to a temblor such as that of Wednes-day," the *Japan Gazette* intoned.

THE GRINDING of tectonic plates below Tokyo Bay was not the only dangerous activity lurking under Yokohama's glittering surface. In ad-dition to being a center of trade and commerce, the port had estab-lished a tradition of intrigue and espionage. In 1899 Sun Yat-sen, the Chinese revolutionary, had escaped to Yokohama after a foiled upris-ing in Shanghai and had lived incognito for a decade on an alley near the harbor, raising cash from wealthy Japanese backers. Smugglers of human cargo prowled the docks, packing steamships full of desperate Asians bound illegally for North America. Gunrunners, Korean inde-pendence agitators, Bolshevik propagandists, Indian anticolonialists, and other activists all conspired in Yokohama, pursued by immigra-tion officials and the secret police.

But the Ellis Affair may have been the darkest episode of them all.

Commissioned a lieutenant in the U.S. Navy in 1903 at twenty-two, Colonel Earl Hancock Ellis had earned a reputation as one of the navy's most gifted—and emotionally fragile—intelligence operatives. In 1922, with what turned out to be astonishing prescience, he made the case to his superiors in Washington that the Japanese navy, driven by a lust for expansion, eventually would seize the Philippines, Singa-pore, the Dutch East Indies, and other territories across Southeast Asia and launch a war against the United States in the Pacific, perhaps as early as the 1930s. The coral atolls and volcanic islets of the Caroline, Marshall, and Mariana Islands, taken from Germany during the Great War, were being fortified with heavy guns and gun emplacements, he maintained, to serve as coaling and repair bases for the Japanese fleet. Tokyo-based U.S. Naval Intelligence officers shared Ellis's suspicions, but several attempts to land spies on the islands had failed. In the autumn of 1922, with the navy's blessing, Ellis concocted a plan to travel to Yokohama, pose as a tea trader for a fictitious New York company, and then visit the Marshall Islands to "find out what the hell was going on down there."

Ellis, however, proved remarkably unsuited to the job. American Naval Intelligence officers shadowed him in Yokohama's Bloodtown, watching with dismay as he reeled in an alcoholic haze from seedy tavern to geisha house, blowing his cover at every turn. "We could never understand how such an irresponsible individual, who violated every rule and principle of proper intelligence, could be entrusted with a mission of this serious nature," recalled Ellis Zacharias, then a thirty-three-year-old U.S. Naval Intelligence officer based at the Embassy in Tokyo. At last, on the order of Lyman Cotten, the U.S. naval attaché, intelligence officers picked up Ellis, escorted him to the American Naval Hospital on Yokohama's Bluff, and placed him in the custody of the chief pharmacist, Lawrence Zembsch. One week later Ellis escaped from his confinement, disappeared into the warrens along the waterfront, then boarded a steamship for the South Sea island of Palau. He died on the island in Japanese custody, and under unexplained circumstances, without ever telling his superiors what he had uncovered.

On a July morning in 1923, two months after Ellis's death, the bizarre denouement played out on the docks of Yokohama. A Japanese steamship berthed at Yokohama port. On board was pharmacist Zembsch, who had journeyed to Palau after Ellis's death to recover his body and to find out how the alcoholic spy had met his end. With great anticipation, Zacharias and a team of Naval Intelligence officers drove to the harbor to meet him. Zacharias pushed open the door to his cabin—and stared in astonishment. The chief pharmacist was sitting on his bunk, near catatonic, with eyes aimlessly gazing into space. "He was unshaved, unkempt, deranged in mind as well as physical appearance," Zacharias observed. "He was completely unmoved by our entrance; failed to rise to greet us. In fact he did not seem to recognize us at all, but continually muttered incoherent words from which we could gather no clue to his amazing condition." In tightly folded arms, like a man guarding a priceless treasure, Zembsch held a white wooden box. Inside were Earl Hancock Ellis's cremated remains. They would prove to be an augury of Zembsch's own fate—and Yokohama's—a few weeks later.

2

The Morning Before

A sudden drop in the water level of the five small lakes near the base of Mount Fuji has caused considerable alarm in the neighborhood, as it is considered a forerunner of a severe earthquake. Yamanashi prefectural officials have ordered an investigation by experts to attempt to discover the cause of the phenomenon.

Article in the *Japan Advertiser*, August 1923

FOUR THOUSAND FEET UP, in the mountains north of Tokyo at a resort called Lake Chuzenji, a thunderstorm raged all Saturday morning, September 1, 1923. Lightning flickered from black clouds that hovered over the water. Mist blanketed the green slopes of the jagged peaks, and the downpour saturated the pebbled and rocky beaches rimming the lakeshore. The faint smell of sulfur wafted from nearby hot springs.

At a few minutes before noon, the U.S. naval attaché, Lyman Atkinson Cotten, sat in a bamboo chair on the wide verandah of his rented house, enjoying the rain beating down on the lake. Every few minutes the mist briefly cleared, revealing a pine-forested shoreline dotted with handsome villas and wooden cottages. Most were owned or leased by Americans and other Western expatriates who climbed the steep slopes to Chuzenji every summer, a 2.5-mile, two-hour journey by rickshaw from the end of the trolley car line in Nikko. (Automobiles remained a novelty in those days, and the switchbacked dirt path leading up to the lake was barely wide enough for a horse or human-pulled cart.) Ernest Satow, a British diplomat, had been the first foreigner to visit Chuzenji, arriving on horseback in the early 1870s and writing a laudatory article about the lake for the *Japan Weekly Mail,* a Yokohama English-language newspaper. In 1889 the Emperor Meiji, the Mikado, had removed travel restrictions on foreigners in Japan and permitted them to own or rent houses outside of the designated "foreign settlements." One year later a railway had opened between Ueno station in Tokyo and Nikko, starting a wave of expatriate migrations each summer. More than forty homes belonging to foreigners hugged the shore and the forested slopes that rose steeply from the water. A fleet of moored sailboats bobbed at the head of the lake in front of the Nantai San Yacht Club, named after a mountain peak topped by an ancient Buddhist temple that loomed four thousand feet above the shore. Next door stood a rickety, three-story guest house called the Chuzenji Hotel, filled to capacity during the summer with military officers and diplomats from Siam, Czechoslovakia, Belgium, and the United States, along with their families.

On this rainy Saturday morning, the Cottens had risen late. Cotten's wife, Elizabeth, a belle from North Carolina whom he had met while a cadet at Annapolis and married in 1908, fussed around the cottage, which she called Momiji-san, or Maple House. A beautiful woman in her mid-forties, with long, lustrous blond hair and a touch of melancholy in her soft-featured face, she suffered from frequent attacks of sciatica and had spent much of the past year confined to her bed. In North Carolina she had served as a leader of both the Daughters of the American Revolution and the Daughters of the Confederacy, raised money for the families of American soldiers killed or injured in Europe during the World War, campaigned for women's suffrage, and been a candidate for mayor of her hometown, Salisbury. Yet the vitality that had characterized her in the United States had given way not only to illness, but also to a generalized frustration about the diplomatic bubble in which she lived. "I often miss the years of work during and after the war, and the feeling that I was not only doing my duty as a wife and mother, but was also giving and accomplishing something for my state and country," she had written to her sister, the chairman of the North Carolina State Democratic Commit-

A family portrait of the beautiful Elizabeth Cotten,
with her sons Lyman and John

tee, earlier that summer. Lyman, she added pointedly, had never offered her encouragement in any of her professional undertakings, and
had even recoiled with embarrassment when she told him about an effort to draft her as a candidate in Salisbury's mayoral race.

The Cottens' eleven-year-old son, John, was also at home, perhaps
playing with the family's Irish setter puppy, Taisho, on a throw rug in
the living room. A large, bright space that looked onto the lake, it was
pleasantly furnished with willow settees, chaise longues, and hourglass
chairs covered with cushions of figured crepe. "John is swimming better
and better," Cotten had written in family correspondence days earlier.

"He now dives between my legs, dives to the bottom and picks up stones and swims awfully well on the surface. . . . I now let Taisho go walking with us and he thinks life is one continuous adventure. The other day we passed the fur shop in the village and Taisho saw all the furs and thought that they were animals. The hair stood right up on his back and he almost barked his head off."

Also at the cottage was John's pretty cousin, Mary Curtis Henderson. Known to the family as Curtis, she had arrived in Tokyo the previous November intending to stay for four months, had become infatuated with Japan, and had received permission from her parents in the spring of 1923 to remain until the end of the summer. "Curtis is usually out for luncheon, tea, dinner, and the evening and always comes back beaming and says she had a glorious time," Cotten had observed earlier that summer. "Of course she is no angel and has quite her share of the faults of eighteen and of the present age."

Four servants—a houseboy and three women who cleaned, cooked the family's meals, did the laundry, and prepared the Japanese bath—bustled about. A fire crackled in the fireplace. Baskets filled with growing ferns, a little bamboo bird cage with two chirping canaries, hanging Japanese lanterns, half a dozen bamboo chairs, and a wooden picnic table with a blue-and-white checkered tablecloth cluttered the porch above the lake.

It was a splendid scene, yet one can sense from his diaries that Cotten felt edgy. Would he finally be able to spend a few days in peace in the cottage? he wondered. The diaries—piles of red leather-bound notebooks penned in blue or black script, accompanied by letters to his family and Elizabeth's even richer correspondence with her mother—give the curve of his desires and frustrations, as well as the settings of a thousand moments. They capture an interlude of calm before the fates intervened, and they offer the most textured look available at one American family's life in early 1920s Japan. In their innocence, in their minute observations and ruminations, they also provide an indelible picture of a soon-to-be-lost world.

The summer had been filled with interruptions, with small and large tragedies. Cotten had first come up to Chuzenji in early July with his family, intending to stay for most of the season. But every time he began to unwind another telegram arrived and dragged him down the mountain to the sweltering plain, where an unprecedented heat wave had lasted for most of the summer. Crisis had followed crisis, obligation had followed obligation. The bizarre and still unresolved Ellis espionage scandal had reached a crescendo in July. On July 15 a typhoon and flood had delayed the train carrying him and his elder son, Lyman Jr., to Nagasaki—where the fourteen-year-old was to sail on an army steamer to boarding school in the United States—and had caused them to miss the ship. "The army quartermaster, a weak, flabby specimen, said he could not hold the transport for us," Cotten wrote. "I was angry, blue, and despondent, I can assure you, but kept my temper as it was too late to accomplish anything . . . I am awfully discouraged." Instead of dropping off Lyman Jr. and returning to Chuzenji, he had spent several more days trying to find a berth for his son on another vessel, finally putting him on a boat at Yokohama in late July. While the steamship debacle had been going on, the new American ambassador, Cyrus E. Woods, arrived in town and, accompanied by his entire staff, had presented his credentials to Prince Regent Hirohito at the Imperial Palace. A young protégé of Cotten's, a language officer at the American Embassy, had shot himself in the head with a forty-five caliber revolver at his home in Tokyo on July 28, leaving behind a distraught widow. The mysterious death on August 2 of President Warren Harding in San Francisco, apparently of pulmonary pneumonia brought on by a case of food poisoning he had contracted in Alaska, further postponed Cotten's return to the lake. Although he regarded Harding as a weak and ineffectual leader, Cotten had been shocked by the president's sudden demise and worried that "radicals" were positioning themselves to take over the U.S. government. "The political future of our country seems very uncertain," he wrote to his parents in North Carolina.

On August 16, two weeks after Harding's death, Cotten and the new U.S. ambassador had received a stream of Japanese officials—princes, noblemen, military officers, and the diplomatic corps in full uniform—at a memorial service for the president held at the Roman Catholic Cathedral in the Tsukiji district of Tokyo. Cotten maintained a dignified front inside the sweltering church, but he felt little emotion over Harding's death, and he could barely hide his impatience to get back to the mountains. As soon as the memorial service ended, he and Elizabeth raced across town to their house in western Tokyo, changed their clothes, packed their bags, drove through the crowded streets to Tokyo Station, and caught the one o'clock train to Nikko. "We ran into a terrific thunder storm, and it was still raining when we reached the foot of the mountain," Elizabeth wrote to her parents. "And not a single rickshaw! So we walked up in the rain." The Cottens spent the next few days in a blissful escape from the terrible heat of Tokyo. Hiking through virgin pine forests, climbing the mountains that ringed the lake, plunging into the clear, icy water, sailing around the islands, and sipping *o-cha*, Japanese green tea, in a little teahouse at the top of the 290-foot-high Kegon Falls, Cotten could only hope that the tragedies of the summer had run their course. "My longest stretch in Chuzenji has been about five days," he wrote in his diary. "Now we hope for a quiet spell for a time."

It was not to be. One week after Harding's memorial service, on August 24, Cotten received another piece of shocking news: the unexpected demise of Japan's prime minister, Admiral Tomasaburo Kato, a pro-Western leader, Anglophile, and longtime friend, from heart failure. Again Cotten headed down the mountain. This time, it was the American delegation's turn to pay its respects to the passing of the old order. Taking his place with a phalanx of Japanese and Western dignitaries at the official residence in Tokyo of the late prime minister, Cotten lay before the casket the branch of a sakaki tree, an evergreen considered sacred in the Japanese Shinto religion and a home for benevolent deities, or *kami*. For the American naval attaché, Kato's death was a personal loss: he had been not only an admirer of the late prime minister, regarding him as a strong counterweight to the right-wing military officers and noblemen who held most of the power in Japan, but also an intimate associate. The two men had spent many evenings together in Tokyo's most exclusive nightclubs, talking politics, sharing sake, and being entertained by the highest-paid geishas in the capital. Now he fretted that Kato's death would weaken Japan's moderates and do grave harm to Japanese-U.S. relations. "Kato was a man of splendid character," Cotten wrote in his diary. "A real leader of his people, and one that can be spared with difficulty."

On the morning of Wednesday, August 29, he finished business on the still "beastly hot" Kanto Plain and ascended the mountain again, hoping for two weeks of tranquility before the summer ended.

IN THE LAST HOUR before the earthquake struck, as tectonic plates located deep below the floor of Sagami Bay strained against each other with unimaginable force, Cotten had ample reason to feel satisfied with his life. Forty-eight years old, an Annapolis graduate, he stood at the peak of a naval career that spanned a quarter-century. A tall, athletic figure, resplendent in his crisp naval uniform, he was classically handsome, with a gray brush mustache, a chiseled jaw, prominent ears, and an air of cool competence. The eldest son of Sallie and Robert R. Cotten, a Confederate Army veteran and cotton and tobacco plantation owner in Pitt County, North Carolina, Cotten, Zelig-like, seems to have been everywhere of consequence in this tumultuous century. He had fought in the Spanish-American War, the Philippine insurrection, and the Boxer Rebellion. He had served as naval attaché in Tokyo from 1912 to 1915 and evacuated Americans from Vera Cruz as lieutenant commander of the USS *Nebraska* in June 1916 during the Mexican Revolution. He had commanded a squadron of seventy-two submarine chasers in the English Channel during the World War and worked for two years after the conflict as chief of staff to the U.S. high commissioner at Constantinople, the former capital of the defeated Ottoman Empire, then under the joint administration of Great Britain, the United States, and France.

After Constantinople Cotten had been hoping for an appointment as commander of a battleship, or a stint teaching at the Naval War College. In January 1922, however, the navy had abruptly called on him for the second time to become naval attaché in Tokyo. "Lyman has been ordered to Japan," Elizabeth Cotten wrote on January 3, 1922, to her parents from Constantinople in a letter that reveals her mixed feelings about the new assignment.

We were ordered to proceed immediately by way of the Suez. We have moved Heaven and Earth to be allowed to return [first] to America. Finally the request was granted. I thought the Navy Department totally lacking in perception to send Lyman out to Japan as Naval Attaché before returning home, when he had been away from America for two years and consequently out of touch with the sentiment of his own country. [We are] sailing on January 8 by way of a Greek steamer, making one stop at Smyrna, then at Piraeus. He was also asked if he'd consider England, but we haven't enough money. We will have two months in America.

In April 1922, Cotten arrived in Yokohama with his family aboard the *Korea Maru* from San Francisco. His return after seven years came at a moment when relations between the United States and Japan—a growing Pacific empire, military machine, saber-rattling new power bent on challenging Western designs in Asia—hovered between cordiality and deep mistrust. Forty miles down the coast from Tokyo lay the epicenter of Japan's military power: the naval base of Yokosuka, where rows of gleaming battleships, destroyers, cruisers, and submarines stood ready to embark for Asian shores at a moment's notice. Japan's fleet, a constant source of worry for her Western allies, had led the island nation to epic victories on the Yalu River in the Sino-Japanese War of 1894–1895 and at the Straits of Tsushima in the Russo-Japanese War of 1904–1905. In April 1922 Japanese troops were occupying a broad swath of Asia, from Siberia to the Manchuria railway, from China's Liaodung Peninsula to the South Sea Mandated Islands, and seemed ever hungry for more territory. "There were cliques and cabals in every official building in Tokyo, pulling the nation now to the right, now to the left—but always toward expansion," observed Naval Captain Ellis M. Zacharias, the Jacksonville, Florida–born son of a tobacco grower, who was to become one of Lyman Cotten's principal aides in Tokyo. Zacharias, who had decided on a naval career as a boy after watching U.S. battleships cruise past Jacksonville harbor on their way to Cuba during the 1898 Spanish-American War, was one of an elite circle of Japanese-speaking intelligence officers based in Tokyo under Cotten's command. "All eyes were strained to the west," he wrote, "across the sea, toward the Asiatic continent, where white spots on the map of China marked the stepping stones of this plan."

Japan had fought, briefly, on the side of Great Britain, France, and

U.S. naval attaché Lyman Atkinson Cotten, whose tardy response to the disaster would result in his reassignment.

the United States during the Great War and had captured territory from Germany in both China and the South Pacific. But "Japan was never really an ally of the Allies," declared Dr. Karl Reiland, rector of St. George's Episcopal Church in Manhattan and a self-professed Far Eastern specialist, in December 1922, in a prescient and highly publicized warning about the country's ambitions. "Germany and Japan are destined for a friendship through which [they will try to] master the whole world. Japan is no longer the Land of the Rising Sun, but the Land of the Rising Hun."

Weeks before Cotten's arrival, Japan had agreed at the March 1922 Washington Conference hosted by Harding to limit its fleet of battleships and submarines to three-fifths the size of Great Britain's and America's fleets. Right-wingers in the Japanese cabinet, in the Japanese navy, and in the press had condemned the accord as treason. They saw the conference as one more attempt by the Western Allies to thwart Japan's ambitions, a repeat of Teddy Roosevelt's mediation of the Russo-Japanese War in 1905 that had forced Japan to hand back hard-won territory to its Slavic enemy. Following Japan's 1922 "capitulation" in Washington, radical militarists had called for declaring immediate war against the United States. "If all possibilities of economic and cultural development in China and Siberia are to be stopped, and Japan is to be left an undefended and isolated archipelago in the Pacific, what remedy can there be for Japan but . . . war," declared one columnist in the *Nichi Nichi,* a widely read Tokyo newspaper. "We must make up our minds to jump into the most painful struggle the world has ever seen with the firm determination to go through the ordeal for however many years it may last."

To the navy in Washington, Cotten must have seemed like a natural choice for the job: an old hand at both gathering military intelligence and engaging in the diplomatic Kabuki that the position so often required. Smoothing the rough edges of the sensitive U.S.-Japanese relationship, stroking the egos of his Japanese counterparts, cultivating moderates within the government, joining in the peculiar rituals that the Japanese seemed to value above all else—all were deemed as important as surveying the country's far-flung naval bases and making sure that Japan lived up to its Washington Conference obligations. "Perhaps the most important duty given to any naval officer abroad is the post at Tokio," proclaimed Cotten's hometown weekly in Bruce, North Carolina, announcing his visit to the family plantation in February 1922 and his second appointment as naval attaché. "Cotten is regarded as one of the ablest and best furnished officers of the American navy."

Cotten was a man, in short, who had displayed calm under fire, proud of his achievements and given to quiet heroics. A man entrusted with great responsibilities at a moment of extreme sensitivity in the relations between East and West. A man a government would want on hand in the event of a crisis. Yet, something would go terribly wrong for him in the dramatic hours and days that lay ahead. The trauma that would unfold over the next week would serve as a telling example of how times of testing can evoke the most surprising responses. Many would rise to the occasion, performing heroically in the face of great suffering. Others would fail miserably, including those from whom much had been expected.

The storm blew all morning on September 1, 1923. Perhaps during those hours Cotten was thinking of his planned hiking trip to the resort of Karuizawa with his son John, who had been born there in 1912. They had mapped out a three-day journey through the mountains, past rice paddies, idyllic Japanese villages, hilltop Shinto shrines, and Buddhist temples, all of them rarely visited by Westerners. Japan had opened itself to the world less than seventy years earlier, and foreigners in almost any part of the country still provoked stares of wonder and thrilled cries, from adults as well as children, of "Gaijin! Gaijin!" (literally, "outsider"). Cotten loved the Japanese countryside, ventured into it as frequently as he could, relished it as an escape from the stuffy formality that often defined his work. The previous autumn he had spent an exhilarating day in the rice paddies north of Tokyo, shooting snipe with a friend, and he was eager to introduce his sons to the sport. "One has to have the training of a contortionist, the perseverance of a Chinese beggar, and the habits of a mud turtle," he wrote in his diary about the experience, displaying the self-deprecating humor that had helped to make him one of the most popular members of the diplomatic corps.

> If Charlie Chaplin could have seen me attempting to walk on top of a rice paddy dike three inches wide and as slippery as an eel, ten inches high with soft mud a foot deep on each side, I am sure he would have been overcome with jealousy. . . . Just as my right leg would slip off the left side of the dike with a splash into the foot-deep ooze and my left leg ditto on the right side of the dike, a snipe would rise broad off my port beam and sail away with a snippy sneer, unless perchance I were contortionist enough and lucky enough to shoot him, which I seldom was. . . . In one particularly

oozy paddy I saw an eel trap. Could it have been a trap for eels and rice, that most delectable and highly prized Japanese dish?

Or perhaps Cotten ruminated over his prickly relationship with Ambassador Woods, a Republican political appointee and former corporate attorney from Pittsburgh who had kept the naval attaché at arm's length since arriving in Tokyo two months earlier. "I should say from my limited observation that he is a typical political boss," Cotten wrote to his wife after meeting the ambassador for the first time in July. "Fairly clever, very forceful, not over scrupulous, ambitious and with a well-developed ego. This is, of course, for your private information." To his parents he offered a slightly different assessment: "He has the reputation of being rather hard to get along with. But we have so far seen no signs of this. The kind of chief one has at a post has so much to do with the pleasure or otherwise of carrying out one's duty. Fortunately Elizabeth and I usually have the knack of getting along with almost anyone."

Lurking in the back of Cotten's mind almost certainly was a warning he received just after Woods's appointment in May: a colleague at the Office of Naval Intelligence in Washington had sent the naval attaché a letter advising him to watch out for the new ambassador, who had engineered the removal of a naval attaché during his previous tour of duty in Madrid. "I believe that [Woods] is jealous of anybody in his office who has independent dealings with another Department of the Government, and, being of a naturally suspicious nature, he probably thinks that they are reflecting on him," the colleague had written. Cotten had responded to the note with professionalism and a touch of bravado: "You may be sure that I will cooperate with him fully," he wrote, "and the fact that he eats a naval attaché raw every morning before breakfast will neither frighten me nor deter me." Yet the warning surely added a layer of tension to his dealings with Woods and would have significant implications for what was to transpire over the next two weeks.

It is impossible to say for sure what was on Cotten's mind that morning, because his diary entries are often impersonal, lacking introspection—like the man himself. Cotten prided himself on being a man of action, not words, a man so disinclined to probe his own inner life or the inner lives of other people that he had attributed the July 1923 suicide of his young protégé, Ensign Walter Magoon, to "the awfully depressing weather" and to the stress of studying Japanese. All that can be known for certain is that he felt relieved to be here, in his rustic enclave by the lake, and hoped that he would encounter no unpleasant surprises.

AT THE SAME MOMENT that Cotten was admiring the thunderstorm from his verandah on September 1, 1923, another American was going about his business on a typical late summer morning in Japan. A few minutes before the fateful noon hour, he could be found in a crowded Tokyo neighborhood, Shimbashi, west of the Ginza shopping district, in a room on the third floor of a modest hotel. His name was Frederick Starr.

Starr is largely a forgotten figure, but at that moment he was a celebrity in the United States and in Japan. An author, anthropologist, explorer, and Japanophile who had traveled to Japan eight times since 1904, Starr displayed such interest in the country that the secret police, suspecting that he was a spy, followed him whenever he came ashore. Sixty-four years old, never married, he was built like a football linebacker. He had a broad, kindly face, with large ears, a slightly off-center Roman nose, and a halo of white hair framing a bulldog head. A man of great appetites, insatiable curiosity, and limitless wanderlust, he had founded the Anthropology Department at the University of Chicago in 1902 and had held court for twenty-one years before class after class of worshipful students. He had a vast store of material to draw on. Starr had smoked marijuana with Mexican Indians, raising eyebrows when he brought some cannabis home to share with his students in 1905. He had traveled across Sierra Leone, Liberia, and the Belgian Congo; studied the behavior of captive chimpanzees in Cuba and the mentally ill at the State Asylum for the Feeble Minded in Lincoln, Illinois; compiled a glossary of the Kapampangan language in the Philippines; and lived alongside Native Americans in Kansas, New Mexico, and the Pacific Northwest. In recent years, he had devoted most of his time to researching the religion and culture of Korea and

Anthropologist Frederick Starr studied and loved Japanese culture, and his writings introduced the West to the previously closed society.

Japan and had become recognized as one of the West's authorities on Shinto and Far Eastern Buddhism.

Like many anthropologists at the turn of the twentieth century, Starr approached his field with racial and cultural convictions that seem dated and even offensive today. These included an unshakable faith in the supremacy of Western civilization and a condescending attitude toward "primitive," nonwhite peoples. On his first visit to Japan, in 1904, he traveled to the remote island of Hokkaido and took back nine Ainu aborigines, including two small children, to a "living anthropology" exhibition, a sort of human zoo, at the St. Louis World's Fair. They included the group leader, Sangyea, with "graying hair, a gray beard, and a patriarchal aspect," and his wife, Santukuo, "charmingly ugly, with a broad and heavy lower face, prominent jaws, and a fine tattooing on face and arms." Paid a small salary for their services (Starr never stated how much), the Ainu were trundled down to Yokohama by horse cart, ferry, and train. At the conclusion of a short book he wrote about the journey of the Ainu to St. Louis, Starr contrasted the poverty of the indigenous Ainu, a Caucasian people, with the rising power and prosperity of the Japanese. "We white men are fond of assuming an air of great superiority when we speak of other peoples," he wrote. "We take it for granted that all white men are better than any red ones, or black ones, or yellow ones. Yet here we find a white race that has struggled and lost! It has proved inferior in life's battle to the more active, energetic, progressive yellow people with which it has come in contact."

Starr's tendency to classify people by skin color and to look down on aboriginals reached a low point during his year-long trip on foot and by river boat through the Congo Free State, at the invitation of Belgium's rapacious King Leopold in 1904–1905. (It was never established whether the Belgian government picked up the tab for the trip or whether Starr, as he insisted, paid for it himself.) Belgian officials closely supervised him, and he had been duped into portraying the Congo as a colonial paradise. "Debunking" stories of slave labor and the brutal mistreatment of Congolese rubber tappers, Starr wrote a favorable series of articles about Belgian rule for the *Chicago Daily Tribune* in 1907 under the heading "Truth about the Congo Free State." Among his insights: "It is doubtful whether the Congo native has as keen a sense of physical suffering as ourselves. . . . Many a time . . . I have seen a man immediately after being flogged, laughing and playing with his companions as if naught had happened." The articles provoked a backlash. Accused by reformers of being a stooge of the Belgian despot, Starr defended himself with a follow-up preface to the book version of his *Tribune* articles that dug him in even deeper: "It is true that there are floggings and chain-gangs, and prisons. I have seen them all repeatedly," he wrote. "But there are floggings, chain gangs and prisons in the United States. Mutilations are so rare that one must seek for them; and I had too much else to do."

In recent years, however, the controversy provoked by that journey had faded, and Starr had become a pillar of American academia. Some Japanese and American admirers compared him to Lafcadio Hearn, the Greek-born American newspaper correspondent who had traveled to Japan in the 1890s, married a samurai's daughter, and produced books that provided the West with an extraordinary look into pre-industrial and Meiji-era Japan. At a time when most Americans' knowledge of the country was still limited to cliché images—Madame Butterfly, cherry blossoms, and Mount Fuji—Starr dug deeply into and helped to illuminate many facets of the changing society. He called Japan "that great nation which today commands the admiration of the world" and wrote about its cultural sophistication, religion, and natural beauty. In February 1920, Starr held a celebrated debate with attorney Clarence Darrow at the Garrick Theater in Chicago on the subject "Is the Human Race Getting Anywhere?" Arguing the affirmative, Starr laid forth a sunny view of human progress, tracing social, technological, and political advances through civilizations in Mesopotamia, Greece, Rome, China, America—and Japan. When he retired from the University of Chicago in 1923, hundreds of his former students, including the future secretary of the interior, Harold Ickes, purchased a home for Starr in Seattle, Washington, so that he could more easily shuttle across the Pacific to the land that he so admired. Starr's *Strange Peoples,* a collection of essays about his far-flung travels, received positive news in the United States and was to be published in Japanese the first week of September. The desire to promote his book was one reason he had come to Japan at the broiling height of the summer of 1923.

The other reason was to climb Mount Fuji, the sacred 12,643-foot volcano that rises over the Kanto Plain west of Tokyo. The savage power of the mountain, the grandeur and destructiveness that had inspired generations of artists and religious pilgrims, fascinated Starr. He had climbed the volcano more often than almost any other living American—five times since 1916. He knew every step of the several routes up the "splendid cone" by heart. He had amassed one of the world's biggest collections of Fuji memorabilia: color prints, dolls, toys, old coins, pictures, and books. The only individual with a bigger trove was a Yokohama journalist, Ikko Sogabe, who had climbed the mountain seventy times, three times with Starr, and who had greeted the anthropologist at the pier in Yokohama upon his arrival from Seattle on August 14. "I am glad to see him, although he talks no English, as I depend on him for my Fuji ascent," Starr wrote to his mother. Starr was at work on a new book, *Fujiyama: The Sacred Mountain of Japan,* scheduled to be published in the United States in 1924. He intended the work to be the definitive compendium of lore regarding the volcano: its vegetation, geology, role in Japanese myth, religion, and literature, and the fearsome eruptions that had occurred eighteen times in the past two thousand years, most recently during an earthquake in 1854. Starr was intrigued by the role Japan's geological instability played in shaping the national character, forging a sense of national unity, stoicism, and reverence for the earth.

On his sixth climb of Fujiyama, Starr almost hadn't made it to the top. Flabby and out of shape after months of inactivity, he had struggled up the mountain, leaning on Sogabe for support. The view from the summit, as always, moved and thrilled him. Most of Starr's notes from this Fuji expedition were lost in the ensuing catastrophe, but his account of a similar climb up Fuji in 1921 gives a flavor of what he must have experienced. "We looked down into the crater, its sides seem almost vertical," he wrote.

The colors of the lavas are like blotches or stains, there are eight pinnacles or peaks around the lip—which is hence called a lotus blossom of eight petals. Lovely clear views of Odawara and Suruga Bays, Enoshima, Hakone mountains. As we walked we saw hollows scooped out in the volcanic sand . . . and feeling them with our hands, found them hot—eggs can be baked in the hot sand. Climbing some ladder steps, we saw stone Buddhist figures battered and broken, reminding us again of the old days when Fuji was a Buddhist stronghold. At last we reached Kangamine, the sword peak, actual summit of the mountain and highest point in all Japan. We joined schoolboys throwing arms in the air, and crying "banzai, banzai." Then we went down.

Arriving back in the furnace of the Japanese lowlands on August 31, Starr planned to settle down in Tokyo and pull together for the book his notes from the Fuji trip. "I presume except for mountain summit cold, which I have had for moments, that there has been no day that the thermometer has not reached ninety degrees since I came," he wrote. "This morning we are in full view of Mount Fuji, at whose base we slept last night. We were here to see a famous fire festival. We are a little tired, of course, after such a continuous whirl of excitement and travel. But . . . we shall have several days of rest and making up delayed work at Tokyo. So do not be disturbed, all goes well."

Starr's diaries place him in a black-and-white checkered cotton bathrobe, or *yukata,* at a writing desk in his hotel room a few minutes before noon on September 1. Trolley car gongs, motorcar horns, bicycle bells, and laborers' shouts wafted pleasantly into his room from the wide avenue three floors below. The neighborhood, a collision of feudal Edo with robust scenes of Japanese modernity, was one of Starr's favorites in the capital. From his window, he could see the Shimbashi train station, a neo-Gothic edifice of brick and stone topped by turrets, cupolas, and spires, rising dreamlike above a sea of low wooden houses. Remarkably, it is known that the remains of a ripe melon from the night before sat beside him, "a fine cassava, fragrant and beautiful," he remarked in his diary. With him in the room was a young Japanese assistant named Takagi, who had planned to get married the next day but had just postponed the wedding because astrologers had determined it to be a day of bad luck. Takagi had rescheduled the event for October, but he was thinking of backing out of it altogether. "Takagi talked of his matrimonial matter," Starr wrote. "That young girl sent for him to come and see her [last week]. He was shocked at her appearance. [He says] 'she is skin and bones. I suppose it is consumption and I am in doubt what to do.' He says she does not cough, and I advised him to wait and see, hoping that it is something else."

Starr had made only one appointment for the remainder of the weekend: a dinner on September 2 with the mayor of Tokyo to celebrate Starr's sixty-fifth birthday. In anticipation of the event he had sent out his single formal Japanese skirt and jacket, the only outdoor clothing he had brought with him, to be cleaned, and he sat in his Japanese cotton bathrobe, feeling half-naked and vulnerable. "I shall be a prisoner in my yukata until I dress for dinner," he scribbled in his notebook as the hands of the clock atop Shimbashi train station moved toward the noon hour.

NORTH OF STARR'S HOTEL rose the Imperial Palace complex, the heart of the Japanese capital, where the Emperor Taisho, the empress, and their huge staff dwelled in an ancient castle protected by wide moats and high stone ramparts. (Earlier in the week, though, the emperor had moved by royal train to his summer palace in Nikko, below the mountain where Cotten resided, and thus would remain out of touch in the coming days.) Here lay the center of the political drama that morning.

Crown Prince Hirohito, twenty-two years old, the real power behind the throne, had arrived at the palace by motorcade from his residence at the Akasaka Detached Palace at 10:30 in the morning. ("His face displayed a rather low order of intellect," Lyman Cotten had written in the frank style that typified his private correspondence, after presenting his credentials to the regent at the Imperial Palace in April 1922. Cotten had an even lower opinion of Hirohito's father, the mentally enfeebled emperor. "From the first . . . he was nothing more or less than a half wit and for several years now has been an imbecile.") Today Hirohito was going to meet with his privy council—a select group of nobles, descended from Japan's great feudal families, who still held most of the power in the country—on the subject of the new cabinet, which was still being formed. Three days earlier, in a secret session, the emperor and his advisers had anointed Admiral Viscount Gombei Yamamoto to replace the late Baron Kato as prime minister. Seventy-one years old, Yamamoto had resigned from the post in 1914 because of a naval bribery and corruption scandal, and his reappointment had raised fierce criticism among Japan's nascent democratic reformers. Prince Hirohito demanded news: When would the prime minister name his cabinet? At that moment Yamamoto was interviewing contenders at the downtown Navy Club for the most powerful posts: minister of home affairs and minister of defense. As the hour of calamity struck, Japan would be effectively without a government.

PLENTY OF PEOPLE in Japan had earthquakes on their minds that morning. Hydrologists inspecting the five lakes at the foot of Mount Fuji suspected that a volcanic eruption or a temblor was imminent. Scientists at Tokyo Imperial University had noted a surge of seismic activity around the globe in recent months: a tsunami that had swept over the Hawaiian island of Maui, an earthquake near Easter Island in the South Pacific, the back-to-back eruptions of Mount Vesuvius and Mount Etna in Italy. That summer Professor Thomas Jefferson Jackson See of the Mare Island Observatory near San Francisco had announced that a new submarine mountain range was rising from the floor of the Pacific. See had theorized that all of the seismic disturbances were "links in the chain" emanating from an upheaval of the seabed. A famed Japanese prognosticator had recently claimed that a great natural disaster was about to destroy the archipelago. In Yokohama, an apocalypse-minded American evangelist named B. S. Moore denounced the decadence of modern Japanese life—citing licensed prostitution, Bolshevism, and adultery—and warned his Bible students to prepare for a calamity sent down by a vengeful God. Moore quoted Isaiah 24:20: "The earth shall reel to and fro like a drunkard, and shall be removed like a cottage, and transgression thereof shall be heavy upon it; and it shall fall and not rise again." Meanwhile, in the fashionable Hibiya section of Tokyo, the biggest celebrity in town was about to be shown off as a model of earthquake safety consciousness. Two hundred of the most powerful people in Japan—politicians, members of the imperial court, foreign journalists, and diplomats— had been invited to a formal banquet in the celebrity's honor at noon. U.S. Ambassador Cyrus Woods, British Ambassador Charles Norton Edgcumbe Eliot, and French Ambassador Paul Claudel, who had achieved fame as a poet and playwright before joining the diplomatic corps in Tokyo, were among the notables on the guest list.

The celebrity was Frank Lloyd Wright's Imperial Hotel, the most debated, fussed over, praised, and criticized new star of the international capital. After six years, 18 million yen ($9 million), the round-the-clock efforts of six hundred Japanese laborers, and emergency infusions of cash by the Imperial board chairman, Baron Okura, the Imperial at last stood ready to open its doors officially to the public. (Some select guests were already staying at the hotel.) Anticipation was high. The architect and critic Louis H. Sullivan, writing in the *Architectural Record* in the spring of 1923, had hailed the Imperial as a "masterpiece" and praised Wright as a "great free spirit." He had written, "There hovers over all a sense of primal power in singleness of purpose; a convincing quiet that bespeaks a master hand, guiding and governing."

A daring construction that prefigured some of Wright's other cre-
ations, such as the 1936 Fallingwater in Pennsylvania's Monongahela
Valley, the Imperial Hotel had dominated the Tokyo landscape for
months. Crowds came to admire the striking exterior, a mosaic of
kiln-fired yellow bricks and greenish, leopard-spotted volcanic stone,
or *oya*, each piece chiseled from a quarry near Kyoto and carved by
hand. Terraces and cantilevered rectangular slabs protruded from the
multihued facade, all sharp angles and horizontal planes, a bold break
from the bloated Victorian architecture that had came to dominate
modern Tokyo. The Imperial's interior, which to that point only a
privileged few had seen, began at the Main Promenade, a starkly mod-
ernist hall with shimmering lava tile floors and low cement ceilings
that sliced downward at sharp diagonals. Terraced bridges between
the two main guest wings hovered above a complex of inner Japanese
gardens and piazzas. Each of the Imperial's 230 guest rooms was
unique, and Wright had been so captivated by the Japanese "small-
ness" aesthetic that the entrance to each room consisted of a glazed
door barely five feet high.

Reporters and architectural critics also lavished praise on the safe-
guards that Wright had installed against earthquakes: cantilevered
walls and floors tapered to lower the center of gravity, topped with a
lightweight copper roof, rested on a "pin-cushion" foundation consisting of thousands of short cement piles. In the entrance court stood
an immense outdoor pool connected to the hotel's water system, protection against inevitable fires that all the experts guaranteed would
break out in the event of a severe shock. (In the last days of the hotel's
construction, facing cost overruns, the Imperial's board of directors
had tried to eliminate the pool. Wright had argued strongly that it
would be the "last resource" against a conflagration, and the board
had relented.) The hotel had already withstood one test: on April 26,
1922, the worst earthquake to strike Tokyo in fifty-two years had
cracked walls in the Imperial Palace and sent thousands of terrified
people into the streets. Wright had been working upstairs in the Imperial Hotel's architectural studio when the temblor hit and had left a
vivid account of the event. "As I lay there I could clearly see the
groundswell pass through the construction above as it heaved and
groaned to hideous crushing and grinding noises," Wright recalled,

writing in a stilted Victorian style that stands in sharp contrast to his coolly elegant architecture. "Several thunderous crashes sickened me, but later these proved to be the falling of five tall chimneys of the old Imperial Hotel, left standing alone by the recent burning of that building."

One figure was about to move from obscurity to center stage in the drama. Tetsuzo Inumaru, the Imperial's thirty-five-year-old general manager, had lived, until this point, an unremarkable life. Born in Tokyo, he had fallen into hotel work by chance, starting as a bellboy in Shanghai and climbing through the ranks from railway hostels in Russia to the first Waldorf Astoria in Manhattan. Hired in 1917 as a duty manager at the original Imperial, a Victorian firetrap built by a German firm, he had been promoted to general manager following the resignation of his precedessor after an April 1922 blaze that had destroyed the old hotel. He was known to be immensely capable, a favorite of Wright's (who had returned to the United States the previous year), a man who could be trusted to protect the hotel as if his life depended on it. At a few minutes before noon, Inumaru met in his second-floor executive suite with two members of his staff, making final preparations for the reception. It was going to take place in the Central Banquet Hall, one story above the Main Promenade. He wore a formal kimono suit—gray *haori*, black *hakama*—and wooden geta. He sat behind his desk. His executives informed him that everything had been prepared. All they had to do was wait until the dignitaries arrived.

ONE MORE PLACE in Tokyo bears visiting in the hour before noon, September 1, 1923. It lay across town from the Imperial Hotel, in a working-class neighborhood called Honjo, sprawling along the east bank of the sluggish, brown Sumida River. In the days of Edo this had been a fashionable district inhabited by daimyo and their sword-carrying retainers, the samurai. But in recent years, the capital's action had shifted to high ground surrounding the Imperial Palace, and the riverside quarter had fallen on hard times. Factories, warehouses, and modest wooden houses clustered around a squat sumo stadium, where thousands gathered every night to watch pot-bellied behemoths grapple in an earthen pit. A stone's throw from the arena sprawled a huge vacant lot that was, until recently, the site of the Army Clothing Depot. The military had run a factory here that manufactured uniforms for units across the country. But in 1922 the army had relocated the sheds and warehouses and demolished the buildings; neighborhood children used the vacant, fifteen-acre expanse as a playground.

One of those children was Kikue Washio, nine years old at the time of the cataclysm. She told her story in a book of survivor's tales, written in Japanese, compiled many decades later. Not much is known about her. She was an elementary school student in a part of Honjo called Yokoami, a typical neighborhood of tightly packed together, one- and two-story wooden houses built along the river. Her father owned a small tea shop next door to the public bathhouse on a wide street with a trolley car line. The Washios—Kikue was apparently an only child—lived, like many working-class Japanese families, crammed into a pair of tatami-mat rooms on the second floor above their shop. She had spent much of that summer learning how to swim on school-sponsored outings to Enoshima on Sagami Bay, an hour's train trip from Tokyo. She was especially close to her mother, whose cooking she loved. On September 1, the first day of the school's fall semester, her father had gone out of town on an unspecified errand, and, a few minutes before noon, Kikue sat at home eating a lunch of boiled spinach, squid, tofu, and rice that her mother had prepared for her. She devoured the meal happily. In every way it was a typical morning, except for one tiny detail. Just before her father had departed for his trip, he had gazed at the sky and noticed an unusual brown circle rimming the sun. "There is something peculiar about that," he had said. A casual remark, ignored at the time, and yet Kikue Washio would remember it vividly when she looked back on the events of that day, from a distance of nearly seventy years.

3

On the Waterfront

What terror greater to many than a heavy earthquake, and what so soon forgotten?

From an article in the *Japan Gazette*, after an earthquake struck Yokohama at 10 A.M. on April 26, 1922, damaging many buildings and killing a young Chinese woman

EIGHTEEN MILES SOUTH of Tokyo, in the international port of Yokohama, a heavy thunderstorm erupted before dawn on September 1. The rain tapered off at ten o'clock in the morning, and the day then held the promise of clear skies and a break from the oppressive heat. A light breeze filled the sails of the sampans in Tokyo Bay. Freighters and ocean liners crowded the harbor. Stevedores pushed carts piled high with steamer trunks, many emblazoned with colorful stickers from Shanghai, Hong Kong, Singapore, and other Far Eastern ports of call. Rickshaw men, clad in white cotton jackets and bowl-shaped straw hats, sinewy limbs reflecting years of hard toil on the city's sunbaked streets, trotted along the Bund. They jostled for space on the road with black sedans—Dürkopp Wanderers, Maxwells, Minervas, Oaklands, and Fords—heading toward Yokohama harbor. The elegant lobbies of hotels along the Bund filled with a crush of departing guests. On Benten Dori, a famed arcade festooned with paper globe lanterns and dominated by a Gothic clock tower, passengers who were embarking on today's steamship made last-minute shopping expeditions. Inside the world-renowned Kuhn & Komor Ltd., located at 31 Water Street, the owners George Komor, a Hungarian émigré, and his Russian wife also tended to the needs of a pack of souvenir hunters. A large picture window, flanked by Corinthian columns, displayed a bounty of lacquer ware, porcelain, kimonos, screens, chests, samurai swords, carved ivory, tobacco sets, miniature temples, sake cups, and hundreds of other artifacts culled from across the Japanese archipelago.

Directly across Water Street at Thomas Cook & Son, the travel agent, clerks behind a polished wooden counter sold traveler's checks, booked steamship reservations, and arranged tours for new arrivals in Japan. Posters of Mount Fuji, the temples of Kyoto, and other attractions of "the land of the rising sun"—a slogan that agency founder Thomas Cook had coined half a century earlier—covered the wood-paneled walls of the branch office, opened by Cook's son, John, in 1894. One of the clients waiting inside Cook's was Mrs. Lois Crane, who planned to rendezvous at noon there with her husband, Major William C. Crane, the outgoing army attaché to the U.S. Embassy in Tokyo. Mrs. Crane was in an elated mood that morning. After spending the summer at the lakeside hotel in Chuzenji, where they had been enthusiastic sailors and companions of the Cotten family, she and her husband had come down the mountain for the last time on Thursday, August 30. Their two-year tour of duty in Japan over, the young couple were about to start a four-month trip through China, India, Egypt, England, and France before going home to America. The Cranes had originally planned to travel to China from the western Japanese port of Shimonoseki. But something made them change their plans at the last minute and decide to leave from Yokohama instead. The Cranes had spent two nights in Tokyo. Then, on Saturday morning, while William Crane had remained behind to finish last-minute business, Lois Crane had taken the train to Yokohama to complete travel arrangements and book passage on a steamship to Shanghai. Mrs. Crane had another reason to be in excellent spirits. She and her husband had taken first place in the previous Monday's sailboat race on Lake Chuzenji; the prize, which she carried with her, was a miniature crystal Daikoku, the Japanese god of luck.

The Empress of Australia *took on many refugees
but remained stuck, perilously, at dockside.*

* * *

IN AN ERA BEFORE transoceanic travel became routine, the departures of steamships from Yokohama for North America and Europe were special events. Today's sailing was no exception. Docked at the hatoba, the immense steel and concrete pier built in 1894 that extended half a mile into Yokohama harbor, was one of the most elegant liners that had ever berthed at the port. The *Empress of Australia* was 615 feet long and 75 feet wide. Three coal-stained silver funnels rose at a slight tilt above her streamlined black hull and gleaming white upper decks. Owned by Canadian Pacific Lines, she was the most recent acquisition in a fleet of four luxury vessels, the White Empresses, that sailed the lucrative route between the Far East and North America. Competition with other shipping companies for freight and passengers had grown fierce: the American-owned Admiral-Orient Line, with five large, seventeen-knot liners, including its flagship, the *President Jefferson,* began offering a Seattle–Far East service in April 1921, and the Japanese were also angling for a share of the business.

But Canadian Pacific was holding its own. Only the week before, the *Empress of Australia*'s sister ship, the *Empress of Canada,* had set a new speed record for crossing the Pacific: eight days and eleven hours, eclipsing by more than ten hours the previous record set by the *Empress of Russia* in 1914.

The *Empress of Australia*'s short history mirrored the world's journey from bloody conflict to peace. Built by the shipyard Vulcan Werke on the Baltic Sea for the Hamburg Amerika Line in 1912, she had originally been christened the *Tirpitz* after the admiral who had developed the German navy prior to the World War. Kaiser Wilhelm II had selected the boat to carry him on a victory cruise after Germany's expected crushing of the Allies. Instead, following Germany's surrender, the British government seized the vessel and put her to work as a transport ship to bring its soldiers home from the trenches. In 1922, as the postwar world entered a golden age of steamship travel, Canadian Pacific bought the *Empress* and refitted her as a luxury liner. Her features included a gilt-trimmed dining salon, decorated in Louis XVI style, that spanned the top deck; a steambath; an indoor swimming pool; a state-of-the-art gymnasium; an oak-paneled smoking room with Italian plasterwork ceilings, crystal chandeliers, and the finest champagnes and Cuban cigars; and a first-class lounge with a glass dome, carved torchieres, ten large oriel windows, satinwood furnishings, and a concert grand piano trimmed with bronze. She was one of the finest and most luxuriously equipped steamships in the world.

The *Empress* had docked at the hatoba on the morning of August 30 and was scheduled to leave for Vancouver at noon on September 1. She carried several hundred tons of silk, tea, and other Chinese and Japanese goods for sale in the United States and Canada. Her passenger manifest listed three hundred "Asiatics" in steerage (a well-lit and ventilated space near the bow of the ship that was considered to be far superior to similar facilities on other boats) and 170 Europeans, Americans, Chinese, and Japanese traveling in saloon class. A typical mélange of globetrotters in an era when transoceanic luxury travel was still the provenance of a privileged few, they included well-funded missionaries, businessmen, military officers, and affluent tourists. Bad luck had marred the start of the ship's journey from Shanghai. A cholera epidemic had struck the Chinese port during the miasmic heat of August; when the *Empress* arrived at Kobe three days later, immigration officials had forbidden the ship from docking. Instead, doctors inspected passengers and crew, then launches had taken off disembarking passengers in small groups. The tedious process had delayed by hours the *Empress*'s onward sailing to Yokohama.

At ten o'clock in the morning on September 1, Gertrude Cozad left her Yokohama hotel for the *Empress of Australia* with her cousin, Ella Brunner. They traveled by rickshaw, running a few last-minute errands, then arriving at the pier "in good season," Cozad wrote, an hour before the noon sailing to Vancouver. The daughter of Protestant missionaries in Kobe, Cozad, 58, had spent most of her life spreading the gospel in that hilly port city 370 miles southwest of Tokyo. Her cousin had just finished a month-long tour through Asia and had ended her trip with a week-long vacation with Cozad in Karuizawa, the popular resort located three thousand feet up in the mountains northeast of Tokyo. Their stay in Karuizawa had been shadowed by a bizarre tragedy there weeks earlier: the double ritual suicide of two of Japan's most popular writers, Takeo Arishima and his mistress, Akio Hatano, who had hanged themselves on Arishima's rented estate after Hatano's husband discovered their affair. Hundreds of young Japanese had committed suicide in deranged imitation of the writers. At the time of the cousins' stay in Karuizawa, workmen had begun breaking apart the villa with hammers and saws because the landlord didn't want it to become a cult attraction. The cousins may have heard the demolition-in-progress as they ate their breakfast on the hotel verandah or hiked through the surrounding hills.

The hatoba was crowded with ships that morning. The *Empress of Australia* lay twelve hundred feet from the shore, her starboard side against the pier, her bow facing the Bund, and her stern a few yards from the bow of the small American freighter *Steel Navigator,* owned by the U.S. Steel Corporation. Across the pier lay the disabled steamship *André Lebon,* owned by the French company Messageries Maritimes. She had been docked at Yokohama for several days while awaiting maintenance work on her engine. Cozad and Brunner walked up the *Empress*'s white gangplank, steadying themselves on the handrails, and down the corridors to Brunner's twin-bed cabin, well appointed with eiderdown quilts and mahogany furniture. Brunner's luggage had been sent ahead of her and was already neatly stored in the cabin; her roommate, a young Korean woman from Seoul, had settled in, and they introduced themselves. A white-jacketed steward informed Brunner that because the *Empress* was only one-third full, she could move to a private room once the boat got started. Cozad told her cousin that she wouldn't be able to stay for the bon voyage ceremony; she needed to catch a 12:30 train to Tokyo Station to reach her home by 6 A.M. on Sunday to celebrate a "real good" Sabbath with fellow missionaries. "I . . . said my goodbye before the band began to play and the confetti to fly," Cozad recalled. "The last word to Ella was, 'I am so glad that after all the years of planning and the months of travel your trip has come to an end without one unpleasant hitch.' Then we kissed and parted."

As BRUNNER AND COZAD inspected Brunner's cabin on the *Empress of Australia,* guests were gathering for Saturday lunch at the Grand Hotel on the Bund. With its gingerbread facade, balustraded terraces, and a gabled roof ornamented with winged horses, the Grand was either, depending on one's architectural tastes, a gaudy bit of Victoriana or the jewel of Yokohama's seafront. The hotel had been a legendary destination for globe-trotters in the Far East for decades, a place that beckoned travelers as much for its storied history as for its atmosphere of luxury. The original Grand, which had opened in 1873 under British management and was still in use, was a simple two-story brick building with ten rooms. In 1890 the ornate new wood-frame annex, designed by the noted French architect Paul Pierre Sarda, opened adjacent to the old building. The Grand stretched a long block along the seafront, with one hundred rooms, five grass tennis courts, Japanese gardens, expansive lawns, and serene views of Yokohama harbor. U.S. naval officers on shore leave often stayed at the Grand, and in the early twentieth century a group of them had formed a corporation that purchased and ran the hotel. "The Company can safely challenge any Hotel in the East for pleasantness of situation, comfort, and elegance," its turn-of-the-century catalogue proclaimed.

Authors, politicians, and other luminaries from around the world supported that assessment. After a stay in 1889 Rudyard Kipling had praised the service and called the Grand "an open door through which you may catch the first gust from the Pacific slope." In 1882, an Englishman named C. Dresser had written enthusiastically about the hotel's menu and Western charm: "The fish, entrees, and large slices of meat were served one after another, and for a moment I imagined that I was sitting in the Grand Hotel in Paris. Among the items that I was served were preserved meat from Crosse & Blackwell's Co., and marmalade and jam made in Dundee by Keillor & Co." Other famous globe-trotters who had stayed here included W. Somerset Maugham, the French industrialist and Asian art collector Emile Guimet, and William Howard Taft, who had apparently been one of the few guests to have had a bad experience at the hotel. Taft, who had stopped in Japan on a round-the-world steamship cruise with an entourage that included Alice Roosevelt, the president's daughter, had suffered an outbreak of diarrhea after dinner in the Grand's main dining room in 1905. Fortunately for Taft, the party included his personal physician, Major Edie, who, though stricken himself, had nursed the U.S. secretary of war back to health.

Saturday, September 1, began as another typical day in the life of the famed hotel: Martin of the Grand, "the Japanese hotel runner par excellence," according to one contemporary description, dashed around the chandeliered lobby, helping guests with luggage, arranging tours of the countryside, and passing out the cards of local guides and souvenir dealers. Several guests played in the lofty and spacious billiard room. H. C. Davis, a naval lieutenant attached to the U.S. Embassy in Tokyo, leaned back in a chair in the basement barbershop, his face covered in lather, as a Japanese barber stroked his cheeks with a straight-edged razor. Others leafed through international newspapers and a rare book collection in the library. The steam launch *Tourist* sped across the harbor, ferrying guests to and from ocean liners that couldn't find berths at the hatoba. Black sedans rolled through the polished brass main gate on Water Street, one block from the seafront. They glided along a circular white gravel driveway, rounded a manicured garden filled with fountains and cherry trees, and dropped new arrivals in front of the teakwood double doors leading to the lobby. The usual collection of rickshaw coolies clustered outside the brass gate, offering rides to Chinatown, the Yokohama Foreign Cemetery on the

Bluff, and the One Hundred Steps, a ladderlike staircase leading up a cliff to a Shinto shrine and a famous tea shop that had been patronized by Matthew Perry, the Maharaja of Jaipur, and the Prince of Wales.

On the hotel's opposite side, facing the Bund, the seafront lounge was filling up. Bordered by a two-hundred-foot verandah that "affords its occupants a magnificent view of the Harbour and a cool and pleasant residence, even in the hottest days of the sultry season," according to the Grand's brochure, the lounge was a popular gathering place for Yokohama residents and tourists alike. Among those relaxing in the sun-splashed salon was Doris Babbitt, the seventeen-year-old daughter of Ellwood C. Babbitt, the new commercial attaché to the U.S. Embassy in Tokyo. The Babbitt family—also including Ellwood's wife, a "partly paralyzed invalid," according to the *Japan Gazette,* and the couple's nineteen-year-old daughter, Jocelyn—had arrived from San Francisco aboard a Pacific Mail steamer, the SS *President Lincoln,* at seven o'clock on Thursday morning, August 30. They had immediately checked into two rooms in the original brick building facing the Creek, a sixty-foot-wide stream along the original Foreign Settlement's southern border that emptied into the harbor. The trip was a homecoming of sorts. The Babbitts had lived in Yokohama for four years before the war, when Ellwood Babbitt served as a commercial officer at the U.S. Consulate there.

This morning, Babbitt left the hotel early and traveled by train to Tokyo to search for a residence near the U.S. Embassy. His wife and daughters had decided to remain behind to familiarize themselves again with the port and to look up old friends. Mrs. Babbitt, who had grown up in Nagasaki, and Jocelyn rested upstairs in their room, from which they could hear the cries of boatmen navigating the waterway below their window. Doris, in the lounge, may have taken notice of a boyish-looking, twenty-two-year-old naval ensign named Thomas John Ryan Jr. Attached to the U.S. Embassy in Tokyo, the New Orleans–born officer had come to Yokohama for a weekend leave, joining several other navy men who were regulars at the hotel. He sat in an easy chair facing the harbor, talking with a friend. The sun streamed through French windows that looked over the sloping lawn, the sweep of the Bund, and the bay beyond.

Others sipped coffee or tea and leafed through the *Japan Gazette,*

Yokohama's English-language broadsheet. They glanced at the shipping news and the summaries of world events. Five years after the Armistice, the days of trench warfare, poison gas attacks, and mass death seemed, thankfully, a distant memory, though regional flare-ups and economic meltdowns continually reminded the world of how fragile the peace was. The Italian dictator Benito Mussolini's warships and warplanes had bombarded the Greek island of Corfu on August 31, killing fifteen people. The surprise attack had followed the ambush killings of five Italian diplomats by Greek guerrillas at a remote border post in Albania. The German mark had plummeted to 10 million to the U.S. dollar, and in Munich, a rabble-rousing war veteran named Adolf Hitler was stirring passions against the Weimar Republic. Much of the news, however, reflected the age's fascination with diversions of all kinds. The heavyweight boxing champion, Jack Dempsey, was training in Saratoga Springs, New York, in preparation for his bout with the Argentine contender, Luis Angel Firpo, the Wild Bull of the Pampas. Babe Ruth's New York Yankees had beaten the Washington Senators, 4–2, on Thursday at the newly built Yankee Stadium. "Yes, We Have No Bananas" was soaring up the American popular music charts, the paper noted, and a Ford motorcar and one-ton truck had passed Yokohama in their "End to End" journey from the southern end of Kyushu to the northern tip of Hokkaido, the first attempt ever to traverse the Japanese islands by automobile. "Seven years ago [I] made the seven-hundred-mile journey that began and ended at Kobe, and not a single motor car was seen until end of the [ninth day] when a limousine appeared filled with geisha and profiteers," a reporter observed. "Now it is possible—nearly—to get from one Ford agency to another in sunup to sundown. Thus wonderfully have we progressed in seven years."

The *Gazette* reported several notable arrivals and departures at the port that weekend: Professor Henry Fairfield Osborn, the curator of the American Museum of Natural History in New York City, accompanied by his wife, had docked at Yokohama aboard the SS *President Madison* from Seattle. Osborn was continuing to China and Mongolia to investigate the research being conducted by the American Third Asiatic Expedition, which the Museum had bankrolled. The Reverend E. H. Hamilton of Richmond, Virginia, had arrived on the same ship and was met on the hatoba by his fiancée, Estelle McAlpine of Nagoya. The couple had been wed immediately after the docking by Paul Emmott Jenks, the deputy U.S. consul in Yokohama, then had left for their honeymoon in Karuizawa. Afterward, the paper announced, "they will go to China for missionary work." And Mrs. Rupert Hughes, wife of the prolific American author, playwright, and movie scenarist (and an uncle of a teenager with grand aspirations named Howard Hughes), arrived at Yokohama on board the *President Lincoln*. She was en route to Peking with a traveling companion, Ruth R. Sedgwick, to study Chinese calligraphy and write poetry through the winter.

The Gaiety Cinema, the only movie theater in Yokohama exclusively for the foreign community, had two Saturday showings of Mack Sennett's *Molly O,* a "beautiful romance on youth and love," starring Mabel Normand. Tokyo, a forty-five-minute train ride away, offered more extensive choices: *Boomerang Justice* with George Larkin, *Man Hunter* with William Farnum, *The Dictator* with Wallace Reid and Lila Lee, and *The Glorious Fool* with Helen Chadwick. The newspaper's "joke of the day" was set in a barbershop: Customer: Ouch! This towel is really hot. Barber: Sorry sir! I couldn't hold it any longer!

A dozen brass ceiling fans spun in the colonnaded room. Waitresses clad in blue silk kimonos circulated with tea sets in straw baskets. A handful of diners found tables on a balustraded white balcony that overlooked the lounge, getting a bird's-eye view of the bustle on the ground floor.

ACROSS YOKOHAMA on that late summer morning, people were going about their business, enjoying the onset of cooler weather, making plans for the weekend. It was a time of transition, when Yokohama hovered between summer and fall, between lethargy and productivity, when a subtle crispness in the air foretold the season of renewal. Many of the five thousand Western expatriates who lived in Yokohama in September 1923 were still vacationing in mountain and beach resorts or traveling abroad; for a number of those who had remained behind, the port seemed smaller, slower, more intimate than it did during the often frantic autumn. It was, by all accounts, a completely ordinary morning, with nothing to indicate that in a matter of minutes, everything would change.

At Dodwell & Co., a venerable British trading firm on Main Street, one of Yokohama's most popular citizens, Otis Manchester Poole, prepared to call it a day. Poole, the forty-three-year-old general manager of the firm, born in Chicago and a resident of Yokohama since he was eight years old, was looking forward to the twelve o'clock "News Exchange" at the long bar of the United Club on the Bund. After the Saturday get-together would come another series of weekend rituals: lunch with his family at their home on the Bluff, followed by two sets of tennis with a business partner in the afternoon heat. Many United Club regulars had gone down to the hatoba to bid bon voyage to friends, but two dozen of the faithful had opted to skip the ceremony. The men—women were seldom allowed to cross the threshold of the half-century-old establishment—tipped back whisky and British ales served by a Japanese bartender named Jimmy. The friends discussed the weekend sailboat race in Yokohama harbor, Mussolini's surprise attack on Corfu, and a threatened rickshaw strike in Yokohama to protest the government's granting of a license to a private autobus line between the central train station and the waterfront, the most lucrative route in town. The coolies had resolved, reported the *Japan Advertiser,* that "foreigners cannot be allowed to have the use of other conveyances which will put an end to the prosperous days of the pullers of the two wheeled carriages."

At the French Consulate on the lowest spur of the Bluff, south of the Grand Hotel, Marshall Martin, a wealthy merchant and leader of the British expatriate community, conferred with the young French consul, a John Barrymore lookalike named Paul Déjardin. The two men were hashing out a strategy to resolve a long-standing tax dispute with the Japanese government. Edwin Wheeler, Yokohama's physician and one of its original foreign settlers—Wheeler had arrived aboard a British warship in 1862 and had recently delivered his one thousandth expatriate baby—visited patients until 11:30 A.M. Then, as was his custom, the white-haired octogenarian traveled by rickshaw to the Yokohama Auction House at 61 Main Street for a ritual noon sherry with his good friend, the auctioneer Tom Abbey. Jennie M.

Kuyper, an Iowa-born, fifty-two-year-old missionary with the First Congregational Church and the popular principal of the Ferris Seminary, read in her study on the second floor of the girls' school on the Bluff, preparing for the first day of classes the following Monday.

At the American Naval Hospital down the road, Dr. Ulysses R. Webb, the superintendent, escorted the wife of Lawrence Zembsch down the corridor of the main building to Zembsch's hospital room. The previous spring Zembsch, the hospital's chief pharmacist, had traveled to the South Sea island of Palau on a volunteer mission to retrieve the remains of Earl Hancock Ellis, a U.S. Naval Intelligence operative, and to investigate rumors of a Japanese secret military buildup in the South Pacific. In July he had returned to Yokohama, catatonic, possibly drugged, holding Ellis's ashes in a white box. After a month of incoherence and apparent amnesia Zembsch was showing signs of snapping out of it, but the mystery of what had happened to him during that South Pacific sojourn remained unsolved. "For the last few days he has been much improved," Naval Attaché Lyman Cotten had written in his diary after a quick trip to Yokohama to visit Zembsch on August 28. "But I got no information of value from him. Only a large amount of unimportant details about his trip."

More than two hundred well-wishers, meanwhile, had gathered on the hatoba to see off friends and relatives who were leaving for Vancouver on the *Empress of Australia*. Passengers leaned out of portholes and gazed down from beneath a blue-and-white canopy on the top-deck promenade. The ship's band struck up a sprightly tune. On the bridge of the *Empress of Australia*, Captain Samuel Robinson prepared the vessel for departure. A sandy-haired native of Hull, England, Robinson had first gone to sea at the age of fourteen and became a Canadian Pacific commander at the turn of the century. In May 1914, as the captain of the *Empress of Asia*, he set new world records for both a single day's steaming (473 nautical miles) and for crossing the Pacific (nine days, two hours, and fifteen minutes, a record that lasted for only two weeks before being eclipsed by the *Empress of Russia*). Colleagues regarded the fifty-two-year-old commander as one of the trade's most skillful, most competitive sailors.

A tugboat crew fastened its cables to the bow. The *Empress*'s mates unhooked the mooring lines. Robinson leafed through the passenger manifest, reviewed the sailing schedule, and conferred with his engineers about the ship's troublesome steam turbine engines. Plagued by excessive fuel consumption, the ship had managed a disappointing top speed of sixteen knots on her last trans-Pacific journey. That was two knots per hour slower than the top speed achieved by the other White Empresses and a cause for concern about the liner's commercial viability.

The *Empress* had one more stop to make, at the northern Japanese port of Shimizu, to pick up a shipment of tea before beginning its journey across the Pacific. Champagne corks popped. Wads of red, white, and blue confetti filled the air. A straggler, a man in a bowler hat, hustled down the Canadian Pacific gangplank. Crew members raised the gangplank and locked it back into place. The ship's whistle blew three long, resonant notes. People on board and on the pier waved white handkerchiefs for a last farewell. "The weather had cleared, and it was as pretty a scene as you can imagine," recalled Eva Downes, a vacationing student nurse in her twenties from Peking Union Medical College. Downes had arrived from her room at the Young Women's Christian Association on the Bluff with a colleague, Mrs. Macmillan, to bid farewell to a friend. Although it was a sunny morning, both Downes and Macmillan had, at the last minute, decided to slip on thick raincoats, a decision for which they would soon be thankful. The clock on the Customs Quay read 11:58 A.M.

4

The Catfish and the Keystone

The land itself is a land of impermanence. Rivers shift their courses; coasts their outline, plains their level; volcanic peaks heighten or crumble, valleys are blocked by lava-floods or landslides; lakes appear and disappear. . . . Only the general outlines of the land, the general aspects of nature, the general lines of the seasons, remain fixed.

Lafcadio Hearn, *Kokoro* (1896)

UNTIL THE EMPEROR MEIJI dragged Japan into the modern age in the late nineteenth century, most Japanese believed that their archipelago rested on the back of a temperamental creature whose tantrums resulted in convulsions of the earth. Some said that it was a whale; others believed that it was a dragon, a snake, or a spider. The most commonly accepted version of the myth held that Japan perched on a giant catfish. The all-powerful Shinto god of the earth, Kashima, usually restrained the bewhiskered behemoth, pinning his head with a dagger-like slab of rock called the *kaname-ishi*, or keystone. But when the god relaxed his guard, or left the keystone in the hands of an unreliable caretaker, the animal thrashed about in anger, and an earthquake was the consequence.

Great catfish thrashings punctuate Japanese history. The earliest documented earthquake in Japan occurred in A.D. 416, when the Imperial Palace at Kyoto was thrown to the ground. In the year 599 a

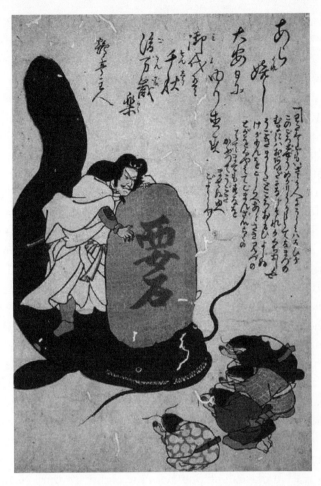

*Ancient Japanese mythology contended that Japan rested on a giant
catfish, and if the Shinto god of the earth, Kashima, was not vigilant,
the catfish would stir, creating the island's frequent earthquakes.*

temblor destroyed buildings throughout the province of Yamato,
now Nara Prefecture, and thousands of survivors offered prayers to
Kashima to stave off further destruction. In 1703, a great earthquake
lay waste to Edo, collapsed the Tokugawa shogun's castle, hurled
giant waves along the coast of Honshu Island, and killed or injured
two hundred thousand people. In 1822, Edo experienced 150 shocks
over three days, and six years later thirty thousand people died in a
temblor that destroyed the city of Echigo, near Osaka. Interspersed

with earthquakes were terrifying volcanic eruptions: the 1627 explosion of Mount Fuji rained black ash for four days on Edo; eighty years later, in November 1707, Fuji let loose a fifteen-day torrent of "hail, great fireballs, smoke, thunder, and lightning," according to one survivor, that destroyed much of the surrounding countryside. Earthquakes followed, and a second crater, Hoeizan, ripped open on the volcano's upper flank. According to the great Japanese seismologist Fusakichi Omori, no fewer than 222 destructive earthquakes struck the Japanese archipelago between the beginning of the fifth century and the beginning of the twentieth century, the vast majority of them originating off the southeast coast of Honshu, Japan's largest island.

The shrine to Kashima is tucked away on the eastern shore of Honshu, in Ibaraki Prefecture, in an area reputed to be immune to earthquakes because of its deep layer of vibration-resistant bedrock. For centuries earthquake survivors have trekked to the shrine on pilgrimages. The eleventh-century Japanese epic *The Tale of Genji* celebrates the Kashima shrine, and archaeologists have dug up shards of ceremonial pottery there that date back fifteen hundred years. Down a path through a forest of birch and pine, in the shadow of a temple that the first Tokugawa shogun built to celebrate his victory in 1602 over rival warlords—the victory that unified Japan—a round gray rock, a foot in diameter, protrudes a few inches from the ground. According to myth, the visible part of the stone is the tip of a sacred shaft, the kaname-ishi, that burrows underneath Japan, holding the catfish's head in place. The poetry of the eighth-century Nara period anointed this rock "the secret place of God."

On November 2, 1855, a powerful shock, the Ansei earthquake, struck the feudal capital, Edo, at ten o'clock at night. The temblor crushed people beneath the heavy tiles of their wooden homes while they slept; fires swept through the alleys of the densely populated city. At least fifteen thousand people died in what was to that date the worst earthquake ever to strike the capital. "Yedo was turned into a rubbish heap, and fire broke out simultaneously in thirty different places," wrote J. J. Rein, a German scientist who interviewed scores of eyewitnesses. "It was light as by day, and black clouds of smoke covered the whole sky. Those of the inhabitants who had not previously thought of saving themselves, perished under beams and ruins; others fell a prey to the flames." In the temblor's aftermath thousands of residents of Edo traveled by boat and on foot to pray at the Kashima shrine for deliverance from future calamities. Artists sold the pilgrims *namazu-e*, fantastic drawings that depicted the epic struggle between god and fish. The anonymous draftsmen conjured up more than two hundred variations on the theme, half-comic, half-tragic representations that were meant as solace to traumatized survivors. The most popular among them sold ten thousand copies.

In one picture Kashima soars over the flattened landscape of Edo, surveying crushed corpses and terrified refugees; a foaming tsunami surges toward the shore. "While I was absent, this catfish caused this problem. I will not forgive him," the deity says. "Now I am back, so be at ease. I won't let the catfish do this kind of terrible thing again." Another image shows the catfish sitting humbly at the feet of the furious, long-haired deity. "I'm going to tear you apart," says the god. The catfish begs for forgiveness: "Sorry, this November it was very hot, and I just couldn't control myself, and I appeared from the ground and caused this mess." A third picture, entitled "What a Lucky Day," portrays the stern god, wearing a formal kimono, perched atop the thrashing catfish and holding the keystone on top of his head. "Since the eel became more popular than me [in restaurants] I made this mistake," says the catfish, "but from now on I'll bury myself under the sand and I will not move again. So please forgive me." One drawing in the series offers a thinly veiled political commentary on the major controversy of the period, the opening of Japan to the "hairy barbarians" in July 1854. The giant catfish, bearing an unmistakable resemblance to one of Commodore Matthew Perry's Black Ships, swims menacingly into Tokyo Bay before a crowd of curious onlookers. The seismic sea monster, the artist implies, represents divine retribution for the Tokugawa shogun's widely debated decision to let the foreigners into Japan the previous year.

(Eleven months before the Ansei disaster, an earthquake and tsunami had wiped out the Izu peninsula port of Shimoda, which the shogunate had just designated as the headquarters of the first U.S. consul to Japan. The catastrophe lent credence to the notion that the gods, or *kami,* were displeased by the foreigners' intrusion. "Every house and building on the low grounds were destroyed; a few temples and edifices on elevations above escaped," Commander H. A. Adams wrote during a visit to the port a few weeks later, the first time that Americans had observed the aftermath of a Japanese seismic disaster. "The water, violently agitated . . . began retreating fast, leaving the bottom of the harbor nearly bare, where there was usually five or six fathoms of water. After this it returned in a huge wave, overflowing the beach and town up to the tops of the houses, the inabitants fleeing to the hills for safety. Numbers were overtaken by the wave and drowned, the accounts varying from 100 to 400.")

At the time of the Ansei calamity, Western scientists knew nearly as little about the causes of earthquakes as the peasants of Edo did. They attributed the quakes to electric currents deep inside the earth that set off explosions of gases; spontaneous combustion of sulfur and bitumen; movements of magma; or vapors generated by water reacting with quicklime and iron pyrites. They had no understanding of the reasons the Japanese islands were more susceptible to earthquakes than any other region in the world. (Modern scientists say that Japan generates 15 percent of the world's earthquake energy; Chile is second with 12 percent.) But in the late nineteenth century the first practitioners of a new science, seismology, began gathering empirical data about subterrestrial forces. Their primary field laboratory was Japan. One of the founders of the science was a British engineer, John Milne, hired in 1876 as a professor of mining and geology by Tokyo's Imperial College of Engineering, later to become Tokyo Imperial University. Milne was one of the many young scientists whom the Emperor Meiji had lured from Europe—Milne was offered twice his British salary—to lift Japan out of its feudal torpor. A minor earthquake disrupted Milne's sleep on his first night in Japan, sparking a fascination for temblors that came to define his life's work.

A man of unflagging energy and intellectual curiosity, Milne wanted to demystify the phenomenon and find ways for the Japanese to live more securely in their unstable environment, perhaps even develop a means of predicting earthquakes. "What the public imagine they would like to know about an earthquake is the time at which it might occur," he wrote. "If this could be stated, and at the same time something about the character of the expected disturbance in earth-quake districts, seismology would be liberally supported." In 1883, in collaboration with another Tokyo Imperial University seismologist lured from England, John Gray, he developed the world's first seismograph. Working on a pendulum principle, the Gray-Milne apparatus consisted of three needles that recorded east-west, north-south, and vertical earth movements on a revolving drum. Milne replicated seismic waves by blowing up dynamite in mine shafts and dropping eighteen-hundred-pound metal and concrete balls from varying heights. He designed Japanese-style buildings that "floated" on their masonry walls to allow flexibility in the event of a seismic shock. (The approach, known as a "waiter's tray" and adapted by Frank Lloyd Wright at the cantilevered Imperial Hotel, has since been rejected by mainstream seismic design.) He became fascinated by the apparent ability of animals to detect earthquakes hours, sometimes days before they happened. Frogs often stop croaking, he noted; geese, swine, and dogs display uneasiness; "pheasants scream" and moles "show their agitation by burrowing." Milne gathered evidence suggesting that the slippage of geological faults, offsets of rock lying both on the surface and below the earth, was the primary cause of earthquakes, not, as most scientists believed at the time, the explosion of subterranean gases. The larger geological forces that cause pressure to build up and the fault slippage to take place, however, remained a mystery.

One clue about those hidden forces emerged in 1874, with the discovery of a huge underwater trench, or deep, running from the Aleutian Islands of Alaska to the Tropic of Cancer and passing just a few dozen miles east of the Japanese seacoast. The U.S. Navy vessel *Tuscarora* had located the trough during an expedition to sound the ocean depths for the purpose of laying a telegraph cable between the United States and Japan. The technological breakthrough would have been impossible only a year or two earlier. In the two decades since undersea cables were first laid, efforts to take accurate soundings in deep ocean water—dropping a measured line through the depths until it hit bottom—had been bedeviled by unsophisticated technology and powerful hydrological forces. "Perhaps no problem ever presented itself to seamen which so long awaited satisfactory solution as that of deep-sea sounding," wrote the *Tuscarora*'s captain, George E.

Belknap. "The great difficulty of sounding in 'blue water' arose from the fact that, as the plummet descended, the weight of the line and . . . friction and action of submarine currents increased to such an extent that the line would continue to run off from the reel after the bottom was reached simply from its own weight; the moment of touch could not be told, and the wildest results were reported." In the 1850s one Captain Denham of the Royal Navy reported finding a depth of forty-six thousand feet, or more than eight miles, in the South Atlantic. A few years later, off the coast of Brazil, Lieutenant Parker of the U.S. Frigate *Congress* ran out fifty thousand feet of twine without, as he thought, touching the sea floor. The equipment presented another problem: When soaked with water, the twine became so heavy that it often broke in hauling back, destroying dozens of hours of work. Sounding engineers had experimented over the years with materials of various textures and strengths—"rope, cod-line, spun-yarn, fine silk lines and strong waxed twine"—all to no avail.

Then in 1872, the British telegraphic pioneer Sir Walter Thomson invented a "wire spooling machine" equipped with a delicate resistance mechanism that braked the reel at the moment the weight reached the ocean floor. Thomson perfected the device in early 1873 and sold it to the U.S. Navy, which fitted it with six nautical miles of Birmingham gauge no. 22 piano wire and placed it aboard the *Tuscarora*. The vessel set sail from Cape Flattery in Puget Sound that September. "[The cable] was wound on an iron reel, fitted with brakes, or friction-bands, for its better control in working, and swivels were fitted next to the sinker and at every thousand fathoms, to counteract the tendency to twist," Belknap wrote. Sounding the Pacific between San Diego and Hawaii in early 1874, the captain observed that "the Thomson machine was as sensitively perfect at three thousand and fifty fathoms [18,300 feet, or three and a half miles] as it had been at lesser depths, and whether sounding at night or by day the results were equally accurate and indisputable."

Departing Yokohama on July 9, 1874, the ship traveled north toward the Aleutian Islands. As they sailed into the Pacific, the *Tuscarora*'s crew recorded a precipitous drop of two thousand fathoms, or twelve thousand feet, over the course of thirty miles. The vessel entered the Kuro Siwo, the black stream of Japan one hundred miles off the coast. There the cable snapped under the strain of the fierce ocean current, but not before detecting the deepest ocean floor ever sounded. "There was no more doubt of the true measurement of the depth at four thousand six hundred and fifty five fathoms, where the wire broke in hauling back," Belknap wrote, "than when a good specimen of yellowish mud, with sand and specks of lava, came up in the cup from three thousand three hundred and fifty six fathoms." They continued sailing north. Off the coast of Tanaga in the Aleutian Island chain, the *Tuscarora* crew sounded another extraordinary depth: 4,340 fathoms, more than five miles. The crew then doubled back and took further casts running southwest toward Japan, all of them revealing depths of more than four thousand fathoms. "These deep casts had been made under the most favorable conditions: light wind, smooth sea, and gentle swell; the wire had run straight down as though sounding in a pond or dropping a plummet into a well, and the indications of the [Thomson machine] were as wondrously perfect and unmistakable as ever," Belknap wrote. "Indeed, there could be no mistaking the instant of touch."

The *Tuscarora*'s findings were considered so remarkable that the scientific community immediately questioned their accuracy. "Several soundings exceeding four thousand fathoms were obtained by the 'Tuscarora' to the eastward side of the islands of Niphon [Honshu] and Yezo [Hokkaido], and another close to the most westerly of the Aleutian islands," reported John James Wild of the civilian scientific staff of the navy vessel SS *Challenger,* which had also been taking soundings in the Pacific. "But as it appears that no sample of the bottom was brought up, there is no evidence of the bottom being reached." The 1874 discovery, however, was soon validated by further scientific investigations, and the area became known as the Tuscarora Deep. Though scientists would not grasp its full significance for nearly a century, Belknap suggested that the deep trough running "under the Japan stream" could have something to do with the region's geological instability. "In view of the remarkable character of the ocean-bed in the entire region of the western North Pacific," he wrote in his 1879 account of the expedition, "a most complete and extended examination of that part of the Pacific basin would undoubtedly be of great advantage to hydrographic science."

* * *

AT THE TIME of the Great Kanto Earthquake seismologists disagreed bitterly about the relationship between the Tuscarora Deep and Japan's extraordinary seismic activity. In one camp stood the "heating and expansion" advocates: they theorized that seawater at the bottom of the trench periodically spilled through fissures in the earth's crust into the lava underneath. In this Jules Verne hypothesis, the reaction of the seawater and molten material created gas and steam, which expanded or exploded internally, generating great convulsions of the earth. "It is not necessary . . . that there should be any definite crack in the ocean floor for water to get through to the hot lava underneath, cause steam, make pressure and necessitate adjustments in the earth's crust, perceived by mankind as earthquakes," Thomas Jefferson Jackson See at Mare Island, California, opined in an interview with the Associated Press. "Most of the ocean floor [is] granite, permeable to water under the immense pressure set up at great depths by that fluid."

The opposing camp argued just as strenuously that the Japanese islands and the ocean trench corresponded to folds in the earth caused by cooling and contraction. As the contraction continued, the theory posited, the ocean trench became narrower and deeper, while the islands rose ever higher. The archipelago was "slowly tilting toward the West," according to Henry S. Washington, chief meteorologist of the Carnegie Institution. "This wrinkling movement is still in progress in the Japanese area," Washington declared. "Harbors [are becoming] shallow, posts at which fishermen formerly tied their boats [are] now hundreds of yards inland." This geological wrinkling supposedly built up great stress that found violent release by slippage along surface or subterranean faults. At some point, the fault would slip and spring back violently, triggering a tremendous release of energy. Although the seismologists' understanding of the root causes of earthquakes was flawed, they fully grasped the mechanisms of destruction. Edgar W. Woolard, director of the U.S. Division of Seismological Investigations, provided a lucid description of the process in a 1923 essay:

> The rocks are held by friction and pressure under increasing strain, until they yield; slipping suddenly, like a spring, they com-

municate an elastic shock or jar to the crust of the earth, and vibrations spread out in all directions with velocities of several miles per second. The slip usually takes place at a depth of one or more miles beneath the surface, but in many cases the break continues right up to the surface; the vibratory motions, together with the sudden displacements of the ground—often amounting to 10 or 20 feet or more, vertically or horizontally or both—cause general destruction over a wide area. Alarming sounds issue from the bowels of the earth; and if the quake occurs near or underneath the ocean, it is followed by a series of great sea-waves (popularly misnamed "tidal waves") called tsunamis by the Japanese.

Fusakichi Omori, Milne's protégé and his successor as chairman of the Tokyo Imperial University Seismology Department, and his colleagues, including his chief assistant, Akitsune Imamura, suspected a link between Japan's ocean trench and other seismically active regions around the globe. "Destructive earthquakes do not take place at random, but originate along weak lines in the earth's crust which may be termed earthquake zones," Omori wrote several years before the 1923 catastrophe. "The most active Pacific zone runs off or along the coast of South and North America, and off the Aleutian and Japan arcs. In the south-western part of the Pacific remarkably deep local basins are found off the arc formed by the islands of New Guinea, New Caledonia and New Zealand, it being exactly there that great earthquakes originate." Imamura identified two distinct earthquake zones running beneath Japan and cited them as the cause of Japan's unrivaled seismic instability. These early seismologists, however, remained mystified about what these "weak lines" signified.

It would not be until World War II, more than two decades after the Great Kanto Earthquake, that researchers would unlock the secret of the ocean trenches. Seeking hiding places for allied submarine fleets, a team of British and U.S. geologists and oceanographers employed newly developed sonar technology to carry out the most extensive mapping of the ocean floor that had ever been undertaken. The scientists verified what the crude soundings of the nineteenth century had suggested: a pattern of long, sinuous ridges in the middle of the Atlantic Ocean and the eastern part of the Pacific Ocean and deep trenches running along the margins of continents, particularly surrounding the Pacific. These troughs, as Omori and others had already shown, were invariably areas of intense seismic activity. Based on the data he collected from these surveys, Professor Harry Hess of Princeton University published a postwar article called "An Essay in Geopoetry" in which he set forth a revolutionary hypothesis: The sea floor is spreading and its movement generates earthquakes.

Half a century earlier the German scientist Alfred Wegner, intrigued by the jigsaw puzzle–like appearance of the Atlantic continental margins, had advanced the theory of continental drift. Widely ridiculed at the time, Wegner argued that until 200 million years ago all of the continents had been joined together in one giant land mass that he called Pangaea. The supercontinent had broken apart, he argued, and has been steadily moving ever since. Hess refined and expanded Wegner's hypothesis, which focused entirely on shifting land masses and ignored the activity of the ocean floor. The sea bed, Hess maintained, is not static, but in a constant state of drift and regeneration. Liquid magma wells up from the earth's mantle on both sides of the midoceanic ridges, cooling and creating new sea floor. The sea floor is then carried in a "conveyor belt fashion" away from the ridges toward the trenches at the speed, he calculated, of two or three inches a year.

An English graduate student, Fred Vine, and his supervisor, D. H. Matthews, provided strong supporting evidence for Hess's theory in 1963. They based their findings on data collected from magnetometers, sensitive, compass-like devices that the U.S. Navy had utilized during World War II to search for enemy submarines. Researchers towing magnetometers over the North Atlantic sea floor had made an intriguing discovery: they detected magnetic particles of equal size and varying polarity running in mirror images to each other along both sides of the midocean ridge. Vine and Matthews were the first to link these findings with Hess's spreading sea-floor hypothesis. Scientists had long known that the earth's magnetic poles had periodically reversed over the eons, and that rocks solidifying during a period of "reverse" polarity would be magnetized accordingly; that is, their magnetic particles would point toward the south. The mirror-image variations in magnetic particles picked up by the magnetometers proved that new floor was constantly being created. As magma poured out of the ocean ridges and cooled, particles froze into place toward wherever the earth's pole happened to be at the exact moment of their creation.

The geologists synthesized their discoveries into a landmark theory: plate tectonics. The outermost layer of the earth, they hypothesized, consists of large slabs of solid rock called plates, each of which extends to a depth of fifty to 120 miles. Each plate moves horizontally, conveyor belt style, sliding along softer rock immediately below it. The boundaries of plates mark areas of the greatest geological instability: the areas where the vast majority of the world's earthquakes and volcanic eruptions occur.

The theory of plate tectonics, which gained rapid acceptance in the geological community, for the first time drew a clear connection between the deep troughs in the ocean floor and seismic activity. The troughs occur where the cooler, denser oceanic plate sinks, or "subducts," beneath the continental plate. As the oceanic plate begins its descent into the earth's mantle, it edges downward at roughly a forty-five-degree angle, to a point four hundred miles below the surface of the earth. There it breaks apart, melts, and transforms back into magma, completing the geological cycle. Stress builds up as the two giant masses, the ocean plate and continental plate, press against each other, with the ocean plate dragging the continental plate down and away from the trench. At some point the ocean plate slips suddenly beneath the continental plate, which rebounds upward and toward the trench with unimaginable force. In the most dramatic example of the past half-century, the sharp upward thrust of the Asian plate against the subducting Indian Ocean plate on December 26, 2004, set off an earthquake measuring a gigantic 9.0 on the Richter Scale, the equivalent of a bomb made of 32 billion tons of TNT. In one cataclysmic lurch, the ocean floor off Sumatra rebounded thirty feet back toward India. The upward rebound of that sea floor created a tsunami that radiated out from the epicenter across the Pacific Ocean at six hundred miles per hour, swamping thousands of miles of seacoast and killing a quarter of a million people.

Nearly a century after the discovery of the Tuscarora Deep, scientists had at last formulated a theory that explained Japan's unique seismic convulsions. Three geological plates, and possibly several more,

Akitsune Imamura, a University of Tokyo seismologist,
accurately predicted the timing and severity of the quake
years in advance, but was repudiated by his superior.

converge directly beneath the archipelago. The Pacific Ocean plate, the Philippine Sea plate, and the Eurasian continental plate are constantly pressing and straining against one another, placing enough stress on the islands to keep them in a constant state of instability. When the pressure finally exceeds the strength of the interface between the plates, which happens somewhere in Japan once every decade or so, it is released suddenly: a massive shift takes place along one of these geological fault lines, directly beneath Japan, with terrifying force.

THE MAN WHO came to understand better than anyone else the dangers posed to Yokohama and Tokyo had never heard of plate tectonics, but his visionary thinking about earthquakes anticipated many discoveries made decades later. Akitsune Imamura was born in Kagoshima, a pottery manufacturing center on the southern tip of Kyushu, in 1870, two years after the Meiji Restoration, at a time when Japan was just emerging from centuries of superstition and feudalism. The son of a trader whose business went bankrupt when Imamura was a small boy, he grew up in poverty: He and his family, he told his biographers, subsisted for years almost exclusively on a diet of rice, miso soup, and *okara*, white, tasteless soybean chaff that remains behind during the tofu-making process.

As a boy, Imamura lived in the shadow of seismic disaster. Two miles east of Kagoshima, Mount Sakurajima, an active volcano shaped much like Italy's Mount Vesuvius, rose 3,506 feet on an island in Kagoshima Bay. The stench of sulfur swept over Kagoshima, and frequent predictions of a new eruption kept the population on edge. Though he doesn't mention the volcano in his writings, Imamura almost certainly hiked up to the steaming crater many times in his youth and must have thrilled to the stories of past explosions known to every resident of the city. "It was so dark that it seemed as though powdered ink filled the air; thunder and quakings came together and the whole world was noise," one feudal-era Japanese eyewitness reported. Another chronicler wrote of the Sakurajima eruption of 1779, "Light stones were blown out from burning holes on the mountain; they fell in the water and would not sink, making the sea look as though covered with matting." (The volcano would explode again, catastrophically, in January 1914, long after Imamura moved away from his hometown. For three days "cauliflower-like" fountains of fire, according to one eyewitness, burst two miles into the air, and pumice and ash rained down on Kagoshima; thirty-five people died, tens of thousands fled the city, and twenty-five hundred houses were destroyed.) Fascinated by the natural sciences, fiercely ambitious, and eager to escape from the poverty of his childhood, Imamura won a coveted scholarship to study physics at the College of Science at Tokyo Imperial University in 1888.

Physics soon fell by the wayside. On October 28, 1891, the greatest inland earthquake in Japan in recorded history ripped through the provinces of Mino and Owari, two hundred miles west of Tokyo. The shock waves destroyed 140,000 houses, killed seven thousand people, and set loose ten thousand landslides. Immediately after the disaster, the university dispatched a team of science students, including twenty-one-year-old Imamura, and Fusakichi Omori, two years Imamura's senior, to gather data from the scene. Traveling across Mino and Owari Prefectures, Imamura observed up close the fissure-ridden landscape, the smashed houses, the death and destruction that the temblor had caused. "It was shocking to see it," he told one biographer. At that point, he said, seismology stopped being theoretical and became something real, with dire consequences for human beings. He decided on the spot to devote his life to earthquake research.

Imamura entered the graduate studies program in earthquake science at Tokyo Imperial University in 1893, the first year of the department's existence. At that moment, seismology was in its infancy; the vast majority of the Japanese people still believed that mythological creatures and angry gods caused earthquakes. Imamura was part of an optimistic new generation of Japanese scientists, trained by Western experts, who cast off the ancient myths that had imprisoned their ancestors and prided themselves on their ability to think rationally. They approached earthquakes and other seismological events not as acts of God but as problems that demanded a solution. They were convinced that, if they put their minds to the challenge, they could not only understand the causes of earthquakes and tsunamis but also develop the expertise to predict them with reasonable accuracy, much like meteorologists forecast the weather. The primary vehicle for their efforts was the Imperial Earthquake Investigation Committee, founded by the Emperor Meiji in 1892, just after the Mino-Owari disaster. Chaired by Fusakichi Omori, the committee set about searching for a "predictive model" for earthquakes, a search that took on greater urgency for them in August 1896, when an earthquake beneath the Pacific Ocean floor sent an eighty-foot-high wall of water crashing against the coast of Honshu Island. The Sanriku tsunami, as it became known, swamped dozens of villages, destroyed seventy-five thousand homes, and drowned twenty-four thousand people, nearly as many as those who had died in the tsunami caused by the eruption of Krakatoa volcano in 1883.

The committee looked at a range of factors that might presage a seismological disaster. These included variations in the tilt of the earth, fluctuations in terrestrial magnetism, and sudden rises in underground temperatures. Imamura, who played an increasingly active role in the investigations, spent hundreds of hours both in the field and in his laboratory, charting geographical patterns in past seismic activity. He tried to identify abrupt changes in topography—including rock up-heavals, rock subsidences, and alterations in springwater flow—that signaled that an earthquake was coming. He sought links between the timing of temblors and the timing of volcanic eruptions.

In 1901, at age thirty-one, Imamura became an associate professor in Tokyo Imperial University's tiny Seismology Department, then under the chairmanship of thirty-three-year-old Fusakichi Omori. The relationship between the two young scientists was a difficult one. Imamura felt that Omori treated him like an errand boy during the research field trip they had taken together to the Mino-Owari earth-quake zone when both were physics students at the university. He considered himself as talented a scientist as Omori and loathed the idea of working beneath him. Compounding his resentment, Omori refused to pay Imamura a salary, a common arrangement for associate professors, forcing Imamura to support his large family by teaching mathematics at a military school. Imamura, an outspoken, sometimes abrasive figure whom some colleagues considered too straightforward for his own good, didn't hide his displeasure at the arrangement.

Then came professional disaster. In January 1907 readers of a pop-ular newspaper in the capital, the *Tokyo Nichiroku Shimbun*, woke up to a front-page profile of Imamura in which he predicted that a "great earthquake" would soon destroy the city and the neighboring port of Yokohama. The story had originated as an article Imamura had written for an obscure scientific journal the previous August; the Tokyo paper's editors had seized on the most sensational aspects of the piece and, without Imamura's permission, trumpeted them below the lurid headline "Imamura Says Tokyo Will Be Destroyed." Basing his prediction on patterns of seismic activity over thousands of years, Imamura had even identified the probable epicenter of the next major earthquake: Sagami Bay, a curving sweep of warm water, rich in ma-rine life, that lay twenty-five miles southwest of the capital and seven miles southwest of Yokohama. A large seismic upheaval along the fault line that lay beneath the bay, Imamura maintained, would topple thousands of buildings and ignite a conflagration. It would hurl giant waves against the Sagami Bay coast, including the ancient capital, Kamakura, and a string of popular hot springs resorts, such as Atami and Ito. The worst damage was likely to be suffered by Yokohama. The soft alluvium on which the port had been built made it especially vulnerable to earthquakes and all but guaranteed the city's destruction in the event of a major temblor. Imamura warned that the earthquake and subsequent fires would kill "between one hundred thousand and two hundred thousand people."

The article hit Tokyo with the force of a tsunami. Imamura's superior and ostensible nemesis, the brilliant, imperious chairman of the department, Omori—by then a Nobel prize nominee praised by one American seismologist as "the foremost living authority on these terrifying manifestations of Nature"—accosted his subordinate on the campus and, in front of his students, berated Imamura for his "act of foolishness." Accusing his underling of gratuitously frightening the populace, he ordered him to stop talking to the press. Weeks later Omori rushed out his own article, dismissing Imamura's prediction as a "trifle" and assuring Tokyo's jittery residents that, according to Omori's meticulous research, a major earthquake wouldn't strike the city for another three hundred years. The incident proved so harmful to Imamura's reputation that his own father admitted he felt ashamed of him. "At the time when I published my prediction I was the butt of scathing criticism and jeers and derision," Imamura recalled in an interview years later. "The Department of Education ordered me to recant, on the ground that it frightened the citizens. I would not give in and went on fighting, but things grew so hard that I was weak enough to be silenced."

For many years afterward, the incident haunted him, filled him with bitterness, and infected his relationships with his superiors at Tokyo Imperial University, government officials, even his wife. Lying awake at night in his small bedroom in his modest home in Tokyo, he would close his eyes and relive the painful episode over and over. Had he made a mistake by going public with his convictions? Would it have been better to remain silent? He believed that saying nothing would have been an inexcusable abdication of responsibility. Yet Imamura's public dressing-down had been "the biggest shame that I ever received," he said. "It damaged my dignity as a scholar." Although they continued to work together in the Seismology Department, attended many of the same scientific conferences, and even collaborated on articles and studies, he and Omori barely spoke to each other.

TRAGEDIES PURSUED IMAMURA over the next few years. In 1908, the year his second daughter was born, his first daughter fell down a flight of stairs while playing hide-and-seek with her older brother, broke her neck, and died. Two more of Imamura's eight children, his first son and his second daughter, died within the next two years. Imamura escaped from his grief in his work. He drew detailed maps of Tokyo, Osaka, and other Japanese cities and plotted the effects of hypothetical earthquakes on the underlying geological material and the buildings above it. He identified two main "earthquake belts" running through the archipelago, which, though he knew nothing of plate tectonics, roughly corresponded to the collision points of the Eurasian plate with the Pacific plate and with the Philippine plate.

He also became one of the country's leading advocates of earthquake preparedness. If the Japanese had the misfortune to live on top of the most unstable land mass on the planet, Imamura reasoned, then he was going to do all he could to ensure that they were prepared for the worst. He advised the Japanese to build the supporting pillars of their houses out of pine, because the wood was denser than cypress and cedar and thus less prone to seismic vibrations. He recommended covering roofs with lightweight sheet metal, asbestos shingles, or natural slate rather than thick and heavy tiles, which could become fatal missiles if shaken down. He urged the government to toughen its zoning laws, keeping out of residential areas apothecaries, photography labs, and other establishments that stored large stocks of combustible chemicals such as yellow phosphorus, which catches fire upon contact with air, or sodium and potassium, both of which ignite when exposed to water. "Should inflammable liquids, such as alcohol, ether, and benzene, be kept near them, an instantaneous large fire is likely to be the result," he warned.

A photograph taken of Imamura from the late 1910s shows a beanpole figure with thinning hair and a drooping black mustache, towering over family members at a gathering in Kagoshima. Clad in a high-collared black suit, he bears a severe, even haunted expression, as if consumed by visions of impending apocalypse. Fiercely driven, he filled hundreds of notebooks with his scribblings, ceaselessly jotting down logarithmic formulas, densities of various types of woods, suggestions for safeguarding homes and offices, data from the dozens of volcanic eruptions that he witnessed across Japan. He was, it seemed to his friends and colleagues, incapable of letting go of his obsessions; on one occasion, when his wife begged him to take a week off and visit a hot spring resort with her, he pulled out a map of Japan, pointed to the resort, and told her to close her eyes and imagine that she was soaking in the warm mineral baths. "That should do it," he said. Yet at the same time, he could display a warmer and more sensitive side. He was capable of acts of generosity; he was known for taking science students from Kagoshima under his wing, and even developed a dictionary for these denizens of distant Kyushu to help them master the Tokyo dialect. His children and grandchildren adored him; his self-deprecating sense of humor endeared him to colleagues. He attributed his baldness to his "sweating profusely" underneath his hat while climbing up volcanic slopes in the broiling summer sun, his "sharp eyes" to a career spent "reading the squiggly lines" on seismographic wave charts.

Imamura's concerns about a forthcoming cataclysm tormented him. Everything about the capital, from its dense sea of wooden houses to its unpredictable winds, from its fragile water mains to its undermanned fire department, made it likely, he believed, that fires would burn out of control in the event of a large earthquake. The city, as the seismologist was well aware, had a long history of calamitous fires; during the feudal era conflagrations had occurred with such frequency and created spectacles of such fearsome beauty that they had gotten the nickname "The Flowers of Edo."

In Imamura's era, Tokyo authorities had made substantial firefighting progress: they had installed fire stations in all of the capital's thirteen wards, imported steam fire engines, connected hundreds of hydrants to the aqueduct, and ordered every household to install a fire extinguisher. But, in Imamura's view, the city remained a tinderbox. Narrow alleys lined with two- and three-story wooden houses pro-

vided ideal conditions for updrafts. Chemical works, petroleum de-
pots, and factories often stood in the middle of residential neighborhoods. The capital lacked basic equipment for pumping water out of
canals, moats, rivers, and the bay in the event of a collapse of its water
mains. The fire department consisted of eight hundred men, compared with five thousand in New York City. Statistics compiled by the
police provided an indication of how easily the city could be set alight.
A Tokyo police blotter from 1909 listed 139 major fires between October and December of that year: "6 incendiarisms, 3 lightning, 15
chimneys, 38 lamps, 6 *kotatsu* [quilt warmers], 12 hibachi [charcoal
fire boxes], 9 embers in ashes, 8 candles, 11 burning fires for warm-
ing, 3 rushlights, 4 fireplaces, 2 matches, 2 explosives, 6 cigar ends,
7 cinders of charcoal, 1 fire extinguishing pot, 2 portable cooking
stoves, 2 fireworks, 1 gas light and 1 wire of electric light."

Imamura's own statistics were just as frightening. Based on his study
of the 1891 Mino-Owari disaster, he concluded that the average loss
of life in an earthquake amounted to one person for every eleven
houses that collapsed. But the number of dead "grew dramatically"
whenever fire broke out, to one death for every three houses burned.
The recent San Francisco earthquake, which many survivors referred to
as "the Conflagration of 1906," provided a textbook case of the dangers from fire. "Owing to breakage of the mains conducting the water
supply to the city," Imamura wrote in an analysis of the disaster, "and
to breaks in the distribution main in the city itself, the fire continued
unsubdued for four days until an area equal to nearly four square miles,
including the business section and the older residential quarters, had
been wiped out." San Francisco invested hundreds of millions of dollars in a water system for firefighting, built between 1909 and 1913,
that city officials believed to be earthquake-proof. The system included
three reservoirs with a total capacity of 11.5 million gallons of water,
two pumping stations built on firm rocky ground, 143 underground
fire cisterns, each containing up to seventy-five thousand gallons of
water, and fire hydrants on every block in the urban area. Compared
to San Francisco, Imamura knew, Tokyo and Yokohama remained
woefully unprepared. "The fire departments of large [Japanese] cities
rely entirely upon the city mains for their water supply, and thus in the

event of a breakage in the mains, they are helpless," Imamura wrote, "while the efficiency of the citizens as fire-fighters is practically nil."

On February 20, 1913, a blaze broke out in a Salvation Army hall in the Kanda district of central Tokyo, a neighborhood north of the Imperial Palace, packed with secondhand book shops and publishers' warehouses. High winds fanned a rain of sparks onto adjacent buildings. Within thirty minutes, according to a newspaper report, the neighborhood became "a sea of fire." The flames turned book shops, schools, movie halls, hotels, and big stores to ashes. Three hundred soldiers from the First Division of the Imperial Guards came out to help the fire brigades. By the time they put the fire out at 7:40 A.M. it had burned to the ground an area one mile long by one-half mile wide. Fifteen hundred houses had been destroyed, ten thousand people had been left homeless, and several had burned to death. It was the worst fire to hit Tokyo since the conflagration that followed the 1855 earthquake—and a sobering reminder of the capital's vulnerability.

IN MID-AUGUST 1923, during the sultry height of the Tokyo summer, Fusakichi Omori traveled to Melbourne, Australia, for the Pan-Pacific Scientific Conference, a month-long symposium sponsored by the Australian National Research Council, bringing together the leading geologists, biologists, and physicists from across the region. He sailed from Yokohama filled with a sense of well-being, confident that both Tokyo and Yokohama had survived the worst that nature could deliver. On April 26, 1922, a severe earthquake had struck Tokyo and Yokohama at 10:11 in the morning, causing widespread damage. Based on his studies of historical patterns and his field research, Omori had believed for a decade that the fault zone underneath Sagami Bay and Tokyo Bay would "almost certainly" be the focal point of Japan's next significant earthquake, but he insisted that Imamura's estimate of between one hundred thousand and two hundred thousand deaths was wildly off the mark. To the great relief of Tokyo's citizens, Professor Omori had stated at a press conference at Tokyo Imperial University that the earthquake he had predicted had just taken place, and he guaranteed that the area would not experience another one like it in the foreseeable future.

The same week that Omori sailed for the conference in Australia, Imamura journeyed north by train and ferry to carry out field research at his own expense on the slopes of Mount Tarumai, one of Hokkaido's most terrifyingly active volcanos. (Still bearing the taint of his 1907 public embarrassment, the seismologist rarely received invitations to prestigious overseas gatherings; he had traveled outside the country only once in his career, to a conference in Rome the previous year.) Two huge eruptions, in 1667 and 1739, had blown off much of the volcano's cone, leaving a mile-wide caldera, or crater, on the summit. Roughly once every three years for the next two centuries, the volcano had gone off, spewing short bursts of hot pumice, a light, porous lava, which settled on the surrounding countryside. In recent months loud rumblings from deep inside Tarumai's magma chamber and belchings of ash and sulfur dioxide had led Imamura and his colleagues to believe that the biggest eruption in two centuries was coming. Tarumai's stirrings to life were consistent with an unusual amount of seismic activity around the globe during 1923, including the successive eruptions of Italy's Mount Etna and Mount Vesuvius. Along with many other seismologists, Imamura was curious about whether a hidden relationship existed among these eruptions, and he had rushed north to investigate the matter firsthand.

He was not disappointed. "With bare gray top and blasted forest on its sides," the travel writer Isabella L. Bird had observed in 1878, Mount Tarumai loomed over a landscape of "mountains within mountains . . . tumbled together in most picturesque confusion, densely covered with forest and cleft by magnificent ravines, here and there opening out into narrow valleys." Hot clouds of sulfur spewed from crevices on the volcano's flanks, and from deep within came mysterious noises—hisses of escaping vapor, the crashing of what sounded like thousands of tons of glass—that hinted at the powerful geological forces roiling beneath Japan. "One fissure was completely lined with exquisite, acicular crystals of sulphur, which perished with a touch," noted Bird. "Lower down there were two hot springs with a deposit of sulphur round their margins, and bubbles of gas, which, from its strong, garlicky smell, I suppose to be sulphuretted hydrogen." The journal from Imamura's trip gives a flavor of his hike on the steep slopes and around the jagged crater, 4,331 feet above sea level. "Beautiful day," he wrote on August 23. "I decided to climb the mountain again. I had a backpack, and Mr. Ito [his assistant] and I took lots of photographs. We met two young men, but I advised them not to go to the top of the volcano, because it might explode. But they would not listen to me. At 2:50 in the afternoon, as I expected, I saw another eruption, so I took photographs. I felt great!" Imamura and Ito watched in awe as plumes of smoke and ash shot several hundred feet into the sky. "But then I remembered—oh no, these two men are on the slopes near the crater," Imamura wrote. "I felt bad, but I had to go back down the mountain. At eight o'clock in the evening, these two young men returned to the inn, covered in blood. They had fled for their lives down the volcano after it spewed forth hot ash. 'If only you had told us you were Dr. Imamura, we wouldn't have climbed so far,' one told me."

Imamura, exhilarated, returned to the sweltering capital on August 31; the next morning he rose early and bicycled, as was his custom, from his home in the western Ichigaya quarter to his laboratory at Tokyo Imperial University, a distance of about three miles. He pedaled down wide avenues crisscrossed by telegraph and telephone wires and bordered by blue-gray tile-roofed, two-story wooden buildings. Tokyo in 1923 was "a great city that is a gigantic village," wrote Frank Lloyd Wright in a contemporary account, and a city in frantic transition. New concrete and stone government buildings, theaters, and department stores built by European and American architects loomed over ancient shrines and teetering teahouses. Trolley cars and imported automobiles shared the streets with "moving masses of sober-robed people, hand-carts, back-boxes and horses, picturesque strollers and heaving bullocks, innumerable gaily clad children . . . shuttered sedan chairs, scarlet and gold . . . slung to long back beams carried on the thick shoulders of stout naked legged coolies, two in the front, two in the rear." Imamura's route took him past the Imperial Palace in the heart of the capital. At Hongo Dori, the hilly, wide avenue beside the campus, he turned left, crossed the trolley tracks, and entered the university through the Red Gate, a wooden torii arch, more typically found before Shinto shrines. He pedaled along a series of paths shaded by leafy gingko trees to the yellow brick Department of Seismology. He climbed to the second floor, looking forward to a restful day in the office after his grueling excursion on the volcano's slopes.

Imamura sat behind his desk down the hall from the laboratory, where seismographic recording drums fed constant data of the fifteen hundred tremors per year that shake the Japanese archipelago. He sorted with satisfaction through a packet of snapshots from the volcanic ascent on Hokkaido. Sun streamed through open windows that looked over the serene campus, reminiscent of an Ivy League university in the United States. Verdant lawns glistened from the early morning rainfall. Founded by the Emperor Meiji in 1877 on the former estate of a feudal lord, the daimyo of Kanazawa, Tokyo Imperial University consisted of one hundred acres of promenades, ponds, and brick and granite buildings, many with graceful arches and Corinthian columns adorning their facades.

The college's Western ambience extended far beyond its architecture: university officials had hired scores of European and American professors of engineering, chemistry, physics, and other sciences, with the objective of turning out a home-grown generation of Japanese scientists and rapidly improving Japan's technological expertise. "To have lived through the transition stage of modern Japan makes a man feel preternaturally old," Basil Chamberlain wrote in his landmark study of Meiji Japan, *Things Japanese,* in 1907, "for here he is in modern times, with the air full of talk about bicycles and bacilli and 'spheres of influence,' and yet he can himself distinctly remember the Middle Ages." Only a few vestiges of the university's feudal origins remained. Its best-known landmark, the ornate Red Gate, or Akamon, was a relic from the Edo period, built for the twenty-first daughter of the eleventh Tokugawa shogun to celebrate her marriage to a member of the feudal lord's family. Fifty years after its creation at the dawn of the Meiji era, Tokyo Imperial University was Japan's proudest manifestation of the country's phenomenal progress, the fledgling Seismology Department one of its most dynamic new additions.

The Department of Seismology was housed in one of the most sturdily constructed buildings on the university campus. Thus, it perhaps took a fraction of a second longer for the dozen scientists, administrators, and secretaries working inside to sense what other residents of Tokyo and Yokohama were already experiencing. At 11:58, the building started to shake violently. Roof tiles crashed down into the laboratory. As panic took hold, Imamura took notes and studied his watch. After fifteen seconds, the seismologist and his colleagues began to feel a second phase of more intense vibrations coming from the northwest and southeast. For one split second, it seemed to those present that the maximum severity had passed and that the shaking would subside. Then the vibrations intensified, and many felt that they were aboard a ship in a storm, tossed about by colossal, angry waves.

5

Inferno

Jishin, kaminari, kaji, oyaji
[earthquake, thunderstorm, fire, and father].

Japanese proverb identifying the four major forces
of nature

SIX MILES BENEATH the floor of Sagami Bay, under thick layers of silt and sedimentary rock, the Philippine Sea plate begins a forty-five-degree descent toward the liquid mantle of the earth. As it strains silently against the softer and more malleable Eurasian continental plate, creeping, edging, sliding forward by two or three inches a year, the massive slabs gradually build up pressure, until the interface between the two plates can hold no longer. At that moment, an event that occurs roughly once a century in Japan, a portion of the ocean plate lunges forward, forcing up the continental plate and releasing a burst of destructive energy. It was precisely this scenario that occurred at two minutes before noon on September 1, 1923. A sixty-mile-long by sixty-mile-wide segment of the Philippine plate suddenly ruptured, fractured, and thrust itself forward and downward to a point thirty miles below Tokyo. If a witness could have observed the movement from on high, he would have watched the entire Miura Peninsula, east of Tokyo Bay, plus the Kanto Plain and the surrounding regions—the upper side of the plate interface—rear upward and southward by twenty feet over a period of sixty seconds. The lower side of the plate interface, Sagami Bay, slid simultaneously downward and to the north. The initial seismic vibrations—primary waves— raced from the fault zone on a diagonal path to the surface of the earth at a speed of eighteen thousand miles an hour. Behind them came slower and more destructive vibrations—shear waves—moving at roughly seventy-five hundred miles an hour. These vibrations traveled with a lateral motion, shaking the earth violently as they burrowed through the crust. A third and fourth set of vibrations—Rayleigh and Love waves—then shot directly up from the fault and followed the contours of the earth's surface. The waves shook the ground in rolling vertical and horizontal motions, similar to the action of ocean swells.

The first seismic waves reached Yokohama at thirty-four seconds past 11:58 A.M. At that moment Captain Ellis M. Zacharias was standing on Yokohama's pier with hundreds of other well-wishers, seeing off a friend on the *Empress of Australia*. "The smiles vanished, and for an appreciable instant everyone stood transfixed at the sound of unearthly thunder," he recalled years later, contradicting the accounts of others who said that the shock hit without any warning. The thunder "signaled to the paralyzed minds the catastrophe that was already engulfing them." A "tremendous jolt" knocked people off their feet, recalled Eva Downes, the student nurse. It felt, she recalled, as though the *Empress of Australia* had slammed head-on into the pier. Downes tried to stand. Then a series of hard bumps that lasted for between forty and sixty seconds—the estimates vary considerably from witness to witness—knocked her down again. "The huge pier became an undulating sea," wrote Zacharias, "with a strong lateral motion that made standing impossible. People scrambled to their feet only to be thrown down again. . . . It was as though one were riding inside the large wheel of a steam roller over the rockiest road."

A traveler aboard the British Blue Funnel Line's *Philoctetes,* moored inside the breakwater, reached for another metaphor. Reading in his cabin below deck, he was thrown off his bed by a series of jolts "similar to that experienced when one rides on an 'electric horse.' " He ran into the corridor, convinced that the boilers of the vessel were about to explode. "One of the Japanese winchmen, more experienced in these things, suggested it was an earthquake," he recalled. "There was no possibility of error."

On the hatoba Downes watched in horror as fissures opened in the asphalt, then snapped shut, swallowing three automobiles. A quarter-mile-long section nearest the shore collapsed. Rickshaws, cars, and human beings cascaded into the shallow water. Zacharias tried to leave the pier, but a second shock came with renewed force. He felt himself falling through space. Somehow, tumbling toward the water, he grabbed hold of a section of ladder. He clambered back to the top and leaped to a portion of the pier that still stood. "Another quake like that and there won't be a Yokohama," a man near him proclaimed, in what would prove to be, tragically, the understatement of the day.

On the bridge of the *Empress of Australia* Captain Robinson and his crew, knocked off their feet, lay on the floor. Robinson stood back up in time to watch the third set of vibrations, high-magnitude Rayleigh and Love waves, sweep across the Bund. He stared in stomach-churning fear as the land rolled in waves six to eight feet high like a succession of fast-moving ocean breakers. Dozens of people half-scrambled, half-waded to the shore over the collapsed pier, reduced to a tangle of iron railings and chunks of asphalt sunk in shallow water. Then a dense pall of dust rose hundreds of feet above the town and a terrible roar came from it, probably caused by the simultaneous falling of hundreds of brick and stone buildings in the Foreign Settlement. Moments later a fierce wind whipped up, blowing at gale strength from the city toward the harbor. Nearly every account of the earthquake in Yokohama mentions this windstorm that seemed to appear out of nowhere one minute after the first shock, apparently the front end of a typhoon that had swept in from the southwest by a malign coincidence. "For a moment it could be seen that the buildings on the Bund nearest to us had fallen," Robinson wrote, "then everything was blotted out by the dust which swept over us in a cloud so dense that for a time we were unable to see the foc'sle-head [forward section of the main deck] from the bridge." The *Philoctetes* passenger also watched the arrival of this sinister fog. One minute after the first seismic waves hit, he observed a thin yellow film rising from the ground. The film thickened rapidly into a cloud that enshrouded houses, docks, and the hills behind the city. Soon it formed a continuous strip around the bay, deepening in color to ochre, then dirty brown, and sweeping at rapid speed toward the harbor.

On the remnants of the hatoba, one minute after the earthquake, Eva Downes heard the crash of falling buildings and braced herself before the howling gale. Clouds of lime and dust made it hard to see or breathe. As soon as the initial vibrations subsided crew members of the *Empress of Australia* dangled a rope ladder from an upper deck and set off a scramble to board the ship. Some on the hatoba clambered aboard through portholes. Downes and her friend Mrs. Macmillan, waiting at the periphery of the scrum, were terrified that the rest of the pier would collapse at any second. Because the water was thirty feet deep where they stood, they decided to head for shore instead of waiting to board the boat. The women waded to the beach in water up to their waists. On the Bund, Downes and Macmillan conferred with half a dozen other survivors of the hatoba's collapse, trying to decide whether to venture further inland or turn back to the sea. Neither option seemed promising. They saw smoke rising from the city's wooden buildings, indicating they would soon be on fire.

IN THE SUNLIT LOUNGE of the Grand Hotel, at two minutes to noon, Ensign Tommy Ryan was conversing with his friend Mr. Benjamin and sipping from a porcelain cup of tea. The floor suddenly rocked and reared. At first, Ryan assumed that the tremor marked the start of a minor earthquake, a common annoyance in seismologically vulnerable Yokohama. Then the vibrations gathered force and the chairs and tables began to hop around the room. The ceiling of the lounge creaked, bulged, sagged, and seemed about to come down; Ryan leaped out of the nearest window. Seconds later the three-story structure fell to the ground. A cascade of wood, brick, concrete, and glass thundered down a few feet away from him. His friend, Mr. Benjamin, had disappeared.

Ryan crept along the Bund on his hands and knees. With his view obscured by choking gypsum dust, he headed for the harbor. The ground surged up, down, and sideways. Another shock tossed him over the seawall. Eyes stinging, gasping on air thick with pulverized brick and masonry, he ducked below the water, coming up for breath only as necessary. Oxygen was scarce, and he could barely breathe. The typhoon wind rose up and cleared the powder from the air. He climbed back over the seawall and absorbed the sight of the block-long heap of rubble in front of him—all that remained of what many considered to have been the finest hotel in the Far East.

BACK AT Thomas Cook & Son, Lois Crane cleared the front door of the five-story building just before it crashed to the ground. The collapse killed all six employees—their names appear on a casualty list compiled days after the earthquake—and an unknown number of customers in the Cook office, and buried her in debris up to her waist. Crane's arms and head had not sustained even a scratch, and she dug herself free. Along Water Street, she watched buildings sway and buckle before the destructive horizontal forces that the shear waves exerted on them. Steel-reinforced beams and girders snapped like toothpicks, sending brick, concrete, and wood-frame structures falling earthward in a terrible fugue of obliteration.

GERTRUDE COZAD, the Japan-born American missionary from Kobe, was seated in a tram about to enter Yokohama Station at the moment the earthquake struck. The electric car jumped wildly, swung back and forth, and seemed on the verge of toppling over. Cozad and the other passengers bolted for the door and hurled themselves to the ground. Confused, she looked around, and saw to her astonishment that not a single structure in the vicinity was standing. A cloud of yellow dust rose from the shattered landscape, followed by shrieks of pain and fright, then deathly silence. At least it seemed like silence. Looking back on the earthquake days later, Cozad wondered whether the trauma had been so great that she had gone temporarily deaf.

A tram on the next track had overturned, and passengers trapped inside moaned for help. Live power cables swung through the window, electrocuting those inside. "A merciful death," Cozad would later remark. A redcap seized her bags and led her toward the damaged station building, which appeared ready to fall. While they sat in the dirt plaza in front of the sagging structure, Cozad watched fires break out in every direction. Alone, unfamiliar with Yokohama, and cowering from the aftershocks, Cozad waited passively in the open square for someone to tell her what to do. A flow of humanity, many bleeding or suffering from broken limbs, arrived in the plaza. A Western man told Cozad he would help her, but he soon vanished. Some survivors, as if unable to grasp the immensity of what had happened, retreated into small obsessions. "Another man came saying that he [had been] on the bridge when the shake came, and he [had] lost his handbag," Cozad noted. "He thought someone had taken it and would someone please tell the policeman about it."

AT TWO MINUTES before noon Shigeo Tsuchiya, the twelve-year-old boy who had rushed home from school, was kneeling at a low Japanese table, a *kotatsu,* with his sister and their grandparents and drinking from a bowl of sweet-bean soup. The shock hurled him in the air, threw him sideways, and slammed his lower leg against the hard wooden edge of the table. The family's small Shinto shrine toppled over. Live coals from the brazier spilled and ignited the tatami mat. Tsuchiya's grandmother remained calm and doused the flames with pans of water. "Children, get out of the house," she ordered. She pulled open the *amado,* the wooden sliding door, and hustled the family into the street. Tsuchiya stared into chaos. Hundreds of neighbors had poured into Odori, screaming "Jishin da! Jishin da!" (Earthquake! Earthquake!). A blanket of bluish-gray roof tiles covered the road. Dust whirled in the wind. People milled around, confused and distraught. An inferno was blazing in Isezaki-cho, the entertainment and restaurant district, someone reported minutes later, and was moving toward the residential neighborhood. It seemed that every second house in Odori already was aflame.

AT THE Yokohama United Club, a four-story edifice of brick and granite, twenty regulars at the long bar stood frozen for a few moments in disbelief. Then they turned and dashed as one for the front hall and verandah. At that instant Yokohama's most venerable private club telescoped into a five-foot-high pile of rubble, killing all of them, including several members who had been among the earliest inhabitants of the Foreign Settlement. Forty Japanese employees were crushed to death in that moment as well. (Amazingly, a tumbling window frame collared the Japanese bartender, Jimmy, at the bar, leaving him standing in the open air, unscathed.)

At the French Consulate, an ornately gabled, wood-frame construction on the lowest spur of the Bluff, designed by the Grand Hotel architect, Paul Pierre Sarda, the consul, Paul Déjardin, sat discussing tax policy in a salon facing the sea with Marshall Martin. Déjardin heard a low rumble. He froze. "What's that?" he asked. Seconds later the second floor of the consulate collapsed onto the first. Martin was flung from the compound. Déjardin lay crushed but alive beneath heavy timbers. Martin tried to dig him out. Ribs broken, lungs destroyed, and spitting up blood, Déjardin repeated a phrase or two, lost consciousness, then died.

On the opposite end of the Bund the rickety old U.S. Consulate fell at the first shock, burying Max David Kirjassof, the thirty-five-year-old consul general, an émigré from St. Petersburg, and his wife, Alice Ballantyne Kirjassof, a twenty-six-year-old Mount Holyoke graduate, who was pregnant, in ill health, and lying down. Passersby pulled them out alive, but they were both killed fifteen minutes later when flames overtook them near the Customs House along the waterfront. (A nursemaid dragged the Kirjassofs' two children from the garden and brought them to Yokohama Park, where all survived.) Deputy Consul Paul Emmott Jenks, a sixty-three-year-old Yale graduate from Brooklyn who had lived in Yokohama for decades, and several other members of the staff died trapped in the rubble of the Consulate. Next door, at the British Consulate, Hugh Horne, the forty-six-year-old commercial attaché, a concert pianist, Robert Browning scholar, and married father of two; Vice Consul William Haigh, thirty-two, also a father of two; and two young British clerks died together in Horne's office when the roof caved in.

THE FIRST TREMORS sent Ulysses Webb, the chief administrator and head surgeon at the American Naval Hospital on the Bluff, rushing to the door leading into the corridor outside his office in the main building. Seconds later, the structure crashed down on him. Hurled into the basement, Webb came to rest with a four-by-six wooden beam across his pelvis and abdomen, his legs buried under bricks and masonry. He felt, he recalled, "a great and most painful pressure on my left knee." But his head and arms were free and uninjured, and he could see a glimmer of light piercing the wreckage twenty or thirty feet above him. Minutes later he heard the voices of a rescue party, calling his name. "I'm down here," he yelled.

Nearby, Jennie Kuyper, the Iowa-born principal of the Ferris Seminary on the Bluff, had been working at her desk in an inner room of the hillside school when the shock hit. The earthquake knocked the wood-frame structure down in five seconds. After the dust cleared, a Japanese clerk who had been on the verandah climbed atop the detritus and called to the principal in the darkness. The collapsing building had entombed Kuyper in an air pocket. Her body was free, she replied, staring up at the light, but heavy timbers held fast both of her arms. The Japanese clerk rushed off, promising to find assistance.

OTIS MANCHESTER POOLE had just returned to his desk from a leg-stretching stroll around the ground-floor offices of Dodwell & Co. when the building began to vibrate. A popular, energetic leader of the expatriate community, Poole grasped within a few seconds that this was the earthquake that he and his family had been dreading for decades. The jerking accelerated. Poole ducked in a doorway and held on for his life. For "half a minute the fabric of our surroundings held; then came disintegration," he recounted. "Slabs of plaster left the ceilings and fell about our ears, filling the air with . . . dust. Walls bulged, spread and sagged; pictures danced on their wires; flew out and crashed in splinters. Desks slid about, cabinets, safes and furniture toppled, spun a moment and fell on their sides. It felt as if the floor were rising and falling beneath one's feet in billows knee high. . . . And then, as if heralding the end of the world, the earth seemed to rise into the air and rock; and all around us thundered the deafening roar of cascading buildings."

Poole and his colleagues were lucky: the building that housed Dodwell & Co. was one of the best-constructed in Yokohama, an old wood-frame warehouse, or *godown*, built in the 1860s, with a roof "of natural tree trunks, twisted and gnarled, fitted together and immensely strong." Although the building sustained some structural damage, the roof stayed up and the teak-paneled hall in which Poole and his employees huddled survived nearly unscathed. When the shaking stopped, the general manager opened the front door and stepped outside. The sight was, he recalled, "like a blow to the stomach." Main Street was unrecognizable: a tangle of masonry, beams, roofing tiles, and bricks in sizable mounds. The stone facade of Dodwell & Co. had shaken off, forming a perfect checkerboard pattern on the ground. Immediately Poole and a colleague set off toward their homes on the Bluff, navigating the nearly impassable streets:

> It was here that the full measure of the catastrophe came home to us. What seemed most terrible was the quiet. A deathly stillness had fallen, into which the scraping of our own feet sounded ghostly. Shattered fragments of buildings rose like distorted monuments from a sea of devastation beyond belief. Over everything had already settled a thick, white dust, giving the ruins the semblance of infinite age; and through the yellow fog of dust, still in the air, a copper-coloured sun shone upon this silent havoc in sickly unreality.

TOMMY RYAN clambered onto toppled beams, roof tiles, shards of masonry, plasterboard, smashed timber, electrical wires, shattered dishes, crumpled furniture, searching for his friend. "Mr. Benjamin?" he cried out. "Mr. Benjamin, are you alive?" Nothing but silence. Anyone inside the salon who hadn't escaped through a window had been crushed to death. The grotesquely twisted corpses of victims—kimono-clad waitresses; Doris Babbitt, the pretty teenager who had arrived two days before from San Francisco—lay half hidden beneath heavy roof tiles and other flotsam. Ryan pored through the wreckage. From the basement, amid this landscape of death and destruction, came a voice that Ryan recognized. His fellow officer, Naval Lieutenant H. C. Davis, had survived the collapse unhurt and was calling for help to extricate himself from the barbershop. Before Ryan could react, Davis pried loose the iron window bars and dug himself free. He climbed onto the Bund, brushed the dust off his uniform, wiped the shaving cream off his face, and set off in search of his wife. Mrs. Davis, it turned out, had stepped through the double doors of the Grand Hotel lobby into the circular driveway seconds before the structure crashed down, killing everyone inside.

Like almost all of the other Western-style buildings in the city, the Grand Hotel had been built using inflexible concrete piles embedded deep into the soft, water-saturated soil that lay beneath most of Yokohama peninsula. According to structural engineers, this loosely packed alluvium can be particularly lethal during strong earthquakes, because it loses its cohesive strength when shaken and causes building foundations embedded in it to move, crack, or subside. The jerking foundations transmitted the full effect of shear waves, followed by Rayleigh and Love waves, to the building above them. Powerful inertial forces whipsawed the roof and top floors of the building in the opposite direction from the foundations and lower floors, then yanked them violently back into place. Within a few seconds the severe horizontal rocking motions produced by the earthquake, later estimated to have measured the equivalent of 7.9 on the Richter scale, imposed unendurable stress on the columns, beams, walls, and girders that supported the vertical load of the Grand Hotel's three stories. Like a spoon bent forward and back until it finally breaks, wooden beams weakened and splintered. Steel-reinforced concrete pillars bent, cracked, then gave way beneath the weight of the floor slabs they had supported. Load-bearing walls collapsed inward. The entire structure crumpled.

PROBABLY ONLY the earthquake that leveled Messina, Sicily, and crushed to death eighty thousand people in a few seconds at dawn on December 28, 1908—the most powerful earthquake ever to hit Europe—had, up to that point, knocked down as many buildings in as short a time as did the Yokohama temblor. One police report estimates that ten thousand buildings in Yokohama fell immediately, 10 percent of the total number of structures in the city. Those that remained standing either collapsed during the aftershocks—the second major jolt, three successive shocks, hit Yokohama at 12:20—or were obliterated in the next, even more destructive stage of the disaster: fire.

Survivors who had been walking the streets of Yokohama at the time the earthquake struck provide a kaleidoscopic picture of the Foreign Settlement's near-instantaneous obliteration. One Yokohama newspaperman told a writer for the *Atlantic Monthly* a few hours after the temblor:

> I was right in the entrance of our office when the shake shot me out on hands and knees, and when I tried to scramble up, it threw me down again. And in just that time that it took me to get to my knees and look back, these three shocks, coming rat-tat-tat, the whole city had gone. I had faced a city of square mile on square mile of houses, stores, homes; and when I turned back again, it had vanished as if by some gigantic sweep of malevolent magic. . . . And then it was all blotted out by the dust, thicker than the thickest fog. You could not see a foot before you. And then that was suddenly cleared, as if a curtain had been snatched away, by the typhoon that sprang up just then, the gale that Fate seemed to need to help the flames finish the destruction.

EVA DOWNES, the nurse, and her friend, Mrs. Macmillan, began hiking inland from the Bund. Bent before the roaring gale, choking on smoke, wiping grit out of their eyes, they climbed over hillocks of building scraps and dodged blazes breaking out on many streets. They walked up Nippon Odori, a wide avenue perpendicular to the harbor that led past the remains of the Post Office and the Silk Conditioning House, piles of undifferentiated rubble. Downes and Macmillan joined a mass flight into Yokohama Park, a twenty-acre cricket ground and public garden landscaped by British settlers in 1876 and located at the end of Nippon Odori. Water mains underneath the park had burst during the earthquake, and by the time the women arrived, the green expanse had reverted to its original state: a swamp. Downes and her companion sank nearly to their waists in the muck. The first wave of refugees had decided to encamp here. (More than ten thousand Japanese, and several foreigners, would ultimately find their way to Yokohama Park, which would prove to be their salvation. "By standing or sitting in the water, and covering their faces with mud," Downes wrote, "they were able to save themselves from the terrible

heat of the fires which burned about them all afternoon and night.")
But Downes and Macmillan, afraid of being trapped by fire, kept
moving through back streets south toward the Creek. Streams of Japanese walked beside them, loaded with bundles containing belongings salvaged from their wrecked houses. "The crowd had the same
idea that we had—to reach some open space on the windward side of
the fire," Downes recalled. "The crowd was mercifully quiet. There
was no shouting or hysterical conversation to make the nervous strain
harder to bear." Building skeletons burst into flame as they walked
past; twice they believed that they were out of danger and sat down to
rest, only to find themselves menaced again by fires.

TOMMY RYAN probed the jagged remnants of the Grand Hotel in the
hope of finding Mr. Benjamin alive. As he waded through the wreckage, a Danish acquaintance named Enevoldsen rushed up from the
Bund, pleading for Ryan's help. A woman was trapped in a half-
collapsed hotel room in the original brick building facing the Creek, he
said. Ryan noticed that fires had started further down the Bund, and the
wind was sweeping them toward the Bluff. Enevoldsen led Ryan inside
the room through a window. There they found the ensnared woman,
Mrs. Slack, in a sitting position, with one leg held fast under a pile of
brick and plasterboard and a heavy beam pinning her chest against a
wall. Just in front of her teetered a hulk of chimney eight feet tall and
two and a half feet thick. Ryan and Enevoldsen removed the beam from
her chest with ease, but they stared at her leg with consternation. "If we
dug out around the leg the pieces of brick might slide and crush Mrs.
Slack," Ryan recalled. "So we tried breaking down the brick by hand."

The fire swept to within a hundred yards of the hotel. At 12:20
three aftershocks jolted the room, knocking loose more bricks from
the collapsing chimney and sending Mrs. Slack into a fit of hysteria.
The temperature in the room was rising, and the thickening smoke
made every breath painful. "It was either leave her in there or jerk a
leg off and take the rest of her," Ryan recalled. Calming herself, Mrs.
Slack locked her arms around Ryan's neck, while Enevoldsen took
hold of her beneath the armpits. With one mighty, desperate heave,

they pulled her free. "She made it possible by holding on and helping instead of passing out as she certainly had reason to do," Ryan noted.

Before they could leave the room, there was another matter to attend to: Mrs. Slack was clad only in her underwear. The men pulled a sheet off one of the destroyed beds, wrapped it around her, and hoisted her through the window. "The leg which had been buried was useless, the other was badly bruised and nearly useless, but like a good seaman she put an arm around each of our necks and helped more than you can imagine." Ryan and Enevoldsen, supporting the injured Mrs. Slack, staggered across the collapsed Camp Hill bridge over the Creek, followed the seacoast for a hundred yards, and took refuge on a patch of reclaimed land below the Bluff. There they sat, eyes tearing from the smoke, watching huge flames consume the shapeless heap of the Grand Hotel. "I got out of the hotel about half a jump ahead of the graveyard," Ryan wrote, "and the three of us later got out of the hotel about fifty yards ahead of the crematory." As for Mr. Benjamin, he apparently did survive, because his name does not appear on any of the casualty lists compiled by the U.S. and European Embassies in the days after the earthquake.

AFTER DIGGING herself out of Thomas Cook & Son, Lois Crane decided to set forth alone toward the Bund. She threaded through debris-snarled streets, ignoring the warnings of two Japanese male survivors that a tsunami was sure to follow the earthquake. Crane had hoped to reach the hatoba and climb aboard one of the commercial liners, but the sunken pier looked impassable, so she abruptly turned and headed in the other direction, toward the solid ground at the foot of the Bluff beyond the Grand Hotel, where Ryan, Enevoldsen, and Mrs. Slack had taken refuge. She almost didn't make it. Crane passed one collapsed and burning edifice after another: the Harbor Office and Water Police Station, the United Club of Yokohama, the Oriental Palace Hotel, the headquarters of Jardine & Matheson, the Chartered & International Bank, the Hongkong & Shanghai Bank. Corpses lay flung around the ruins. In some cases whole buildings had gone down, "in others only pillars were left standing, flanked by huge rafters and broken pieces of masonry." Licks of flame danced from the carcasses. Scorching cinders floated in the wind. The Grand Hotel was burning so fiercely, throwing off such heat, that she couldn't pass. Nearing the Grand she was joined by a young American named Oli Olsen who had been in a corner room on the third floor of the Oriental Palace when the structure came down, killing dozens of people. Somehow Olsen's room had hung together, and he had scaled an outdoor metal staircase to safety. The two survivors stood on the seawall. The flames, fanned by a strong wind, grew fiercer and merged into an unbroken chain of fire. They took off their clothes, jumped into the water, and swam into Yokohama harbor.

OTIS POOLE and a colleague continued their flight through the Foreign Settlement, passing one terrible sight after another: an elderly foreigner sitting upright, dead, half-buried in a mound of rubble; the tatters of clothes on the backs of two Japanese coolies submerged in a pancaked godown. A Japanese barmaid yelled for help from the top floor of a teetering tavern, which promptly collapsed and buried both her and her would-be rescuers. As he approached Chinatown—a densely packed neighborhood of eight thousand people built on landfill and cited often by government building inspectors for its shoddy construction—he realized that not a single house or shop in the entire neighborhood had been left standing.

Poole and his companion reached the Creek. The earthen banks on both sides had slid into the water. All three of the sturdy iron bridges leading to the Bluff had fallen. On hands and knees they crawled across the partially submerged third bridge from the seafront and entered Motomachi, a Japanese village, or "native town," squeezed below the Bluff. It was unrecognizable. The initial shock had crumpled the Japanese houses like matchwood. Chunks of the surrounding cliffs had tumbled into the gorge, entombing inhabitants in the ruins of their homes. "All was silent, only here and there a shriek from the depths, or encouraging shouts from some frantically digging group." The earthquake had tossed half of the Cherry Mount Hotel from its heights above the village; thirty guests would be found dead in the ruins. Poole felt a blast of heat. He looked behind him and, he wrote, "gasped."

> In the few minutes since we had crossed the bridge, fire had burst out in Motomachi not eighty yards from where we stood and red-brown flames were spiraling into the air in a vicious whirlwind. The torrid summer blast picked up masses of flame and swirled them straight toward us along the groove of ruins. In an instant the fallen woodwork became alight and new flames raced toward us like a prairie fire. At that a great sob rose from the survivors round about and the anguish in that wail was so pitiful that it seemed to numb one's senses against the impact of any further tragedies to come.

FROM A SAMPAN in the harbor, Ellis Zacharias watched wind-driven blazes sweep across the Foreign Settlement and bear down on the waterfront. "Approaching the warehouses along the embankment, the flames appeared to pounce upon them as a tiger on its prey," he wrote, "and with a loud, crackling roar burst from the buildings, spiraling high into the air and crying out with a morbid joy of destruction." Volatile chemicals exploded in factories, apothecaries, school laboratories, and photography shops. Oil tanks of the Rising Sun and Standard Oil companies, situated on high ground near the Yokohama Railroad Station, burst; oil gushed down drainage canals into the harbor and exploded into flame whenever it came into contact with sparks or embers. In thousands of homes in the sprawling Japanese district, where almost every family had been sitting down to lunch, the temblor had knocked over charcoal braziers and spilled glowing embers onto tatami mats. Terrified residents had rushed out of doors, and unchecked flames had raced through their flammable wood and paper houses. The gale force wind fanned flames through the alleys, creating powerful updrafts and soon engulfing the whole Japanese district, then the Foreign Settlement, in a sea of fire. And the shock had instantly ruptured all of the water mains running underneath the city, paralyzing the port's fire brigades. "Thick black columns and gray smoke were curling upward as far as the eye could see," the passenger aboard the *Philoctetes* observed. "This smoke, combined with the yel-

low dust in the atmosphere, almost turned day into night. . . . The
colour of the sky changed continually, from yellow to brown, from
brown to grey and black, shutting out the sunlight. The sun itself
could at times be seen through the smoky and dusty atmosphere—
a red ball. The colour of the sea changed to a dirty olive green and at
times appeared black. In spots, the reflection of the sun seemed like
a trickling stream of red. It was an uncanny sight, never to be forgotten."

SURVIVORS IN THE WATER, including Lois Crane, watched the Bund
behind them turn into an impenetrable wall of flame, escaping from
the unbearable heat by ducking beneath the sea. These harbor swim-
mers were the fortunate ones. For people who found themselves even
a block or two from the waterfront, a moment's hesitation could be
fatal. Minutes after the earthquake struck, Tom Abbey, the fifty-six-
year-old director of the Yokohama Auction House on Main Street, led
his Japanese assistant and her son out of the heavily damaged building
to safety. Then he turned his attention to Edwin Wheeler. The octogenarian physician could hardly walk because of an ankle injury that
had never properly healed. Abbey helped Wheeler hobble down the
front steps. The pair stood together on Main Street, eyes darting in
fear and confusion as the wind swept the fire toward them from two
directions. Abbey gripped the physician by the hand and led him
down an alley in an attempt to reach the Bund. But a tangle of fallen
beams and bricks in the narrow street and Wheeler's infirmity slowed
their progress. Between Main and Water Streets, the flames and smoke
overtook them. They asphyxiated in the parking lot of a tea warehouse
one and a half blocks from the seafront.

Across the Foreign Settlement, a wasteland where black clouds of
smoke shot through with flame towered over charred vehicles and the
ghostly fragments of banks and offices, people pinned in the wreckage
and their loved ones were caught in a desperate race against the fires.
"All over were people one knew, whom one had danced with, dined
with, played bridge with, reduced, in a moment, to the uttermost
depth of despair," one eyewitness told Henry W. Kinney, the writer
for the *Atlantic Monthly* who, by luck or misfortune, reached Yoko-

hama hours after the earthquake struck. "They were standing, crying wildly by the ruins, clawing at them, desperately, to reach others caught under the bricks, and already, here and there, the flames were leaping forth, coming closer and closer, while the poor wretches in the debris were yelling for help." This survivor observed the last embrace of an unidentified couple who were almost certainly the Komors, the Hungarian owner of Kuhn & Komor curio shop on Water Street and his young wife:

> A man called to me, "Here, help me get my wife out." She was caught by the waist. Her entire body was free, and she was staring at us and straining, slim, jeweled hands pressing frantically at the great beam that held her unhurt, but tightly pinned. Half of the beam was covered by bricks. We might as well have tried to lift a house. We tugged away, helplessly. We caught at men who rushed by, called to them to assist. One or two of them stopped, but most of them shook themselves free. I wanted to hit them. It seemed so damnably callous. And still, they also had wives, children, somewhere, in their homes on the Bluff, and were obsessed by the anxiety to find them, too, but I couldn't leave that woman. And then the flames came and drove us back. I had to half strangle that poor devil to pull him away. The roar of the flames drowned her cries, so I rushed along.

THE PASSENGERS AND CREW aboard the *Empress of Australia* gazed in awe as the fires drew closer to the hatoba. On the bridge Captain Samuel Robinson ordered "every able-bodied male" to turn the fire hoses on the ship's decks. The powerful wind drove heat and cinders into the faces of the fire hose operators, stinging their eyes and obliging them to seek relief from new volunteers. Sparks, "fire flakes," and burning material, driven by the gale, threatened to set alight a two-story wooden freight shed that stood on the undamaged portion of the pier beside the *Empress's* bow. Worse, the ship, Robinson saw, was trapped, unable to advance more than a few feet because of the shallow water, hemmed in astern by the *Steel Navigator*.

Yokohama harbor had become a deadly obstacle course. Large Japanese cargo lighters and sampans came unmoored in the swirling water and collided in the thick veil of smoke. One pilotless vessel, the *Lyons Maru,* bumped into the port side of the *Empress* and lightly damaged a lower deck, then drifted off. Burning cinders settled on the cargoes of many vessels, setting them alight. "There were many of these boat furnaces traveling rapidly, burning fiercely, making straight for ships at anchor," wrote the *Philoctetes* passenger. "Most lighters were laden with logs, planks, and 'baby squares' [small wooden panels used for housing construction], recently discharged from American and Canadian cargo holds and, once ablaze, could hardly be extinguished in the gale." Oil burbled from broken tanks ashore, caught fire as it drifted through the canals, and flowed into the harbor. Dozens of survivors of the earthquake, including Lois Crane, clung to flotsam amid the flaming slicks.

DR. ULYSSES WEBB, the chief administrator of the American Naval Hospital, lay pinned in the darkness. Aftershocks shook his tomb every ten minutes. The welcome cacophony of pickaxes, saws, shovels, and excited dialogue grew nearer as the rescue team tunneled a hole deep into the ruins. The rescue party consisted of a Japanese gardener, Mr. Ito; an unnamed member of the Municipal Fire Brigades who had happened to be passing by; and seven American hospital staffers, several of whom had been injured themselves. C. E. Yost, a naval pharmacist, had been "struck down and pinned to the earth by a beam as he was escaping from the Hospital Annex," Webb recalled, "but when released joined the rescue party and worked with great zeal until he fainted from his own injury." Edith Linquist, the chief nurse, had fallen from the balcony of her quarters when the building collapsed, but suffered only a few bruises and abrasions; she quickly joined Yost and "worked indefatigably, with great bravery, in imminent danger." "A gale was blowing, the whole city was burning, the air was full of smoke and cinders, the British Naval Hospital across the way was blazing," Webb recollected. "These are the conditions under which my men worked . . . nor did they desist until our own piles of debris were ablaze and our escape all but cut off." Mr. Ito, the hospital gardener, reached Webb first. He sawed through the timber that immobilized the hospital administrator's pelvis and freed him seconds before the flames ripped through the building. Lawrence Zembsch, the chief pharmacist, and his wife, who had been visiting him in his hospital ward that morning, lay pinned in the wreckage. Mrs. Zembsch screamed for help, but, one rescue party member recalled, "it was too late, all had to flee from the fire." Two American pharmacist's mates and four Japanese hospital employees also burned to death in the ruins. American sailors sifting through the ashes with shovels days later identified Mrs. Zembsch through her gold wedding band, wrapped around a charred finger bone.

FOR ONE HOUR the Japanese clerk at the Ferris Seminary raced about the grounds of the ruined school, seeking assistance for Jennie Kuyper, the school's principal, still held fast by a fallen beam. At 12:30, the fire leaped across the Creek and advanced up the hillside, destroying everything in its path. Half an hour later, with the fire approaching, the trapped principal begged the clerk to abandon her and save himself. "God's will be done," she cried over the roar of the fire. "Give my love to my friends." Kuyper began to sing a Christian hymn, falling silent only when the flames swept over the ruins.

"WE MUST GO to an open area," Shigeo Tsuchiya's grandmother said. Tsuchiya, his grandparents, and his younger sister set off from their street, Odori, toward Yokohama Station, a brick and stone, double-winged Victorian edifice with a wide dirt plaza in front, located one mile north. They treaded carefully around tiles, electrical wires, planks of wood, and fissures in the earth. The neighborhood through which they walked had been paddy fields before the Meiji era, drained and reclaimed using hard-packed earth and stones, and had absorbed the full force of the seismic waves; Tsuchiya felt he might as well be walking on the moon. In the plaza before the damaged station, Tsuchiya picked his parents out of the crowd, and after an emotional reunion, they heard reports that fires were bearing down on the station. At one o'clock they decided to move again.

Tsuchiya's father carried his daughter on his back. His grandfather hobbled with a walking stick. The six refugees fled down a wide asphalt road. A spider's web of fissures made every step treacherous; they passed a dead horse half-protruding from a crevice. Someone cried out, "Fire is coming," and they abruptly changed direction. Fifty or sixty people had joined Tsuchiya and his family, a frightened scrum of humanity driven by a single impulse: survival. They decided to head toward a cemetery at the southwestern edge of the city, at the foothill of the mountains that formed the city's natural border. The ground quivered from aftershocks, three times knocking the twelve-year-old Tsuchiya to the ground. He saw crushed corpses protruding from the wreckage. A chorus of trapped victims cried out from crumpled buildings, but the earth tremors, the crackling of wooden homes being consumed by fires, and the columns of fire-laced smoke rising from the alleys prevented anyone in the group from stopping to offer assistance. By two o'clock in the afternoon darkness had descended. The rubble thinned out and they began a slow climb through rice fields to the cemetery. One hundred refugees had already arrived. Tsuchiya and his family had no food or water, and dust and smoke had blackened their faces. Tsuchiya dropped onto a toppled tombstone, took a deep breath, and watched a dense cloud of purplish smoke rise over his city.

As FIRES ADVANCED on the plaza in front of Yokohama Station half an hour after the earthquake, Gertrude Cozad, the American missionary from Kobe, who was a visitor to Yokohama, knelt in the dirt until a policeman blew his whistle and said, "Everyone to the hills." She followed the crowd over fractured roads, painstakingly circumventing fissures, and soon fell in step with a handsome Asian man in his early twenties.

"Are you alone?" she asked, in Japanese. Cozad, who had been born and raised in Japan, spoke the language fluently.

"Yes," he replied.

"Won't you stay with me today?"

"Gladly."

"What is your name?"

"Hayashi Shotaro." A Korean immigrant whose father had died

suddenly after bringing him to Japan, he had been left penniless and without friends or relatives, he told her. Cozad and Shotaro (like most Korean immigrants in Japan before the Second World War, he had been obliged to adopt a Japanese name) climbed a hill on the southwest outskirts of Yokohama with hundreds of other refugees and passed through a wooden torii to a serene and green oasis, the Daijingu Shrine. "[It was] strangely intact, sitting there calmly as if it had always been and always would be, while the large buildings [nearby] had fallen," Cozad recalled. "You can imagine how that impressed the people and how many earnest prayers were offered there. . . . The people began to pour up there from every direction." The Korean and the American sat side by side on the sacred ground, with more than a thousand others, praying that they were beyond the fire's reach.

OTIS POOLE and his companion ran through Motomachi in the direction of the waterfront. They leaped over legs and arms protruding from smashed houses, passed bewildered Japanese staring mutely at the inferno as it bore down upon them. At the second bridge from the sea, Maedabashi, they turned to the right, up Hegt's Hill (named after a British resident who had built a grocery store there in the 1870s), and climbed to the top of the ridge. Along the verdant Bluff, the villas of Poole's friends and acquaintances lay in ruins, some pancaked flat, others with facades sheared off like doll houses, a medical clinic sunk "like a hammock between its two wings." The news he picked up from survivors was grim: the two-year-old son of a friend crushed to death in her arms, six European nuns and dozens of their Japanese students killed in the collapse of the convent school on the Bluff, the young wife of the Poole family physician dead in the ruins of her home. Poole's own handsome Victorian house had survived, although the chimney had plummeted through the roof and narrowly missed his wife, Dorothy, and their three young sons. He found them sheltered in the garden of a neighbor's bungalow. With them were the children's Japanese amah, or nurse, Miné; Dorothy's mother, Calla; and her father, W. W. Campbell, the manager of the Pacific Mail Steamship Company and commodore of the Yokohama Yacht Club. They embraced one another, but Poole realized that they had to keep moving: "Although only an hour had elapsed since the earthquake first struck, it was already evident that we were to be given no respite. The billowing canopy of smoke overhead was now as black as a thunder-cloud, shedding burning chips as it swept past. With fallen houses like prepared bonfires on all sides, our danger was pressing, and flight unavoidable. . . . Every minute or two the ground swayed afresh, and crashes here and there signaled continuing demolishment."

The family followed the Bluff Road along the top of the ridge. The road was "like a flight of steps, fissures eight inches wide every few feet, each ledge sagging successively toward the valley opposite." Far below, the Foreign Settlement and Japanese city lay hidden beneath sheets of flame and smoke. Tombstones were scattered like broken teeth about the Yokohama Foreign Cemetery, a sprawling hilltop graveyard containing the remains of sea captains, missionaries, early victims of samurai warriors, and hundreds of other expatriates who had died far from their native lands. The granite Memorial Arch, raised in April 1922 to commemorate Allied World War dead, had shattered into a dozen fragments. A landslide had cut off the dirt road leading down to the Bund, and to the family's yacht, the *Daimyo*, where they had hoped to take refuge. The tiny Japanese village that had filled the gully alongside the road was a "roaring furnace." They pushed on further trying to find a way down to the beach through the last spur of the Bluff. But rock slides and hot smoke stopped them. They huddled together on the Bluff, the fire raging behind them, with nowhere, it seemed, left to run.

AT THE STERN of his ship, Captain Samuel Robinson tried desperately to maneuver the *Empress* away from the hatoba before the freight shed burst into flame. Pressing a megaphone against his lips, he pleaded with the officers of the *Steel Navigator* to "heave up anchors and drop astern." He received no reply. (The silence may have been because the *Steel Navigator*'s commander had been crushed to death at the U.S. Consulate in the first moments of the earthquake, leaving the chain of authority in disarray.) "No notice had been taken, the officer in charge either not understanding or deciding that his vessel was safe where it was and that our safety was a very secondary matter," Robinson later wrote with evident frustration. "In this I cannot entirely blame him. . . . With the gale that was blowing and unable in the dense smoke to see what was going on in the harbor astern, his position alongside the . . . wharf . . . must have seemed to him the safest place."

At 1:30 the shed's roof ignited, and a shower of sparks rained on the *Empress*'s deck. Robinson ordered his crew to start the engines and back down on the *Steel Navigator,* "taking the risk," he wrote, "of damage to our propellers and to her upper works and our own, and force her enough astern for our bow to clear the main part of the shed." The propellers churned the black water into foam. At that moment Robinson got a lucky break: two lumber-laden Japanese lighters, abandoned by their captains, drifted into the narrow gap between the *Empress* and the *Steel Navigator,* and as the vessel inched backward, the lighters wedged her stern away from the pier. The huge ship slid along the port side of the smaller freighter.

> As our stern passed the bow of the *Steel Navigator,* I stopped the engines and used them as little as possible. After the stern was well past her bow and approaching her bridge . . . the port propeller fouled something. . . . On trying it again, it could not be turned either way. The obstruction was presumably the port [anchor] cable of the *Steel Navigator.* The *Steel Navigator*'s port anchor had probably been dragged out of position by the anchor of the *Lyons Maru,* ranging fore and aft alongside us both. [Our bow] was now abreast of the outer end of the freight shed, a roaring mass of flames from end to end.

The heat was intense, the ship immobilized. Though he doesn't mention it in his account of that day, Robinson must have feared deeply for the lives of his crew and passengers. Then, his luck changed again. The two lighters that had become wedged between the vessel and the pier nudged the *Empress* out another twenty feet, so that the *Empress*'s bow was sixty feet away from the nearest flames. The wind abruptly shifted, blowing cinders and sparks away from the *Empress.* "We got every hose we could connect forward and on the starboard side," Robinson recalled, "and nothing caught fire."

It would be only a temporary reprieve.

* * *

FILTHY AND HOT, caked with mud up to their waists, faces and hair black with dust and grit, Eva Downes and Mrs. Macmillan reached the Creek at one o'clock. The murky canal was choked with large and small boats packed with so many Japanese, their cotton bedding, and their household goods that it looked to the two women as if many would sink if more people came aboard. Thousands of these refugees would die later in the afternoon, burned to death by fires that would start from flying sparks that torched their wooden boats. The pair reached a broken footbridge leading to the Negishi Hills, west of the Bluff. Pedestrian traffic had ground to a halt. "A wire cable underneath the bridge floor had come up through the floor to a point about one foot above," Downes recalled, "and this formed a serious blockade to the crowd. But a strong Japanese man stopped to help and soon everything was moving again."

Downes and her companion trudged up Race Course Road, a steep path that wound through verdant open country. In front of a ruined dairy, several Japanese women offered them dippers of warm milk and refused to accept money in return. At two o'clock, after a five- or six-mile circuitous walk through Yokohama, they arrived at a golf course on the hilly road to the coastal resort town of Kamakura. Clouds of black smoke billowed above the city. The gale still blew at full strength. Violent aftershocks rocked the hillside. They joined fifty other foreigners who had come to the golf course for refuge from the fires. After retrieving crackers and bottled water from the lockers of the clubhouse, Downes and Macmillan settled on the grass. Wiping the sweat and grime from their faces with their sodden raincoats, they silently watched Yokohama burn.

6

Tokyo Burning

Great wave movements go shuddering through the body of their land, spasmodically changing all overnight. Whole villages disappear. New islands appear as others are lost. Shores are reversed as mountains are laid low and valleys lifted up. Always flames! The terror of it all faces conflagration at the end.

Frank Lloyd Wright, *Autobiography* (1943)

T HE SEISMIC WAVES that ripped through Yokohama at two minutes before noon on September 1 raced toward the nearby capital, Tokyo, at ten times the speed of sound. If a witness had been hovering above the stricken zone at that moment, he could have watched the destruction unfold like an animated image on a pack of children's flip cards, vibrations carving a path of ruin through one of the most densely populated areas on the planet. The waves sliced fissures in the tarmac highway that followed the course of the ancient Tokaido. Moving north, they buckled the trestles of a railway bridge over the Tamagawa River dividing Tokyo's prefecture from that of Yokohama's. They tossed trains from the tracks of the Tokyo-Yokohama Line, knocked loose giant boulders, precipitated mudslides, and toppled nearly every house in the large village of Kawasaki. Henry W. Kinney, the managing editor of *Trans-Pacific,* a Tokyo-based monthly magazine, was riding a train from Tokyo to Yokohama on his way to join his twelve-year-old son at a summer lodge in Kamakura for the weekend. He was slammed into the seat in front of him and hit the roof. The train screeched to a halt amid cries of "Jishin!" ("Earthquake"). Kinney glanced out the window just as the stone face of an embankment hurled itself onto the tracks. "It did not slide or tumble down," he wrote in his *Atlantic Monthly* account. "It literally shot down, as if compelled by a sudden, gigantic pressure from the top. . . . A four story concrete building vanished, disintegrated in the flash of an eye. Tiles cascaded with precipitate speed from the roofs. The one predominating idea that struck the mind was the almost incredible rapidity of the destruction."

Ten miles further north, in a third-floor room at the Kinokuniya Hotel in Shimbashi, the waves hurled Frederick Starr and his assistant, Takagi, against a wall. Starr wrote in his diary: "[The room] shook and shook; tiles were falling and the air of the room was filled with powdered plaster. The dressing case was overthrown; mouths, eyes, nostrils were full of the dust. The boy took it well. He gave no cry, made no effort to rise or run, sat back as firmly as he could against the upright. I watched him closely and said 'no matter; it will soon end'—a remark which might be taken in either of two ways. As for myself, I believed we were dead men."

When the vibrations stopped, the hotel still stood. Starr, clad only in his wooden clogs and checkered bathrobe, led Takagi "gingerly" down a darkened staircase choked with dust, through the darkened lobby and into the street. Hundreds of people had gathered in front of the hotel. Electric trolley cars had stopped dead on their tracks. In the midst of the confusion, Starr made an odd mental note: the disabled trolley directly in front of the hotel bore the license 1904, the year he had first arrived in Japan. Starr makes no mention of significant damage to the hotel or to the surrounding buildings, though one can assume that it was considerable. Still, by all accounts it was nowhere near as bad as that in Yokohama: the force of the seismic vibrations had weakened slightly as they made their forty-eight-mile journey from the epicenter, and much of the Japanese capital was built on more solid ground. "Terror was on every face and fear in every heart," Starr recalled, "yet there was no shouting or screaming. Confusion and uncertainty—yes." At 12:20, Starr reported, "there was a second sharp shock, which sent people scurrying into the open and felled the

standing street car. It was reported that fires were breaking out. Criers
ran calling that domestic water was shut off." The terrible aftermath
of the 1855 Ansei earthquake, when the water mains had been cut and
fires, spreading unchecked through the feudal city of Edo, had burned
to death thousands of people, had not been forgotten. In those first
few minutes, reading Starr's diaries, one has the impression of an eerie
calm, a shared wait for the next act of the apocalypse.

ALL ALONG the mountainous coast of Sagami Bay, twenty miles from
the epicenter, the powerful seismic waves emanating from deep beneath Oshima Island generated destruction on a scale unprecedented
in Japanese history. Villages and towns vanished in a few shakes of the
earth. Ninety percent of the houses in the seaside town of Odawara
collapsed in seconds, and fires burned whatever remained. There were
countless tragedies that day, but one of the most spectacular occurred
on a local train of the Tokaido Line that was traveling south along the
coast toward the hot spring resort of Atami; 113 people, including
many families from Tokyo on their last outing of the summer, were
aboard. It was nearing lunchtime, and passengers had spread wooden
lunch boxes, *obento,* across their laps. Pine-fringed coves and deep
gorges, sweeping beaches and picturesque fishing villages offered
an exhilarating sight to people beaten down by the sweltering heat in
the city.

At three minutes before noon, the southbound train crossed a five-
span railway trestle. Passengers on the left-hand side could see, 150
feet below the bridge, the fishing village of Nebukawa, a cluster of tile-
roofed houses at the bottom of a precipitous green canyon formed by
the Nebukawa River. To the right, a sheer basalt cliff, veined with
moss, soared several hundred feet above the sea. The train stopped in
the middle of the bridge and waited for a northbound train to pull out
of Nebukawa Station. Suddenly, the coaches lurched forward. Window glass shattered. Luggage tumbled from the racks. Lunches spilled
on the floor. A cry rang out: Earthquake! Passengers screamed. A loud
rumble sounded from the mountain. Seconds later a huge mud slide
hurtled down the slopes and slammed into the train. Coaches slid and
somersaulted down the precipice. They slammed into the shallow

water, landing one on top of the other, embedding in the sand with a sickening crunch of metal and wood. Dozens of passengers died on impact. Others were trapped upside down in crushed cars that rapidly filled with seawater. Perhaps ten people aboard the train survived. Seconds later the landslide that had toppled the train buried the village in muck, and then pushed it into the water, suffocating all three hundred residents. "The Nebukawa, a swift mountain stream and gulch, had formed the channel for the mud flow," one American eyewitness observed the next morning. "The village had swept into the sea. . . . The mud was ice cold, so cold, in fact, that it was 'steaming,' giving us the impression that it was boiling hot. . . . It was of a clayey texture and extremely sticky. All vegetation was gone and the sides of the valley were smooth and slippery."

The sudden upsurge of the continental plate displaced billions of gallons of seawater, which formed into a great wave that headed straight for the bay's cove-sculpted shoreline. The tsunami began as an almost imperceptible swell, no more than three feet high: fishing boats near Oshima Island at the time the earthquake struck reported a minor disturbance, nothing more. Though unseen and barely felt by those at sea, the wave raced across Sagami Bay at a speed approaching six hundred miles an hour. As the swell approached the beaches, it brushed against the shallowing sea floor, which slowed its movement and drastically changed its shape. Like a piece of carpet shoved suddenly against a wall, the wave curled upward, growing to terrifying size. The precise height of the wave when it hit the shore was determined by both the depth of the sea floor and the varying shape of the coastline. The narrower the inlet, the greater the tsunami's size. In Atami, the wave squeezed through a slender cove and reached a height of thirty-five feet, swamping the town minutes after the shock and drowning three hundred people.

A few miles northeast, in a rocky pool at the end of Manazaru Point, an American conchologist, Professor D. B. Langford, and a colleague were collecting shells when the earthquake hit, followed by the tsunami. The shock felt like a series of dull thumps similar to heavy charges of dynamite exploding deep beneath their feet, Langford observed. The sea receded seconds later, drawing back an astonishing quarter of a mile. "Water was spurting from innumerable places along the sea bed . . . as high as four feet," Langford reported. "Immediately after the subsidence of the sea . . . the water rose very rapidly. Very large boulders and large pine trees were tossed about like peas and straws in a boiling pot." A terrific rush of water came through the channel from the direction of Atami. The wave washed over the nearby island of Mitsu-ishi-Shima, fifty feet high, and "caused a roaring noise comparable to the sound of Niagara Falls." (The two conchologists clung to a cliff face, barely surviving the inundation and an avalanche of giant boulders.)

At the same moment, further to the east, the tsunami bore down on Kamakura, the former capital of Japan, summer retreat for the wealthy, and site of the famed thirteenth-century giant bronze Buddha, Daibutsu.

Ian Mutsu, the son of a Japanese diplomat and his English author wife, was one of the first to see the wave approaching the shore. Moments after the earthquake demolished the Mutsu family's beach house, the twenty-one-year-old university student squirmed through a window and crawled onto the sand. The tide, which should have been coming in at that hour, was receding at an unprecedented velocity. Mutsu sat on the beach for a while, his curiosity aroused by the strange phenomenon. The tide continued rushing out, exposing rocks that he had never seen before. Then something else caught his eye. On the horizon, he noticed what appeared to be a solid white wall heading toward the beach. Mutsu turned and ran, across the sand, across the highway, up a road leading toward the giant Buddha. The huge swell—twenty feet high when it hit the shore, fifteen feet lower than the wave that swept over Atami—surged over the town. It raced through the streets, barreling through houses, sweeping up automobiles, road signs, trees. Mutsu saved himself, but three hundred residents of Kamakura drowned or were crushed by the avalanche of waterborne debris. The total death toll in Kamakura from earthquake, tsunami, and fire was more than two thousand, including several prominent foreigners who maintained summer residences in the dunes high above the beach. Jude Madsen, a noted Danish war correspondent and watercolorist, was sitting on the verandah of his summer villa on the dunes, reading and enjoying the sunshine, with "the Shrimp," the twelve-year-old-son of Henry W. Kinney, the *Trans-*

Pacific editor and *Atlantic Monthly* contributor. According to Kinney, who arrived in Kamakura a few hours later, the earthquake brought the house down on top of them, pinning both beneath a huge beam, layers of tiles, and pieces of broken wood. Struck in the spine, Madsen called weakly to the Shrimp, groaned that he wished he'd been killed instantly, then died. Kinney's son, still immobilized, watched helplessly as the tsunami swamped the garden, ripped down the sea wall, and stopped just a few feet from the ruined villa. "I thought for sure I was a goner," the Shrimp told his father, "when I saw the water come on and I couldn't move." He freed himself fifteen minutes later. Recounted Kinney: "The tidal wave swept out a great section of the village near the beach. I saw a thirty-foot sampan that had been lifted neatly on top of the roof of a prostrated house. Vast portions of the hills facing the ocean on both sides of the bay had slid into the sea. . . . The entire beach and the sea-floor had been raised about six feet by the quake and where there had been only a narrow beach strip lay now a wide, wet expanse of sand."

BACK IN THE CAPITAL, the second stage of the calamity was not flood, but fire. One minute after the earthquake struck Tokyo, many witnesses saw four columns of smoke rising in neighborhoods north, east, and south of the Imperial Palace. After five minutes, according to a police report, fifty-two more blazes had started. Twenty-four more after ten minutes. A total of eighty-three locations after fifteen minutes. By 12:30, 136 fires were burning in twelve of Tokyo's thirteen wards. "From every fire tower the alarm was quavering," reported Joseph Dahlmann, a Jesuit priest and professor of German literature at Tokyo Imperial University. "Lambent tongues of fire began to be plainly visible . . . this combination of smoke, fire and clanging bells made an impression utterly indescribable." Dahlmann lived in a Catholic seminary on a hilltop in Akasaka, a prosperous district located just southwest of the Imperial Palace, with a nearly panoramic view of the low-lying city to the east. For the next several hours he stood on his rooftop overlooking the great sea of wooden houses, documenting the fires' advance. By 2:30 the situation had worsened: "Dark masses of smoke, shot through with tongues of fire, filled the sky in every direction and each new gust of wind gave new impulse to the fury of the conflagration."

Hour by hour, the fires spread for exactly the reasons that seismologist Akitsune Imamura had predicted they would. Across this tightly packed city of 2 million people, 90 percent of whose half-million structures were made of wood, glass vials containing combustible chemicals shattered, charcoal braziers and gas cooking stoves overturned, fuel tanks erupted. The earthquake knocked the tile roofs off many traditional houses, exposing the highly flammable wooden roof footings underneath and hastening the incineration of flimsy homes. As in Yokohama, the earthquake broke the city's fragile system of water mains, initially paralyzing the fire department. A desperate shortage of manpower, the absence of a backup system to replace broken water mains, the lack of apparatus to draw water out of Tokyo's canals and rivers—all contributed heavily to the spread of the flames.

One key difference, however, between the Yokohama and Tokyo conflagrations may have been the role played by the wind. Accounts of its behavior vary. Dahlmann writes of "strong breezes" that "quickly spread fire through the densely populated streets." Another witness refers to winds that "shifted back and forth" throughout the afternoon. K. Takahashi, author of an account of the earthquake published in 1923, says that when the earthquake began, a light southerly wind was blowing, but it changed to a stiff west wind, and then became a northerly gale, causing confusion and setting new fires. Yet Starr makes no mention of a violent wind in his diaries. And curiously, M. W. Pett, the head of the Shanghai Fire Brigade, who came to Japan after the earthquake to inspect the damage and make recommendations about future fire prevention, said witnesses told him that, at least during the fire's early stages, there was no wind at all. "The Manager of the Imperial Hotel was very positive about it," he wrote, "and he had a fire very close to him, of terrific heat, but ascending straight up into the air. It seems extraordinary that this should be the case when a typhoon was blowing at Yokohama, so nearby, but the conditions of some half-burnt posts that I saw bears it out. They were burnt quite evenly instead of the tops being cut down by the flames as they would have been in a wind." Whatever the case, the sixty-mile-per-hour

southerly gale that turned Yokohama into charred rubble in three
hours must have diminished by the time it hit the capital. Instead,
Tokyo was subjected to periodic gusts that changed direction several
times in the course of the afternoon. As a result, the Tokyo conflagration took on a markedly different—but no less terrifying—character.
It moved by stealth, slowly closing a trap around tens of thousands of
unsuspecting people. The Tokyo fire didn't reach its peak until many
hours after the initial shock. But it grew, over the course of its forty-
six-hour duration, into the worst conflagration in history.

FREDERICK STARR was slow to appreciate the danger bearing down
on Shimbashi. During the first hours after the earthquake, he shuffled
around the street wearing his checkered bathrobe and strap-on
wooden clogs, observing the scene with more curiosity than alarm.
With his young assistant, Takagi, he calmly watched smoke and flame
rise from the north of the city. Takagi, on the other hand, was terrified. His family lived in Kanda, the book store neighborhood that had
burned down in 1913 and had been one of the first parts of central
Tokyo to go up in flames after the earthquake. "I urged Takagi to go,
especially as reports began to come in that . . . Kanda had especially
suffered," Starr wrote. "But Maebashi [another assistant] had not yet
come and the boy seemed to feel a responsibility in his absence. So we
waited. The streets were full of people hurrying home. They walked,
ran, any mode of convenience was in demand."

The fires inched closer and the hotel staff grew increasingly anxious. Starr, still playing the role of detached investigator, asked to borrow a rickshaw to inspect the conflagration; the manager told him
sharply that "it was sheer folly to think of using a *kuruma* [rickshaw]
for careless viewing, when they were in demand for necessary things,"
Starr noted. "Kurumas went by with passengers and wads of household goods—mountains of stuff, every kind of cart was in requisition;
humans were loaded with all their earthly possessions. . . . Smoke
could be seen rising in various directions. The boy could finally stand
it no longer and begging to be excused, hurried away homeward."

At four o'clock Joseph Dahlmann, the Catholic priest, noted from his rooftop observation post west of the Imperial Palace the convergence of two "rivers of fire" near Shimbashi. One strand swept east through Akasaka, the neighborhood known as Embassy Row, on a path toward the U.S. and British Embassies, the villas of Tokyo's counts and barons, and the homes of hundreds of foreign residents. Another moved south along the Imperial Palace's eastern flank, burning canals, centuries-old wooden bridges, and the Ginza, Tokyo's Fifth Avenue. "The two burning streams became merged near Shimbashi," Dahlmann observed, "and made of that district a lake of fire." Starr, in the middle of it, at last grasped that his life was in danger. Just across the Shimbashi canal, within sight of his hotel, a large conflagration was sweeping toward him with astonishing speed. The Kinokuniya staff, clearly agitated, urged Starr to gather his belongings as flight appeared all but certain. He stuffed a few notebooks into his black satchel, pulled out his gold watch from his steamer trunk. "Everything in the street was a wild flight before the red advance," Starr recalled. "The clerk summoned a truck, my trunks and the baggage of other passengers were heaped up on it. Some other customers and I clambered up and we were a part of the fleeing crowd. Where? To any open space where [we could find] safety."

Two miles to the north, another life-or-death drama was unfolding at Tokyo's most famous new landmark: Frank Lloyd Wright's Imperial Hotel. Manager Tetsuzo Inumaru had been meeting in his office with two employees just before the opening-day banquet when the earthquake hit.

> The building was shaking up and down and left to right. Three of us screamed "earthquake. This is huge!" We all put our hands against the wall and managed to stand up. Then I rushed to the kitchen . . . The electric ranges had fallen over and were all aflame, because some fat had been on the stoves. There were small fires on the floor. Fire was coming out in every direction. . . . I called "is anybody here?" Three cooks came out from under the tables where they'd been hiding. I asked them, "Can't you put the fire out?" . . . We soon succeeded in dousing the flames. In another ten minutes, the walls would have taken fire.

Enod San, who had been the chief assistant to Wright during the construction of the hotel and lived on the grounds, provided another account of the chaotic first minutes. In a report he prepared for Wright on September 8 about the damage suffered by the hotel, San described the scene:

> First came the shock without any previous signs of any kind. Rolled out of the house and ran to Imperial rear court. . . . Down came the restaurant across the street in the park, and fire broke out next moment. Horror-stricken people running to and fro, women weeping like little children. . . . Went to front of the building right after the shock ceased. Four stone figures fell, two of them along the pool. . . . Big corner piece of dining room showing cracks, but not serious. Banquet [Hall] on top as glorious as ever. Just when I was on this floor, up forty feet high above the ground, slam-bang business came again with such horrible roar swept me off my feet to floor; tottering and uneasy came to post and sustained myself and watched. Promenade, horizontal cracks in north half, but similar cracks used to be in south half. No signs showing of effect of shock.

After returning to his second-floor executive suite, Inumaru removed his ceremonial kimono and put on a jacket and tie. The hotel manager knew that he would need mobility in the hours ahead. The banquet, scheduled for noon, was forgotten. All efforts of the staff focused on saving the hotel from the fires. Mains across Tokyo had broken, cutting off the hotel's water. At one o'clock, Inumaru walked out the rear exit to check on the surroundings. There he observed a terrible sight: flames shooting from the windows of the Tokyo Electric Company, a six-story building directly behind the Imperial. Cinders fluttered over the hotel, igniting cloth blinds hanging from open guest room windows. Inumaru summoned his employees. "Since there is no water, we have to extinguish the fire by ourselves," he told them. "No matter what happens, this building should not burn down. Protect this building, risk even your life." It's unlikely all of Inumaru's employees felt the same zealous call to duty as the general manager.

Frank Lloyd Wright's new Imperial Hotel was one of the few structures in Tokyo to survive the quake relatively unscathed.

Nevertheless, dozens of staff members raced from room to room, ripping curtains down and stamping out the blazes.

The pool in the entrance court, as Wright had predicted, became the Imperial's salvation. Employees filled buckets, formed a relay team, and extinguished a dozen small fires that had broken out on the roof as a result of the Electric Company blaze. No sooner had the rooftop fire been doused than a life insurance company on the north side of the hotel went up in flames. The Imperial bucket brigade remobilized. Guests milled about the darkened Main Promenade; the power in the city was out, and Inumaru had turned off the hotel's generator as a precaution. The wife of an executive with Universal Pictures in Hollywood wandered, hysterical, looking for her young daughter, from whom she had separated in the initial panic. Outside the front entrance refugees trooped toward Hibiya Park, a sprawling complex of woods, gardens, and ponds opposite the Imperial. Inumaru ordered his cooks to prepare rice balls for the homeless, then, with fires breaking out all over the neighborhood, tried to comfort hundreds of anxious employees and guests.

* * *

AT LEAST ONE MEMBER of the local populace was entitled to a much more complicated response to the tumult. At Tokyo Imperial University, Akitsune Imamura, the noted seismologist, paced the laboratory, watching the needles scribble on his recording drums, bitterly cognizant that the catastrophe he had long predicted had arrived. By triangulating the data from three seismographs spread around the region, Imamura was able within minutes to calculate the precise epicenter of the earthquake. "For years I had believed that the region around Sagami Bay was a zone where a great earthquake should have been expected to occur, but history failed to record such a phenomenon," he wrote in his diary that day. "At this moment I was startled to discover that the expected had at last happened." Twenty Japanese and foreign correspondents who had reached the campus despite the outbreak of fires and the collapse of the city's transportation system surrounded him thirty minutes after the earthquake. "At eleven fifty eight and forty four seconds," he intoned, as an aftershock rattled the windows of the lab and shook the floors and smoke seeped in from nearby fires, "a powerful earthquake occurred, originating south of the Izu Peninsula near Oshima. Tsunamis will strike Sagami Bay in a few minutes, but Tokyo and Yokohama will be spared." (Imamura may have based that prediction on another major slippage along the Sagami Bay fault line, in 1703, which had sent huge waves crashing against the Sagami Bay coast but spared the Kanto Plain.) At 12:40, while Imamura was wrapping up his press conference, the most powerful of the aftershocks occurred, and several journalists rushed from the building. When assured of their own safety, the handful who remained continued to ask questions. In a wry acknowledgment of his second-class status in the Seismology Department Imamura wrote, "I admired, in particular, the foreigners who even assured themselves of my name, which I had to spell for them, and of my position in the university." Then, his pen dripping with sarcasm, he added, "Some of the Japanese journalists took me for Doctor Omori and so reported. Poor great Doctor Omori!"

What was going through Imamura's mind? After the years of rejection and ridicule, he must have felt a deep sense of vindication. At the same time, it could hardly have been very satisfying for him. The capital was in flames, thousands had already died, and his own family's fate remained unknown. In a candid interview a few days later with a Tokyo newspaper, the seismologist bared his relief at being exonerated, his sorrow at the destruction and death, and his lingering resentment—toward the superior who had belittled him, the institution that had failed to back him, the government that had ignored him. "When I [made my prediction] initially everybody from every direction critized me," he said. "I was totally smashed down. 'You have to take it back, because this really caused panic among the people,' they told me. So even though I thought my prediction was right, all I could do was keep silent. If I had insisted on that prediction to the end, and kept warning the public, maybe this terrible disaster could have been avoided. I feel very sorry about that." Imamura would never mention Omori by name in connection with his disgrace, but he left no doubt whom he blamed. "There was even an eminent scientist who ridiculed my opinion once at that time [1907] and again in 1915, as nothing other than a rumor which might cause a general panic," he would write two months after the earthquake. Perhaps—though there is no evidence for it—he experienced a touch of schadenfreude at the thought of the humiliation that awaited his superior, away at his conference in Melbourne. Only one year earlier "poor great Doctor Omori" had confidently reassured Tokyo's citizenry that there was no danger of an imminent catastrophe. It had proven to be one of history's most egregiously inaccurate predictions. Omori's exile in Australia during the greatest seismological event of the twentieth century almost certainly gave Imamura a twinge of satisfaction. "Contrary to Professor Omori," he would later write, barely concealing his delight in his rival's absence, "I have been very lucky. I was just in our institute at the moment of the great shock, could appreciate fully the earth movements, and after half an hour was able to give to more than a score of journalists some brief information about the exact time of the earthquake and the position of the epicenter . . . which now I find to have been not so much in error."

Descending the staircase after the press conference, Imamura found the exit of the Seismology Building blocked by fallen tiles. He cleared them and stepped outside. Walking toward the main gate of the uni-

versity at Hongo Street, he stared in horror at the collapsed Center for
Law and Literature and the burning Laboratory for Applied Sciences.
"Hongo Street was packed with frightened people. . . . Fires were visible in the distant south and a strong wind was blowing. I realized the
terrible situation but I hoped for the best." The seismologist returned
to his laboratory and packed his negatives and other research materials. With alarm, he realized that a fire from the adjacent library threatened to leap across the pathway to the Seismology Department.
"With the aid of two other men we carried out all the important
things to a safe place," he wrote. "The fire was now fast approaching
but not a drop of water was to be had. There appeared to be no hope,
but just at this juncture the direction of the wind changed and we
were out of danger." Imamura's eldest son reached the campus on his
bicycle in midafternoon, bringing word of the family's safety. But
Tokyo Imperial University's fate was less certain. Imamura saw that
twenty buildings were blazing on and next to the campus. "The
sight," Imamura wrote, "was too awful for words."

ALL AFTERNOON the city burned. People fled through the streets,
looking for open ground, a safe haven, the river, a field, a vacant lot,
a public park, a canal, anywhere that they believed the flames wouldn't
reach. Western diplomats, foreign tourists, members of the royal Japanese court, politicians, laborers—all were thrown together in a desperate flight for safety. There are only a handful of English-language
testimonies available, but the account of an American Lutheran missionary, Deaconess Knapp, conveys a sense of those frantic hours.
Knapp—her first name isn't known—had had the bad luck of arriving
back in Tokyo at eleven o'clock on the morning of September 1 following a month-long vacation in the hills. After checking her bags
into a hotel near the Imperial Palace, the missionary had gone to a
restaurant for lunch. She told her story to Elizabeth Cotten, who recounted it in an emotional, sometimes overwrought, letter to her parents in Salisbury, North Carolina. After crawling out of the damaged
but still intact restaurant, Knapp decided to head for Tsukiji, at the
mouth of the Sumida River in eastern Tokyo, to take refuge at her
church. Unable to find a rickshaw, she set out on foot but almost im-

mediately encountered fires. "As she walked they pursued her," Cotten wrote. "Behind her they came—down a side street she would start, but in front of her was a street of flame. She would turn to the left, the rush and the roar of the flames blocking her way. To the right—this time a little headway could be made, only to find she must retrace her steps and take another alley that seemed to lead her to safety. And so for miles this hideous race, this game of hide and seek with her all powerful pursuer. But she won the game."

Knapp's story ends there, though one imagines that she must have had much more to tell. According to Dahlmann, at about the time Knapp arrived at the church mission in Tsukiji, two distinct fires, from the north and the west, roared over the bayside neighborhood. They swept across the waterfront, even leapt to a small island a few hundred yards offshore. The Catholic cathedral where Lyman and Elizabeth Cotten had attended the memorial for Harding, the Presbyterian church, seminaries, Westerners' houses, English-language schools— all burned to the ground. Knapp eventually made it out of Tsukiji and resurfaced in Lake Chuzenji, where she told her tale of survival to Elizabeth Cotten. But how she escaped from the inferno in Tsukiji is a part of the narrative that will never be known. (Knapp's survival story took a while to reach her family. On September 20 a telegram arrived at the U.S. Embassy in Tokyo from a "Knapp" in Paris, asking, "HAS DEACONESS KNAPP SURVIVED CABLE REPLY MY EXPENSE." Ambassador Woods cabled back, "DEACONESS KNAPP SAFE.")

Greed and exploitation did not disappear in this hour of common danger. Less than a mile separated the elite foreign enclave of Tsukiji from the densely packed slums further north along the sinuous Sumida River, including Yoshiwara, Tokyo's largest and most famous red-light district. The government had established the quarter during the Edo period in a corner of Asakusa, Tokyo's tawdry entertainment district (often referred to as the Coney Island of Japan). One hundred seventy-five brothels employing three thousand prostitutes lined six main streets and a score of crooked alleys. A procession of "show rooms" faced the street, where, each evening, "young girls draped in purple and red kimonos expose[d] their painted faces for onlookers and shamelessly smoke[d] their long bamboo pipes," according to a guidebook to Tokyo from the early 1920s. On September 1 most of the young women were sleeping when the earthquake struck, after entertaining their clients until the early hours of the morning. As the nightgown-clad prostitutes fled in panic down rickety staircases, they were met at the exit by madams and their muscle, who pushed them back inside. The brothel owners locked the doors and the twin gates leading from Yoshiwara to the world outside, fearing a mass defection of their sources of income. At last, in the late afternoon, with fires burning on the edge of the red-light district, most of the madams relented. Hundreds of prostitutes followed them to a small park and pond within Yoshiwara. "If the fires come closer," the women were told, "you can jump into the water." One teenage survivor recalled, "Some people brought their samisen [a stringed instrument, originating in Okinawa in the fourteenth century, that courtesans and geisha were required to master]. Some brought tatami mats. The houses surrounding the park caught fire. I heard girls say, 'it's very hot—help!' and people began to jump into this pond. I was about to jump in, but I couldn't reach the edge: so many people were crowded around the water. Somebody shouted, 'if you cannot jump into the pond, then you should leave this place.' Someone had unlocked the gate and I ran away toward the hills. And right after I left this park, the whole brothel area around Yoshiwara caught fire."

Those who surveyed the bodies the following day believed that, at four o'clock, the women leaped, one after another, into the muddy pond to escape the flames and sparks. The water was twelve feet deep. Few knew how to swim. They clung desperately to the slippery edges, but others jumped into the water on top of them, and more on top of those. The women lost their grip, flailed in a panic, grabbed hold of those nearest them, and pulled them down. Glowing ash from surrounding buildings landed on hair that had been laquered with oil and wax, a traditional beautification method among Japanese prostitutes, and set it on fire. The pond became a churning, fiery mass of humanity. Some drowned, others burned to death, others suffocated beneath the tangle of bodies. Police pulled 490 corpses, 440 of them women, from the pond the next day. Few of the victims were over twenty years old.

* * *

IN HONJO on the east bank of the Sumida and in Asakusa on the west bank, tens of thousands of refugees fled down alleys crackling with fire, converging into a few passable avenues that led to the river. Laden with cotton bedding and bags filled with clothing, rice crackers, and thermoses of tea, they moved toward the water consumed by a single thought: Safety lay on the other side of the river. Relentlessly driven forward, the crowds surged toward the Sumida from both banks. At the river's edge a huge traffic jam developed. The first licks of fire began to appear in the rows of flimsy structures abutting each side of the Sumida. The flames grew fiercer, nearing the wooden bridges that spanned the eight-hundred-foot-wide waterway, filling the air with cinders and sparks. Rather than a salvation, the river had become a trap.

At a bridge called Eitabashi, a man named Shin Kumihara found himself shoved and pressed by hundreds of people toward the center of the arched wooden span. Pillars of smoke from across eastern Tokyo had merged into a fluffy, charcoal-colored cumulus cloud that hovered low over the Sumida, blocking out the sun. In the semidarkness the air reeked of sweat and burning wood, and the cries of children mingled with grunts and curses of people immobilized by the mob. Kumihara described to a Japanese newspaper reporter what happened next:

> People were rushing in both directions. I was being pushed from both sides, I couldn't move. Children and women screamed, kids fell down and were crushed. The houses on both sides of the river started to catch fire. Those people on the edges of the bridge couldn't stand the heat, so they tried to push people and go to the center. Fifty, maybe one hundred people fell into the water—they just disappeared. I noticed poles under the bridge—so I climbed underneath the bridge and I shinnied down the wooden pole until I reached the river. Luckily it was ebb tide. I put my body under the water, my head above the water so I was able to breathe. Then the bridge caught fire. Men, women, old people, and children began to jump into the water. People in the river were drowning. They were grabbing, and fighting to survive. It looked like hell. . . . I looked around, it was a sea of drowned bodies. I couldn't even see the water. And finally the whole Eitabashi dropped down into the river.

At the same time that thousands of Honjo residents were making for the bridges over the Sumida—five of which collapsed and burned that evening—an even larger number headed to the grounds of the Army Clothing Depot, two blocks east of the river. Honjo's chief of police encouraged this migration, eventually steering more than forty thousand people to the twenty-acre patch of bare earth and scruffy grass in the shadow of the sumo stadium. It would prove to be a tragic misjudgment.

Nine-year-old Kikue Washio and her mother left their home at 12:30 after several other houses on the block had begun to burn. Kikue wore thick socks, *tabi,* and carried on her back a *furoshiki,* a square cloth wrapped around the few personal belongings she had managed to gather: a doll, a packet of rice crackers, and a bottle of water. Others from her block pushed handcarts piled with futons and luggage. A ten-foot-high barrier of corrugated tin surrounded the depot, which was in the shape of an irregular rectangle, but the fence was open in many places. Because they traveled light, and because they had arrived early in the afternoon, Kikue and her mother found a spot in the center of the depot grounds, where they believed they would be safest. They sat on a patch of dry yellow grass and tried to make themselves as comfortable as possible.

One of Kikue's neighbors, ten-year-old Shin Nakamura, had been watching a Charlie Chaplin movie at an Asakusa cinema when the earthquake struck. Arriving home at 12:30, he discovered the door open and the house deserted. His parents, siblings, and most of his neighbors, he learned, had followed the advice of the police and taken refuge at the depot grounds. Nakamura picked up a rice container in the kitchen and rushed out to search for the rest of his family. He found the grounds packed with people and luggage. He stood at one of the many entrances and waited, until, by chance, his father passed by an hour later. "He grabbed my arm, and he took me to a place in the center, where I found my mother, grandmother, and younger sister and brother," Nakamura recalled. "I felt so guilty. I knew my father had been worried and waiting for me to come."

The atmosphere on the grounds of the Army Clothing Depot remained festive in the early afternoon. Groceries did a brisk business selling the hot, thirsty refugees *karupisu,* a popular summer drink made from yogurt, milk, and sugar. Some people sang songs. Others spread rice balls, dried fish, and pickled radishes on their furoshikis—brightly colored fabrics used for wrapping, storing, and carrying—and held impromptu picnics. A few played board games such as chess and go. Some who lived nearby felt secure enough to venture back to their houses to fetch more belongings: tatami mats, *tansu* (wooden wardrobes), futons, cooking utensils, and rice. Newspaper photographers snapped pictures of the crowd. One image that survives, taken at two o'clock, conveys a sense of calm. The grounds are packed, but here and there one can spot individuals: a pretty young girl clad in a polka-dotted kimono, an elderly woman with a white scarf wrapped around her head. Another woman climbs on top of the large wooden wheel of a cart piled high with roped-together boxes and strains to grab something with her left hand. A young boy draped in a white kimono at the bottom of the image seems to have his hands clasped in prayer. People hold black or white umbrellas against the sun, chat with neighbors, confidently waiting out the storm. It felt, one survivor recalled, "like a big neighborhood block party."

Things changed quickly.

At 2:30, Saburo Hasebe, a twenty-three-year-old schoolteacher, tried to take refuge at the depot but had to turn away because of the crowds. The neighborhood fires had grown stronger: on his way to the depot Hasebe noticed that the Honjo ward office was ablaze, and a wall of flame was sweeping toward the river, bearing down on the unsuspecting people trying to cross the bridges. The streets were devoid of people, he recalled, "just a lone hound dog running around." When Hasebe arrived at the southern entrance to the depot, "I saw so many people, and so much luggage, wardrobes, futons, clothes, piles of things [that I left]. The place was entirely full. Two police officers sat on horses at the edge of the crowd, but they couldn't move." Over the next hour, the temperature at the grounds soared, fueled by body heat and the approaching conflagration. The sky darkened; an artificial pile of cumulus clouds higher than Mount Everest filled the sky above the city. Joseph Dahlmann, the Jesuit priest, described what happened next:

Suddenly the fire from the opposite bank seized upon two bridges and pounced upon the narrow strip of houses separating the open space from the Sumida River. Within an incredibly short time the cordon of fire around the Army Clothing Bureau was drawing closer and closer; in every direction billows of flame were raging and screaming. . . . By three o'clock the wide space was so packed with people that they formed a solid block, within which individual movement became impossible. An unbroken circle of fire was raging in every direction. Every exit was closed by fire. The ground was glowing with heat, the air became a . . . furnace.

A description by Takahashi captures the final minutes: "The flames were singeing people on the outer edge [of the depot], while the goods heaped all over the place had become as dry as could be. Frantic cries for help and prayers in frenzy now came, from tens of thousands of throats, making a tremendous din that rose even above the cracks of combustion and roar of fiery tempest."

At a few minutes before four o'clock, people near the Sumida watched in terrified amazement as a pillar of black smoke spun along the west bank of the river in the direction of the Army Clothing Depot. The phenomenon was a "dragon twist," or fire tornado, which, like its thunderstorm-generated counterpart on the Great Plains of the United States, requires a set of peculiar conditions in order to form. The first requirement is a large, intense conflagration that generates violent updrafts of superheated air and hurricane-force winds. The second is an artificial cumulus formation of smoke high above the fire. If these two violent air systems—turbulent clouds and superheated updrafts—collide, often they will spin off rotating vortices of smoke and flame. The twister-like phenomena form high in the sky but sweep across the ground, generating cyclonic winds, sucking up oxygen, and burning everything in their path. Until the 1923 earthquake, the most lethal such funnel had taken shape during a massive forest fire outside the logging town of Peshtigo, Wisconsin, in October 1871; it swept over the town in two minutes, suffocating and burning to death eight hundred people, including many children whose parents had lowered them into wells for safety. "[People] saw a large black object, resembling a balloon, which revolved in the air with great rapidity, advancing above the summits of the trees towards a house which it seemed to single out for destruction. Barely had it touched the latter when the balloon burst with a loud report, like that of a bombshell, and, at the same moment, rivulets of fire streamed out in all directions," wrote Father Peter Pernin, a survivor. "Strange to say there were many corpses [later] found, bearing about them no traces of scars or burns, and yet in the pockets of their habiliments, equally uninjured, watches, cents, and other articles in metal were discovered completely melted."

According to Akitsune Imamura, who gathered data from survivors, the Tokyo dragon twist may have been the largest one ever recorded: "It was 100 to 200 [yards] high and its width was about that of the Sumo Stadium [300 yards]. It swirled counterclockwise and swept off little barges two or three [yards] from the surface of the river. The smoke and flame of the School of Industry on the Asakusa side added to its strength. It then moved over to the opposite side, toward the Clothing Depot. . . . The approximate [rotational] velocity of the whirlwind must have been seventy to eighty [yards] a second [approximately 150 miles an hour]."

The sky grew suddenly as black as night and smoke from four directions formed a thick blanket over the Army Clothing Depot. A strong wind whipped up, blowing flaming cinders into the faces of the refugees. People tried to shield themselves with whatever they could find—a blanket, a futon, a suitcase. "There were terrible sounds," one witness recalled. "The fire extended up to the sky." Scientists who visited the scene afterward calculated that the twister moved along the ground at twenty to thirty miles per hour, taking a leisurely three minutes to cross from one end of the grounds to the other. Some survivors said that it made a single pass; one claimed that the tornado swept over the depot grounds three times, back and forth, at intervals of two to three minutes. Shin Nakamura, ten years old at the time, saw members of his family disappear into the vortex of the whirlwind. His first sensation was an intense stinging in his face caused by hot cinders in the air. The discomfort spread to his neck, the backs of his hands, anywhere his flesh was exposed. The family—Nakamura, his parents, grandmother, three-year-old brother, and baby sister—huddled together, covering their faces and grabbing onto one another for protection against the strong, searing wind. Then Nakamura observed suitcases and bedrolls begin leaping and somersaulting as if they had a life of their own. Corrugated metal roofs swirled lethally through the air, sometimes striking down people near the family. Nakamura's mouth and nostrils filled with searing hot cinders, and he plucked them away. He grabbed his grandmother, who was trembling like a leaf in the wind. Then, with disbelief, he watched the twister sweep his younger brother off his feet and carry the terrified little boy to his death. Instinctively, Nakamura reached out and grabbed his younger sister by her *obi* (a wide sash fastened in the back of the kimono with a large bow). The obi unraveled, she twirled around once, then was gone. "People panicked, they tried to run in different directions, they collided into one another," Nakamura recalled. "They grabbed whatever they could—human beings, luggage, so they wouldn't get sucked up by the whirlwind. People were trying to survive. I saw the expressions on their faces— they looked like devils."

A fourteen-year-old factory worker who had become separated from his parents and taken refuge at the depot with a friend recalled:

> People, horses, tin roofs and futons were flying in the sky. The household goods started to burn with a big crackling noise. My friend and I kept moving left and right, stepping over burning bodies, and suddenly this tin roof flew straight at us. My friend fell. I tried to wake him up, then I realized that his head was gone. I was still holding his hand. I pried his fingers off mine and managed to leave him. I stepped on luggage but I fell down. I had a burned face, burned palm, burned left leg, burned back. I think I fell unconscious. When I woke up, I was on a stretcher of the army and I was taken to the elementary school.

The next thing Shin Nakamura remembered was silence. He found himself on the bottom of a pile of bodies. He tried to wriggle free, but realized he was trapped. Drained of energy and feeling intense pain, he squirmed for what seemed like hours. The whimpers and moans of the dying filled his ears, burned and charred limbs dangled in his face. Determined to survive, he wrenched himself free at last and took a long look around him.

> Everybody was totally motionless. People lay in stacks. Ten, twenty people on top of one another, dead. The smell was terrible. . . . I wondered what had happened to my father, my mother. But I couldn't find them. I had to get out of this place. I started to walk to the Ryogoku Bridge along the river because it seemed like there was less fire. There was a small shelter there. I stayed there, taking a rest. . . . I was alone.

Kikue Washio remembered that, as the tornado approached, her mother tightly held her hand, murmured prayers, and told her daughter not to be afraid. At some point Kikue fainted. She woke up in darkness, lying in her mother's lap, surrounded by the dead and the dying. Faint voices begged for sips of water and relief from pain. A man wearing tall rubber boots climbed over the fence into the grounds of the Yasuda mansion, home of one of the neighborhood's wealthiest residents (he and his entire family had died in the depot fire). He filled his boots with water from a pond in the Yasuda garden and passed them to Kikue and a few other survivors. "But many people convulsed after they drank water and died in front of me," she recalled. Kikue, slightly burned, and her mother, who was severely burned on her face and back, climbed over piles of dead bodies—some charred beyond recognition, others seemingly untouched—and slipped through the remains of the corrugated tin fence. They came upon an ice works nearby, and her mother placed pieces of ice on their burns. As they walked on, "Whenever I saw the dead bodies of small children, I put ice in their mouths, to revive them," Kikue remembered.

A female neighbor carrying her baby on her back—apparently oblivious to the fact that the infant was burned and dead—joined them. They started walking east. It was five o'clock, and the wind had changed its direction and driven the flames away from Honjo. The fire subsided. They passed canals choked with dead bodies. Kikue stared at her mother. She resembled, Kikue thought, an *oiwa,* a female demon from a famous ghost story, murdered by her philandering samurai husband, who roams the earth with a blistered scalp, an empty eye socket, and a face the color of charcoal. Kikue and her mother walked along the Sumida River, clogged with the corpses of the drowned and boiled, and took refuge at a Japanese army-run relief center. Of forty-four thousand people who had fled to the depot grounds, Kikue and her mother were among three hundred survivors. Learning of the dimensions of the catastrophe, the Honjo ward police chief was overcome with shame and remorse. He was the official who had directed thousands of neighborhood residents to take refuge at the Army Clothing Depot grounds, mistakenly assuming that the large open space in the heart of the city would keep them safe from the advancing fires. The night after the holocaust, he committed *seppuku*, disemboweling himself with a samurai sword, to atone for his monumental misjudgment.

IT WAS NEARING DUSK when the hotel truck dropped Frederick Starr and his assistant, Maebashi (who had taken over from Takagi after the boy rushed home), in front of Shiba Park, an expanse of ponds, forests, and fields two miles south of the nearest fire. On a hill beside the park rose the Zen Buddhist temple Zojoji, built in 1393 and the former private enclave of the shoguns. Thousands of Japanese had taken refuge in the park by the time Starr arrived. "Lanterns, awnings, mosquito net camps, heaps of baggage, groups of refugees were anywhere and everywhere," Starr wrote. "We found an unoccupied hut and our stuff was unloaded and piled. . . . We hung our lanterns on the trunks to show our location. Our nearest neighbors were a family with children under a mosquito net—apparently a happy picnic. No one complained." An hour later, though, Starr and Maebashi realized that they would have to flee again.

> The glow from [the north] came nearer. Doubts as to whether we were secure grew. The first to break was the little family under the mosquito net. They began to pack, took down their shelter, and fled. In a few minutes we were all moving, seeking some place of safety further on. The clerk from the hotel was now with us and said something about a gate. We saw but one, to the grounds of Zojoji. Many were pushing through. . . . To me it looked like a trap. If the

fire came and leaped across the road we were crowded into a narrow space between a high and solid fence and temple buildings.

While Starr hesitated, a young priest beckoned to him and Maebashi through the red torii at Zojoji's entrance. "He was an old friend of Maebashi," Starr recalled, "and he was delighted to learn who I was and begged to take us to a place of perfect safety." Starr and Maebashi followed the priest across wide courtyards, blanketed with smooth white pebbles, bordered by centuries-old plain wooden temples in which the Tokugawa princes had celebrated themselves and their military prowess. Stone lanterns lay shattered. In a tatami room inside a temple complex, other priests arrived, greeted them warmly, and begged them "to rest, to have no fear." The temple, normally a place of serenity and contemplation, throbbed with a sense of urgency. Outside Starr could see that the glow from the fires was spreading. "It extended around almost a third of the horizon. Presently they came again. 'It is best to go: we will take you to a place of safety.'"

Starr, the six-time climber of Mount Fuji, set forth on what must have been the most harrowing ascent of his life. Still exhausted from his ordeal on the volcano, he limped up a steep set of steps leading to the highest temple of Zojoji. Priests carried his belongings and led him by the hand. Young acolytes struggled beneath the weight of a sacred stone slab from ancient Japan that they were bringing to a "secret place" of refuge. The climb must have seemed to Starr a mocking counterpoint to all of the exuberant pilgrimages that he had made to the fiery lip of Mount Fuji. And yet the priests around him seemed serene, reconciled to the savage forces of the earth. The group passed under a bridge, then hiked up another flight of steps that curved to the right and led to the gate of the inner temple. On the top step, a priest set down a chair for Starr. High above the city that he loved, Starr watched the fires consume the last remnants of feudal Edo. "We sat there through the night, looking at the brazen sky," he wrote. "The city suffered and writhed in agony, [while] we remained in our place of safety at the inner temple of Zojoji."

7

Rescue

Bodies, more bodies, without clothing, without skin, red and black forms, twisted like vines. . . . A bank, a shop, reduced to its bare essentials: an iron safe standing on its throne of stone. A frightful odor of burning matter and corpses. We arrive at the sea.

Paul Claudel, "Across the Cities in Flames" (September 1923)

A T TWO O'CLOCK in the afternoon on September 1, Otis Manchester Poole gathered his family at the end of Bluff Road high above the burning city of Yokohama. Sheets of fire approached the last surviving houses on the Bluff. A landslide blocked a dirt path leading down to Yokohama harbor, where his father-in-law had moored his yacht, the *Daimyo*. A cloud of smoke and flame cut off an alternative route descending to Fransuyama, the lowest spur of the Bluff and home to the French Consulate, a burning ruin. The Pooles had only one option: to flee into the grounds of the adjacent British Naval Hospital, a villa and bungalows perched at the edge of a two-hundred-foot cliff.

After a few moments of hesitation, the Poole clan—Otis, his wife, their three young sons, his wife's parents, and their Japanese amah Miné—hurried through a red *torii*, a ceremonial gate commonly found at the main entrance to a Shinto shrine. Fissures had split the ground, bungalows lay smashed. Dozens of expatriates, some with severe injuries, had taken refuge on tennis courts built on terraced lawns

*The Grand Hotel before it was smashed to pieces and
then burned to the ground.*

that extended to the edge of the precipice. "Some were disheveled, some bandaged, many dazed," Poole wrote. A cluster of White Russian émigrés, recently arrived on freighters from Vladivostok, huddled together. Two dozen of their confreres had just been killed in the collapse of a Bluff apartment house. "One fair-haired girl of seventeen," Poole observed, "clad only in a nightgown, was standing on a grass hummock beside the path so bewildered as to be unaware that her torn garment was revealing a lovely young figure. Against the swirling black smoke she might have been a Grecian statue."

Poole watched the flames approach a line of houses along Bluff Road. Pine trees crackled; a friend's home exploded into flames. The fire, he realized, would soon leap across the road and ignite what was left of the hospital. Poole turned to his father-in-law. "We'll have to go over the cliff now, whether we like it or not," he said.

He walked to the edge of the Bluff and gazed over Tokyo Bay. The beach lay two hundred feet below, a near-vertical drop along a grass-

and-weed-tufted wall of basalt, covered by ravines and knobby out-
croppings. To the left, looking north, the shapeless remains of the
Grand Hotel, the Oriental Palace, and the other buildings along the
Bund, landmarks of Poole's world since his childhood, spat fire into
the rust-brown sky. Three British sailors had stripped the nets from
the tennis courts, tied them together, and dragged them down the
terraces to the cliff's edge. They lashed one end to a cottage and
hurled the rest over the side. The knotted ropes came to rest above a
narrow rock ledge fifty feet over the beach. The refugees, Poole saw,
would have to maneuver down the cliff, hanging onto the net for support, then inch across the rock shelf for fifty yards to a steep landslide.
There, by sliding down the dirt and gravel moraine, they could safely
reach flat ground.

Poole's good friend and pastor, the Reverend Eustace M. Strong,
chaplain of Yokohama's Christ Church, clambered up the cliff at
almost the same moment that Poole and his family prepared to go
down. A beloved figure in the expatriate community, Strong had almost been killed at the YMCA Seamen's Club on Water Street ninety
minutes earlier. After leaping from the broken building, the chaplain
had walked down an alley past the Oriental Palace Hotel to the Bund,
the last man to make it through before the hotel burst into impassible
flames. He had swum parallel to the burning waterfront, surfaced on
the reclaimed ground beyond the Grand Hotel, and scaled the rock
face to the top of the Bluff. For the next hour, until the flames swept
in, Strong would help evacuate three hundred foreigners and Japanese
down the cliff he had just ascended.

Ulysses Webb, superintendent of the American Naval Hospital, and
the seven members of the rescue party that had pulled him from the
basement, arrived at the same time as Strong. Making a run through
the flames to the British Naval Hospital grounds, Webb and his colleagues had reached the precipice with their faces scorched and their
uniforms afire. "By ropes and by clinging to grass roots and shrubs, by
digging in our fingers and sliding and rolling," Webb recalled a week
later, "we lowered ourselves over the cliffs to the reclaimed grounds
at the water's edge."

Poole's wife, Dorothy, was the first member of the family to go over
the cliff. He watched her dangle and swing down from foothold to

foothold. "Hold tight!" he yelled. "I'm all right," she answered. "I climbed trees as a child and I can do this now." Minutes later she landed safely at the bottom. The sailors looped a rope around Poole's eldest son, Tony. The ten-year-old clung to his father's back. Poole lowered himself to the first foothold. The men on top gingerly belayed Tony down the precipice, paying out the line while Poole worked his way along the net. But after thirty feet, Poole recalled:

> The cliff face grew steeper, the descent tougher, and [since we were] out of sight of those above, they could not tell how fast to pay out Tony's rope and it began to cut into his shoulders. . . . The pain of the rope made him cry out and I had to swing him off my back to my chest, where I could partly support him with one arm and tug at the rope for more slack as we dropped from one foothold to another. Bit by bit we worked down to the end of the net [to the] perilous ledge . . . it was little more than two feet wide, irregularly humped, while immediately below the cliff was undercut and dropped invisible, fifty feet to the beach. A slip would be fatal.

They inched their way across the lip until they reached the gravel moraine. Tony slid safely down the slope to Dorothy, who was waiting for him on the flat ground. Poole clambered back to the top of the precipice, where he retrieved his second son, David, and descended again. A cascade of Japanese and foreigners followed in a desperate flight, kicking clots of damp earth into Poole's face. As he crossed the lip for a third rescue—that of his youngest son, Dick—Poole saw that his father-in-law, the commodore, had already roped the boy to his own back and had started his descent. But near the bottom of the net, the line securing Dick came loose, and the boy dangled fifty feet above the ground, three fingers hooked to his grandfather's shirt collar. Poole leaped across the ledge, grabbed his son, tightroped back across the lip, and slid with him down the moraine. The Poole family stood, reunited, on the fissure-laced ground. Poole looked up.

> Red-flushed billows of smoke were swirling over the cliff top, and out of the murk figures scurried, scrambling over the edge in a fran-

tic stream . . . tongues of flame laced the smoke; some of the figures silhouetted along the cliff-top began to hurl themselves over. At first I thought they were bundles of salvage, but . . . one spread-eagled in mid-air and came shrieking down to sudden silence. Others followed, like rag dolls, hopelessly pinwheeling down the cliff face and dislodging yet others until there was a motionless fringe at the foot of the cliff. . . . It was too gruesome and I retraced my steps downward, sick at heart.

WHILE OTIS POOLE was bringing his family down the cliff, Gertrude Cozad, the American missionary, watched the city burn from the Buddhist temple Daijingu on Yokohama's southwest outskirts. All through the afternoon refugees flowed into the hillside compound. People with crushed limbs and blistered skin rode the backs of relatives and were laid on the grass. A man lugging a kerosene can full of *mizu-ame*, a glutinous starch syrup used for making Japanese sweets, arrived, covered with melted goo from his hair to his knees. Mothers and their famished children set upon him, scraping the syrup off his body, pulling fistful of it from the can. Hayashi Shotaro, Cozad's Korean companion, made a foray out of the compound and returned with an injured teenage girl whom he had found lying in the road. He had plucked her up ahead of the approaching flames. Were the fires that close? Cozad wondered. Cozad and Shotaro made her as comfortable as they could, "with my pillow and a piece of matting, and a part of my ice water poured into her raspberry vinegar."

The reassuring presence of Buddhist priests and government officials, as well as the tranquil surroundings, Cozad observed, lulled most of the refugees into a sense of security. But Cozad didn't share their confidence. Disoriented and passive in the hour after the earthquake, the American missionary was growing to trust her instincts more and more as the day progressed. From her vantage point within the hillside enclosure she could see that the typhoon wind had pushed the fires toward the temple from two directions. Gusts carried cinders and the acrid smell of smoke over the grounds. After an hour of deepening anxiety, she approached a pair of worried-looking men who looked like officials and confided that she was concerned. They seemed passive, paralyzed.

"It looks pretty bad here, doesn't it?" she said.

"Yes, but what can we do?" one replied. "We can't get away from here and where is there a safer place?"

Cozad returned to Shotaro. "Let's get out of here," she said.

The Korean hesitated. "How can we leave these people?" he asked her. "They will be terrified." But Cozad was resolute. Heartbroken, she cast a final glance at the people whom she had been closely observing and conversing with for the past three hours. All of them, she realized, faced certain doom. There was the eight-year-old girl who had been praying ceaselessly since arriving at the temple; the elderly, white-haired couple who hung onto each other desperately—already, it seemed to Cozad, on the verge of giving up. One family of five, well dressed and refined looking, huddled together on the grass, exhausted, their faces drained of color. A young man sat beside his mother, his wife, and their days-old infant, staring vacantly into space. "Still, I could not help them," the missionary wrote. "We stole away, hoping they would not see us go."

They crept out the main gate. Fires approached from the east and the north. The only possible way out was up a steep valley to the southwest hemmed in by precipitous slopes on either side. Rocky horse trails wound along the valley's flanks. As they traversed the narrow neck of the valley, the flames advanced to within three hundred feet of them, and the heat was intense. The fire crossed the trail behind them a few seconds later, shutting off the only escape route for the other refugees inside Daijingu. Shotaro, the nimble young Korean, dragged Cozad's suitcases along a barely visible trail. The fifty-eight-year-old missionary hiked up her skirt and scurried after him. "He would go on and place [my baggage] and find the best footing, then come back for me," she recalled. "In going down he would place his foot, then have me step on it. In going up, he would pull or push me and at last we reached the top." Cozad surprised herself, clambering along the rocky path with growing confidence. Soon they reached an abandoned villa at the top of the valley and rested for a while beside the villa's pond. The aftershocks continued; seismologists would count 150 of them on September 1, an average of one every ten minutes. At every shake of the earth, Cozad feared that the villa would slide into the valley and take her and Shotaro with it.

The flames pursued them. They climbed up the next hill, under fallen trees and over debris of houses. People followed them, shouting, "Hurry! Hurry! We will all be burned!" They reached the city reservoir, the highest place in Yokohama, before sunset. "The whole city was burned up to it on one side, clear over to the Bluff, which was burning fiercely," Cozad observed. Daijingu, the hilltop temple where they had first taken refuge, had become an inferno. "Had we waited ten minutes," she wrote, "there would have been a panic: the strong pushing the weak in their frenzied efforts to get away, and many trampled underfoot. It was heart rending to watch those beautiful, cruel flames, and to think of the many [we had met] who could not get away." A pall of smoke hung over everything and in every direction, "except Fuji, smiling, shall I say beautifully or cruelly?" Cozad spotted a sand pile, enclosed in a brick bin, climbed inside, and lay down to rest. Soon Japanese survivors trickled in and threw together a shelter made of sheets of corrugated iron they had salvaged from the grounds. Twenty people, including Cozad and Shotaro, found their refuge there that night. Cozad remembered every detail of what transpired.

> Against the glare of the burning city there was a constant procession of dark silhouettes, calling the names of those from whom they had become separated. . . . One fine appearing young man was brought there, wounded and scorched. He had been dragged out from the debris and his wounds bound up, and then left where he fully expected to be burned. His father found him and brought him to our camp. All the afternoon I thought he was dying, but . . . rejoiced to see him open his eyes, and when I left he was sitting up.

Late in the afternoon Henry W. Kinney, the *Trans-Pacific* editor, glimpsed the port in its death throes. He had spent much of the past few hours trying to get to Kamakura, where his twelve-year-old son, known in Kinney's account only as the Shrimp, had been staying at the time of the earthquake. Walking south over broken railway tracks, past smashed villages, he stared in awe at giant cumulus clouds of smoke spiraling into the sky both behind him and in front of him. These were the conflagrations, he realized with horror, of Tokyo and Yokohama. Beaten down by the heat, Kinney skirted the western edge of the city, then hiked up a steep road that switchbacked through the hills.

> We came to a point where a main road, running obliquely down to the city, gave a view of the entire scene. . . . Yokohama, the city of almost half a million souls, had become a vast plain of fire, of red, devouring sheets of flame which played and flickered. Here and there a remnant of a building, a few shattered walls, stood up like rocks above the expanse of flame, unrecognizable. It was as if the very earth were now burning. It presented exactly the aspect of a gigantic Christmas pudding over which the spirits were blazing, devouring nothing. For the city was gone.

It was 4:00.

WITH A FINAL SPASM of destruction and death, the spread of the fires through Yokohama slowed. The relentless wind that had blown all afternoon and fanned the flames through the port died down. Tens of thousands of buildings were still fiercely ablaze, but with the gale subsiding and little combustible material left to burn, the flames in the city had passed their peak. From a sampan in the inner harbor Ellis Zacharias watched as the waterfront turned to embers. At five o'clock he decided that it was safe to come ashore.

Chaos ruled the waterfront. The Japanese army had not yet arrived to assert control. Scattered clusters of refugees—some dying, many injured—sat along the smoldering Bund and the reclaimed ground. Dozens of Japanese and foreign vessels raced confusedly about the inner harbor. The first, unconfirmed reports of murders and vigilantism circulated: Captain Samuel Robinson wrote that "one thousand prisoners had been let out of jail during the earthquake, and a number of these commenced killing and looting. Bands of Japanese, armed mostly with long knives lashed to bamboos, were formed to hunt these down." Choking billows of smoke poured from the British

Naval Hospital atop the Bluff throughout the late afternoon, and the reclaimed ground proved to be inhospitable terrain. Long fissures three or four feet wide sliced the surface, and the concrete blocks of the seawall had tumbled into the water. "A couple of thousand Japanese had succeeded in finding sanctuary on these few acres of reclaimed foreshore," Otis Poole observed, "and many of the wounded were being placed in a long bathing shelter made of rushes, which offered some protection from the heat overhead." Tommy Ryan, Mrs. Slack, and the Dane, Enevoldsen, waited there for rescue—throats parched, faces blackened after hours of exposure to whirling ash, cinders, and dust. Japanese launches and tugs passed near the shore constantly, but none of them stopped to take the women and children to ships in the harbor. Recalled Ryan: "They were steaming around like chickens with their heads cut off." A Japanese had tumbled off the cliff and impaled himself on the fork of a tree high above the beach. His screams and yells continued until dusk. By then the fire in the British Naval Hospital grounds had died down, and someone lowered a rope and retrieved him.

The dead lay everywhere—clogging the canals, crushed under debris, piled up in doorways, floating in the harbor. Dozens of charred corpses were heaped around the locked front doors of the Yokohama Specie Bank, a three-story granite building that must have held the promise of sanctuary from the fires. (It was a false promise: rescue workers would discover two hundred more bodies suffocated in the bank's basement.) Hundreds of injured clustered at the water's edge below the Bluff. Others staggered like ghosts through the smoldering city. More were tucked away in less accessible places, waiting for search parties to rescue them. At six o'clock, in gathering darkness, Reverend Eustace Strong ascended the Bluff again and brought down a teenage Russian girl with a broken leg who had somehow survived the fire that had swept the Naval Hospital grounds. Strong was too late for the Dutch Legation's elderly chancellor, Ernest Van Der Polder, and his wife, both of whom, burned and asphyxiated, lay dead beside her.

Slowly, haltingly, an organized rescue effort took shape. Robinson ordered lifeboats sent ashore to pick up survivors. Attacks against Koreans suspected of looting, arson, and poisoning wells had apparently been reported, because Robinson kept anyone of Asiatic appearance on board the vessel. "All the Europeans among the ship's company who could be spared, and several passengers who volunteered, formed search and stretcher parties for the injured." Ellis Zacharias was one of those volunteers. All through the evening the naval officer helped guide the disoriented and frightened to safety, freed people trapped under debris, revived the unconscious, gave first aid to the injured, and calmed, as much as he could, survivors whose loved ones had disappeared or been killed. The Japanese customs and harbor police were also pressed into service, reluctant participants in the rescue effort. "It took a half hour of requesting, begging, and threatening before one of the launch captains agreed to take Mrs. Slack aboard," reported Ryan, who, with Enevoldsen, joined her on the boat. At nightfall, Ryan and Enevoldsen passed Mrs. Slack to the *Empress of Australia,* then Enevoldsen stayed with her while Ryan returned to the launch. Ryan expected the Japanese crew to resume the rescue effort, but the "damned Japs" steamed in, refused to land, then steamed out to one of their ships. "Tied up to the boom I was madder 'n a hatter so I went down to the cabin and corked off."

Lifeboats worked through the evening, silhouetted against the flaming coast; they ferried the injured and the newly destitute to the crippled *Empress of Australia* and the disabled *André Lebon* along the hatoba, and to other boats that lay in the outer harbor. Abandoned sampans, lighters, and barges still drifted, many in flames. Thirteen large steamships, including the *London Maru,* the *Korea Maru,* and the Blue Funnel Line's *Philoctetes,* lay safe at anchor past the sunken breakwater after a dangerous dusk exodus through the burning inner harbor. The anonymous passenger on board the *Philoctetes,* whose recollections of September 1 in the *Chronicle* would be among the first detailed eyewitness accounts to reach the world, offered a doleful appreciation of the destroyed city: "From this point hardly anything could be seen of Yokohama excepting the spurts of red flames occasionally through the smoke. The ships in the foreground in the harbor were silhouetted on a dark brown and beyond, smoke and flames. The sky for miles around, reaching from almost horizon to horizon, was covered by a blanket of blackest cloud."

Robinson commanded the rescue effort from the bridge of his vessel. By nightfall the *Empress of Australia* had taken hundreds of refugees aboard, but still could not move because of its fouled propeller. *Empress* relief teams in motorboats navigated Yokohama's corpse-clogged canals—braving fire, oil explosions, and reports of gangs of thieves—to bring help to thousands stranded inland. "At the suggestion of the Acting British Consul General [Boulter]," Robinson wrote, "we sent several boatloads of fresh water, in breakers, for the refugees, mostly Japanese, in Yokohama Park, who had been without water since noon. Mr. Boulter had arrived on board early in the night, the Consulate having been destroyed and three [*sic*] of the Staff killed or missing. He himself was badly cut and bruised, but he worked hard through the night directing and helping in the relief work."

Otis Poole found a dinghy and rowed his family to the *Daimyo,* the commodore's yacht, which was still moored to a buoy in the harbor. Later that evening they took a small boat to a larger yacht, the *Azuma,* where Poole's wife and children bunked down in a spacious cabin below deck for the night. Poole couldn't sleep. He leaned against the mast in the darkness, poured himself a glass of whisky from a bottle discovered in the hold, and, as the boat gently rocked at its mooring in the inner harbor, watched the spectacle ashore. Fuel tanks ruptured and exploded through the evening, sending mushrooms of gas and fire into the sky. "In the enveloping summer night, the relentless roar of flame sounded like heavy surf, with frequent crashes of thunder," he recalled. "We seemed to be in the center of a huge stage, illuminated by pulsing, crimson footlights."

Lois Crane had spent hours clinging to flotsam in the oil-slicked water of Yokohama harbor. Finally swimming to the *Empress of Australia* after dark, she wandered anxiously across the crowded deck and the saloon-class dining room, where many refugees were bedded down beneath crystal chandeliers, in a futile search for her husband, William, the former American military attaché.

Eva Downes and Mrs. Macmillan ate two crackers apiece and lay on the grass of the golf course. Both nurses were caked with mud to their waists, their faces black with the dust and grime that had filled the air of the city as they passed through it. As evening approached refugees raided the lockers of the clubhouse for warm garments, and the two women put on pairs of men's trousers to keep out the cool of the night. The men invited the women and children to sleep inside the clubhouse, but none of them were confident that the structure would remain standing through the night, so they spread themselves on the grass. Sleep was difficult. "Wherever we looked great clouds of black smoke rolled up, behind us in Yokohama, before us in the little village, across the bay where the [Yokosuka] naval station burned. Violent shakes would make us fear that the first one was to be repeated. The weather was, however, clear and balmy and the wind had died down, so that spending the night on the grass was not at all a hardship."

Not far from the spot where Downes and Macmillan camped for the night, twelve-year-old Shigeo Tsuchiya and his family lay on the hard ground at Kuboyama Cemetery on the southwest outskirts of Yokohama. They had brought nothing with them except the clothing on their backs, and though their light loads had been a blessing during their escape from the city, they gazed with envy at those who had managed to flee with blankets and futons. Tsuchiya and his parents nibbled on raw, tasteless sweet potatoes that a farmer had dumped on the ground for the refugees. He sat in the growing chill, arms squeezed around his knees, surrounded by mothers trying to nurse their inconsolably wailing infants.

As night fell Gertrude Cozad and Hayashi Shotaro shared a four-day-old muffin, a hotel dinner roll, a small bunch of grapes, and a bar of chocolate. She gave away her thermos bottle full of water and half her chocolate. The Korean ventured down into an unscathed valley in search of food and returned with a small package of caramels and fifty green bananas. Cozad distributed twenty-five of the bananas and kept the rest. They were green and barely edible.

That night, lying in his berth on board the *Philoctetes*, finally free of danger, the passenger who had watched the catastrophe unfolding and had documented it in lurid detail crafted a eulogy for the great port that had ceased to exist:

> Yokohama, the proudest city of Nippon, the Eastern Gateway of the mighty Pacific, a City and its inhabitants known the world over . . . is today in ruins, overtaken by a destructive visitation of Nature, a precedent for which cannot be recalled. Tonight, thousands are homeless, Japanese and foreigners alike, taking refuge on

the ships of all nationalities standing by both within and without the harbour, on the hills beyond: anywhere away from the burning city. . . . The burning of Rome in its day could not have been more magnificent, more terrible, more heartrending and appalling than the catastrophe which has overtaken Yokohama. Thousands of lives and homes, millions of yen and property have been [destroyed] by just a few moments of Nature's wrath.

The calamity had passed; the fallout was just beginning.

8

Massacres

I found myself looking at a man who said in a strange rasping voice, "Have pity on me. My leg is broken. If they find me, they will kill me." . . . I heard people shouting outside, "He ran into the graveyard. Catch him! Kill him!" Footsteps of the vigilantes came into the temple. "Here he is!" I heard a terrible cry.

Interview with a boy who discovered a Korean hiding beneath the floor of a Buddhist temple in Tokyo, September 2, 1923, cited in *Two Minutes to Noon* by Noel Busch

O N SUNDAY MORNING, the sun rose over a brutish landscape. Only six buildings still stood in all of Yokohama. Burned and decomposing corpses lay in heaps. Desperate survivors scavenged through the ashes, searching for nourishment. Food and water were scarce. Escaped convicts stripped valuables at knifepoint, jimmied charred safes in the ruins, and stabbed several people to death. Hundreds of policemen had been killed by the calamity; many others had fled to the hills. The Japanese army—paralyzed by conflagrations, debris, broken bridges, and destroyed roads—had not yet arrived from Tokyo to reimpose order. And large fires still burned in parts of the city.

A few minutes after dawn on the oddly bright morning of Sunday, September 2, Lieutenant Ellis Zacharias stood on the deck of the *Empress of Australia*, still moored along the hatoba, breathing air thick with the odor of charcoal, diesel fuel, and burning bodies. In the early morning sunlight, the waters of the harbor were still roiling, and they were covered by a thick film of oil that continued to gush from the shore and spread as far as the eye could see. Zacharias was exhausted. All night he had ferried survivors on a sampan from the shore to the crowded ocean liner, under the blinding glare of deck-top spotlights. Nearly two thousand refugees, both Japanese and expatriates, filled every berth and crowded the corridors. But within this sea of misery and despair a few hopeful stories had emerged. At one o'clock that morning Zacharias had caught a sampan from the shore back to the wrong ship, the *André Lebon,* and there, with serendipity, he had stumbled across the former American military attaché, Major William Crane, frantically searching the deck for his wife. Crane had been traveling on a train six miles north of Yokohama, heading for the rendezvous with Lois Crane at Thomas Cook & Son, when the earthquake struck, and he had spent ten and a half hours dodging fires and following the torn-up railroad tracks to the port. Arriving in Yokohama at 10:30 at night, Crane had first searched the ruins of the Bund for his wife, then had caught a lighter to the French vessel in the hope of finding her there. Having just seen Mrs. Crane on board the *Empress of Australia,* Zacharias placed the military attaché in a launch and brought him to the ship. At 2 A.M., the couple found each other on the *Empress*'s deck. "It was," Zacharias wrote, "a joyful reunion."

Such joy was rare. At 7 A.M. on September 2, Zacharias noticed a new fire gathering force on the oil-saturated water halfway down the Bund, in the direction of the ruins of the Grand Hotel. Hundreds of people stood on the deck of the *Empress* with Zacharias, growing more agitated as the flames rose higher and the black smoke grew thicker. Half an hour later, a light breeze nudged the flames closer to the ship. Again maintaining an air of calm in the face of impending catastrophe, Captain Robinson went aft to hold a meeting with the acting commander of the *Steel Navigator,* which remained stuck astern of the *Empress,* its anchor chain snarled around the ship's port propeller. The commanders swiftly came to a decision: They would cut the cable that had fouled the *Empress*'s propeller, then lash the stern of the crippled *Empress* to the bow of the *Navigator.* The *Navigator* would throw its engines into reverse and tow the *Empress* out of the path of the fire. Zacharias recalled:

Just as the work was begun, the most terrifying sight I was ever to witness was revealed to my incredulous eyes. The fire, now at the corner of the pier and engulfing the Bund, burned fiercely, the heat reaching the ship. Suddenly the fire began to whirl. Faster and faster it turned; higher and higher it spread; until it took the cyclonic form of a waterspout at sea. As those on board watched it, panic-stricken, praying that it would subside, the huge mass, now roaring like a thousand furnaces, started to move, driven by the force of its own whirling in our direction. The crowd on the deck surged back and forth in uncontrolled panic. We all knew that if this fire, now a hundred feet in diameter and reaching five hundred feet in the air, were to pass over the ship it would strip her clean.

Robinson watched the oil-fed fire change shape as it moved toward the ship, "sometimes rolling up in thick greasy-looking masses and then suddenly shooting up into a whirling column." For the second time in twenty-four hours, Robinson had to think fast and move with precision to save the lives of everyone on board the ship: 592 Westerners, 705 Chinese, and 604 Japanese, plus his crew, according to Robinson's count that morning. The unwieldiness of his huge vessel, the length of two football fields, the confusion aboard the *Steel Navigator*, the *Empress*'s chain-fouled left propeller, and the burning ghost ships in the harbor complicated his task unimaginably. As the fire roared closer, a member of Robinson's crew leaped off the *Empress of Australia* into the oil-slicked harbor and swam to the *Steel Navigator*. Working beside the *Navigator*'s first mate, he sawed through the freighter's anchor cable. The American freighter drew the Canadian ship from the wharf without difficulty, then steamed off.

But the crippled *Empress* was still not out of danger: "We tried the engines again carefully and found that the starboard engine and propeller worked but the port one would not move. We realized that the flames were creeping out on the ruined wharf in our direction in several large masses from 50 to 150 feet in diameter, roaring violently and presenting a most terrifying sight. We had then over 2,000 people on board and I was very anxious. All the fire service was turned on deck again and we hove up anchor and drove the ship full speed [toward the shore] with the starboard engine."

Driving the huge vessel toward the shore was Robinson's only option. With the *Empress*'s port propeller still ensnared by the *Steel Navigator*'s anchor and its rudder unresponsive, the vessel would not
steer. He could move the boat in one direction only: straight ahead.
But a steady wind was blowing, and Robinson had a plan. Aboard the
Daimyo, to which they had returned from the *Azuma* that morning,
Otis Poole and his father-in-law had an unobstructed view of the
struggling vessel.

> As the water shoaled rapidly towards the shore, we expected to
> see [the *Empress*] stop and turn, but to our amazement she kept
> right on. Could her skipper be mad? Straight ahead, a group of
> lighters and a launch lay at a mooring. . . . To our horror the ship
> cut right through them, with a crashing of timbers and clamour of
> shouting as their crews were pitched into the water. . . . A minute
> later, with unnatural suddenness, she came to a stop. Was she
> aground? No; her bow began to swing slowly around in the strong
> wind. Gradually she went broadside on, then bow on, and we real-
> ized she was now coming dead at us.
>
> The Chief Officer, standing in her bow, raised a megaphone to
> his mouth and howled, "Cast off that buoy!" The Commodore
> shouted back, "Be damned if we will! Go around us!" Up went the
> megaphone again, "Cast off, I say, or we'll run you down! We can't
> help ourselves!" Having seen the fate of the lighters, we needed no
> further spurring and instantly cast off. . . . We inched away just as
> the huge bulk of the ship swept by, washing us aside like corks.

AS THE HARBOR was still threatened by rampant fires, many of those
onshore were menaced by an equally insidious, though more human,
danger: rampant xenophobia. Shortly after dawn, in their shed beside
the reservoir high atop the city, Gertrude Cozad and her Korean companion, Hayashi Shotaro, awoke to gunshots, screams, and the shouts
of vigilantes chasing quarry through the rubble. The immediate cata-
lyst for the violent pursuit was a mass jailbreak the previous afternoon
from Negishi Prison, a large brick and wood fortress in the southwest
hills, a stone's throw from Cozad and Shotaro's shack. The prison had

caught fire soon after the earthquake struck, the fleeing guards had declared an immediate amnesty and thrown open the cells, and one thousand inmates had spilled out of the shattered front gates to freedom. At five o'clock on Saturday afternoon, according to the *Japan Weekly Chronicle,* a European who lived on a hill in Negishi had been told by a neighbor that "three Koreans" who had escaped from the prison were setting fire to houses in the neighborhood. The European had heard "yells, shouts from many directions, rifle volleys, seventy to eighty firing at once." All of the Koreans had been hunted down and killed, the *Chronicle* reported, the first known incident of anti-Korean violence in the city that day. The word spread quickly that bands of Korean prisoners who had broken out of the Negishi fortress had embarked on a crime spree in Yokohama. "Armlets of red cloth began appearing [identifying people as Japanese], with the idea of protecting people from attack," wrote the *Chronicle* correspondent. "Rumors of attacks by Korean [prisoners] developed into an attack on all Koreans."

As Shotaro huddled, terrified, in his hut on the night of September 1 and the morning of September 2, hundreds of Japanese youths, most of them unemployed and uneducated, carried swords, spears, and rifles across the burned-out port on a frenzied search for Korean "criminals." "Koreans who had escaped from the burning prison . . . were thought to be looting, shooting, and what angered the people most, poisoning the wells and reservoirs," Cozad wrote. "If the rumors had been well founded they would have deserved their awful fate, but at such time as that, credence is given to tales, however bad, if only they are gruesome." The handful of Japanese officials and police who remained at their posts sometimes affirmed these rumors, egged on the mobs, and even joined in the killing. "It is said that three hundred Koreans have come to Hommoku to set fires," the police chief of one bayside community near the Bluff warned vigilante leaders on the morning of September 2, according to a document that was later offered as evidence at his trial. "If you talk and they don't answer, we consider them all Koreans, you can kill them. Be careful." The Japanese refugees who had camped with Cozad and Shotaro in their shack at the reservoir "knew he was a Korean but were kind to him and tied a red cloth on his arm, which signified that he was a Japanese," she recalled. "My boy lay with his face in the sand, beside me, all through that time."

At the time of the earthquake, two hundred thousand Koreans lived in Japan, including about twelve thousand in the Tokyo-Yokohama area. Almost all of them were young men, and they were the most despised—and most vulnerable—members of Japanese society. The Japanese had occupied Korea in 1895, after destroying the rival Chinese naval fleet at the Yalu River dividing China from the Korean peninsula; this was the final victory in the Sino-Japanese War and an extraordinary display of military prowess that had marked Meiji Japan's emergence as a Pacific power. In the years since then Japan, the expanding empire, had tightened its stranglehold on the weak and undeveloped country, deposing the emperor, declaring Korea a protectorate in 1907, and annexing the peninsula three years later. The Japanese occupiers had forced Korean schools to teach Japanese, shut down all newspapers, seized private property, banned political activity, and jailed thousands of dissidents. Ferryboats overloaded with desperate Korean men like Shotaro crossed the Straits of Japan daily, some coming to Japan on labor contracts, others lured by friends and relatives who had found jobs in the archipelago. Deprived of economic opportunity in their own country, the Koreans were willing to work cheap, which made them popular among contractors but hated by Japanese laborers. "The Japanese viewed the Koreans as taking food out of their mouths," the *Japan Weekly Chronicle* observed in 1923.

In the half-decade before the earthquake the position of Koreans living in Japan had grown more precarious. Tens of thousands of people had poured into Seoul, the Korean capital, to attend the funeral of the deposed Korean emperor, Grand Prince Yi, on March 1, 1919, a gathering that had quickly metastasized into a national uprising. Students, laborers and others had marched peacefully in defiance of the Japanese army and distributed copies of a pro-independence manifesto. Cries of "Man sei!" ("Hooray!") had echoed through the streets. "Two hundred Korean students forced their way into the Tokuju Palace in defiance of Japanese guards and police officials," the *Tokyo Jiji* reported. "They proceeded as far as the gate in front of the hall where Prince Yi's body was lying in state, shouting 'Long

Live the Korean nation.'" "Troops, as well as a large police force, were called out to pacify the mob, who did not disperse until night-fall," another Japanese newspaper reported. "According to a report from Seoul 112 ringleaders have been arrested, and the city has been virtually placed under martial law." Left undescribed by the Japanese press was the full Japanese response to the peaceful protests: according to Western newspaper reporters and the *Japan Weekly Chronicle* correspondent, Japanese troops machine-gunned and bayoneted to death six thousand demonstrators in Seoul, wounded fifteen thousand, and jailed at least fifty thousand. The brutal crackdown failed to extinguish the flames of rebellion. On September 2, 1919, a Korean secessionist threw a bomb at the Japanese governor of Korea and his inspector general during a military parade in Seoul, injuring the latter. The attack stoked a deep suspicion not only of Koreans on the peninsula, but of the growing number of immigrant workers in Japan.

A steady drumbeat of allegations, most of them farfetched, of anti-government plots by Koreans living in Japan dominated Japanese newspapers in the months before the earthquake. In the summer of 1923 police said that they had uncovered a Korean conspiracy to assassinate all Japanese officials in Kyoto, "but nothing more was heard of it," reported the *Chronicle,* "so presumably it was only a product of official imagination." On the eve of the earthquake, Japanese attitudes toward Koreans had congealed into a toxic mix of guilt, fear, and resentment.

ON THE AFTERNOON of Sunday, September 2, while Captain Robinson was coaxing his huge steamship toward the outer harbor and Hayashi Shotaro was hiding inside his flimsy shelter, the newly formed government of Admiral Gombei Yamamoto held its first meeting at the Detached Palace in the Akasaka district of Tokyo, an opulent replica of Versailles that had somehow survived the earthquake. Many buildings were still aflame, the nearby British, U.S., and Dutch Embassies had burned down overnight, and reports of Korean marauders had begun to filter through the capital. Half a dozen members of the newly formed cabinet couldn't be located. As firemen dynamited burning buildings in the neighborhood in an effort to halt the fire's advance, the new prime minister obtained the permission of the privy council, the emperor's advisory body, to declare martial law. The imperial decree gave the army the power to ban meetings and newspapers and other publications considered "dangerous to national security"; to seize from civilians property and vehicles "deemed necessary for military purposes"; to confiscate firearms and other weapons; and to censor all letters and telegrams. Japan's supreme military commander, Fukuda Taisho, assumed absolute authority over the Tokyo-Yokohama earthquake zone.

What steps did the Martal Law Authorities take to halt the spreading violence against Koreans? The evidence suggests that, for several days, they did almost nothing. Special military units were packed with fanatical hard-liners who had served on the Korean peninsula and had helped put down the March 1919 rebellion. Some army commanders may have viewed the Great Kanto Earthquake as an opportunity to purge the country of troublemakers, to vent their hatred of all Koreans, to cower the population, or perhaps even to nip in the bud a would-be rebellion. Although the killings appeared to have started spontaneously—certainly in Yokohama, where the military was absent on September 1 and 2—the army in Tokyo and other areas whipped up rumors about Korean well poisonings and arson and for several days gave vigilante squads known as Self-Defense Committees freedom to patrol the streets and exact what justice they saw fit. An amalgam of volunteer fire brigades and neighborhood youth groups trained in paramilitary activities by the police, the Self-Defense Committees threw up roadblocks across the earthquake zone, usually a piece of rope strung tautly across a street. Teenagers and young men manning the barricades carried out identity checks of anyone who tried to pass. They ordered suspected Koreans to sing the Japanese national anthem, to name the railway stations on Tokyo's Yamanote Line, or to repeat telltale Japanese phrases such as "Ju go en, go ju go sen" (fifteen yen, fifty-five sen), which most Koreans mispronounced as "Chu go en, go chu go sen." A failure to answer correctly would bring about instant execution, usually from a swift cut across the throat with a sword. "When the fatal story got [out] that the Koreans were raping, robbing, and burning, the fiercer spirits regarded it as a call to arms," the Chronicle reported. "The work was . . . popular be-

cause it was perfectly safe. The supposed ruffians are not recor
any instance to have put up a fight. They were attacked in ones and
twos wherever they were met, and done to death with the first
weapons that came to hand. In some cases the police were infected
with the scare and encouraged the work."

Stoking the fears of the Japanese population toward the Koreans
was not difficult. Although the evidence compiled by the *Japan
Weekly Chronicle* and other sources suggests that few, if any, Koreans
were guilty of the misdeeds that the vigilantes and the government accused them of, the rumors took on a life of their own. Tokyo and
Yokohama were seized by a pathology that has often emerged in the
aftermath of natural disasters: the singling out of "others" as the per-
petrators of the most foul crimes. During the Black Death that swept
Western Europe in the fourteenth century, for example, the break-
down of law, the trauma inflicted by mass death, and the desperate
yearning for explanations led to the targeting of Europe's traditional
outcasts: the Jews. Rumors coursed through Switzerland, France, and
Germany that Jews had spread the pestilence by poisoning the wells—
a common accusation in times of mass panic—and massacres followed. In Strasbourg in 1348, wrote one eyewitness, Jews "were led
to their own cemetery into a house prepared for their burning and on
their way they were stripped naked by the crowd which ripped off
their clothes and found much money that had been concealed." Even
in our own, supposedly more civilized era, people have not been immune to mass panic and paranoia. In the wake of Hurricane Katrina
in September 2005, reports proliferated through flooded New Orleans that gangs of African Americans had embarked on a murder and
rape spree—reports that turned out to be entirely false. Terrified
groups of armed whites held vigil in front of their houses, waiting for
the invasion that never came.

The scale of the violence that followed the Great Kanto Earthquake
may have approached that of plague-beset Europe. On the evening of
September 2 Japanese vigilantes massacred 103 Koreans at Yokohama's Hachiman Bridge, according to Yoshino Sakuzo, a Tokyo Imperial University professor who interviewed scores of eyewitnesses and
survivors and meticulously documented the killing campaign. One
hundred fifty-nine were murdered in front of the train station of

Kanagawa. At the Kanagawa Iron Bridge, three miles north of Yoko-hama, mobs reportedly stabbed and shot to death five hundred Kore-ans in a single afternoon. An American expatriate, Captain Hedstrom, the assistant dock superintendent of Yokohama, claimed to have wit-nessed one of the most horrific mass killings. "Hedstrom vouches for the fact that on Sunday, September 2, 1923, 250 Koreans were bound hand and foot, in groups of five, placed in an old junk, covered with oil and burned alive," according to the *New York Times*. Other wit-nesses reported that the corpses of one thousand victims who had been killed in Yokohama were burned in the crematorium of the Kuboyama Cemetery on September 3, where Shigeo Tsuchiya and his family had taken refuge. The *New York Times* also reported that on the night of September 3, "an American citizen, W. H. Stevens, hired an automobile to take himself, his wife, [and] his sister in law . . . to Nikko. The automobile was stopped by Japanese soldiers and Mr. Stevens and his party were compelled to witness the preparation for execution of eight Koreans who were to be shot. The soldiers, apparently enjoying the horror of the party, instead of shooting the Koreans, bayoneted them, compelling them to die by inches. The mutilated bodies were then thrown into the highway and the party was forced at the pistol point to drive the automobile over the dead bodies."

JOHN W. DOTY and W. W. Johnston, two American passengers aboard the *Empress of Australia,* bore witness to the spreading anti-Korean fervor after setting out from the *Empress* at noon on Monday, September 3, in a rainstorm, each carrying forty pounds of food and water, to volunteer their services to the U.S. ambassador in Tokyo. It was a terrifying journey. The first units of the Japanese army, ferried down from Tokyo, were coming to shore in Yokohama, but the vigi-lante groups still controlled the port. Volunteer civilian patrols armed with rifles surrounded the Americans and their two Japanese inter-preters as soon as they landed on the filled-in ground under the Bluff. The vigilantes insisted that Doty, Johnston, and their two assistants wrap green or white bands around their arms, as thousands of other residents of the port had already done, so that they wouldn't be mistaken for Koreans and slaughtered. Doty and Johnston threaded their way through a landscape of the dead—some earthquake victims, others butchered Koreans; the only moving objects were armed men on the prowl. Walking from the filled-in ground to the Yokohama Railway Station, they passed many corpses of people who had suffocated and burned in the open; other bodies floated in the harbor. The stench of burned flesh of victims trapped in the still smoldering ruins saturated the air. Japanese survivors dug through the rubble for valuables and carted off galvanized iron for temporary shelter.

Along the way to Tokyo, Doty and Johnston passed roadblocks, broken bridges, ox and horse carts loaded with rice being taken to Yokohama under heavy military guard. Four miles out of Yokohama, terrified of being mistaken for Koreans, their interpreters turned back. The Americans continued their journey alone. In the southern Tokyo neighborhood of Shinagawa, reached after six hours, they flagged down a car and rode the rest of the way in darkness to the Imperial Hotel, four miles further north:

> During this ride we were halted many times by what appeared to be volunteer guards or vigilante committees composed of very excited and terrified young men who were armed with swords and sharpened bamboo poles, with here and there a musket. These bands seemed to have no leader and each man insisted upon questioning, in an excited manner and at the top of his voice, any passers-by with whom he was not personally acquainted. In one instance they climbed into our car and tried to take the chauffeur from it by sheer force, all the time shouting "Korean." Fortunately one of them understood English and this is the only reason, in our judgment, that the chauffeur was not instantly shot.

They arrived at the hotel at ten o'clock at night, finding the building nearly undamaged but shrouded in darkness and surrounded by detachments of troops. A squad of machine gun–toting soldiers patrolled the grounds; snipers had taken positions on the rooftop. Guests huddled in the lobby, illuminated only by candlelight, or waited in their rooms, terrified by rumors spread by the army of an imminent Korean uprising. Bolsheviks, backed by the Soviet Union, were also reported to be planning a rebellion. At 10:20 that evening the clerks and managers of the hotel went from room to room, notifying guests that the military had ordered all candles extinguished. The "Koreans and Reds," the hotel employees warned, were going to invade the hotel within ten minutes. The attack, like so many other rumored assaults by Korean marauders, never materialized.

So Insung, a twenty-two-year-old Korean who had arrived in Japan in search of a livelihood in the winter of 1923, provided one of the most chilling eyewitness accounts of the massacres. On September 1 So had taken the day off from his job in a rice warehouse and was resting at his uncle's home in Tokyo's Yanagashima district. After the earthquake hit, he sought refuge on the weedy banks of the Arakawa River with twelve other Koreans. At ten o'clock that night, axe-wielding volunteer firemen surrounded them in the bushes, bound them with ropes, and herded them onto a long bridge. Instead of killing them on the spot, however, the firemen, for unknown reasons, left them tied up and warned, "Keep quiet, or you're going to die. Stay here without moving." So recalled:

> In the darkness, at midnight, we heard gunshots and cries coming from the other side of the river. We waited on the bridge until dawn, roped together, soaked by the rain. Then the volunteer firemen came back for us and said, "It is better to go to the police or you're going to be killed." On the bridge there were so many bodies that we couldn't pass without stepping on them. The eviscerated bodies were piled up like fish. The ground was slippery with blood. As we stepped over the corpses one member of our group, Chong, noticed a body that resembled his brother. "My brother is dead!" he cried, breaking the thick straw rope to which he was attached, in order to throw himself on the corpse. The firemen tried to catch him with their pickaxes. Seized by fear, he threw himself into the river.

The firemen marched So and his comrades, now sixteen in all, across the river toward police headquarters. At the end of the bridge a gang of armed youths attacked, stabbing three of the Koreans to death with bamboo spears. The firemen shielded the others. "A black fog covered my eyes. I felt I was going to faint," So recalled. "But I told myself that I'd die unless I stayed lucid." He and the survivors arrived at the station. Officers kicked them and herded them roughly inside. So remained there with four hundred other captives, including dozens who would die from untreated knife and bullet wounds, for the next fifteen days.

THE FIRST PRONOUNCEMENT by the Martial Law Authorities in response to the massacres was a tepid call for restraint on the afternoon of September 3, just as Doty and Johnston were reaching the outskirts of the capital. "Most Korean residents [are] good and peaceful," a statement by the Ministry of Foreign Affairs declared. It warned against "violence to Koreans without due reason." But vigilantes—and many officials—continued to find their reasons. Sometimes strong neighborhood leaders reined in the Self-Defense Committees and even provided Koreans with bodyguards. Japanese soldiers rounded up thousands of Koreans and herded them into police stations and heavily guarded military camps, where most survived, albeit in terrible conditions. More often, however, the self-defense groups operated with impunity, egged on—and in many cases joined—by police and military units. "On the second night, in Ushigome [a neighborhood in western Tokyo] groups of teenagers and students worked closely with the police and army to prevent acts of arson and poisoning by unruly Koreans," reported the *Tokyo Nichi Nichi* on September 4. "Armed with clubs and short or long swords, they stood guard the whole night, using ropes strung tightly across the street, stopping anyone who passed. They created the impression of a fully mobilized volunteer army. . . . On the morning of the third day the guards discovered two Koreans throwing rat poison down a well and took them into custody." (The fate of these alleged miscreants can only be imagined.) Authorities in Saitama, a city near Tokyo, sent out this memorandum to village mayors on September 3: "Koreans, organizing themselves into extremist bands, have seized the occasion [of the earthquake] to achieve their ends and a wave of criminal acts from them may be expected. In such circumstances, the authorities must work closely with reservist militias, volunteer firefighters, and youth associations to keep a constant guard. Emergency measures should be anticipated in necessary cases." There were plenty of cases of mistaken identity. In one incident verified by Japanese reporters, vigilantes surrounded two teenage boys who had been searching for their parents in Tokyo's ruins. When the boys proved unable to answer the questions hurled at them, the gang slit their throats and impaled them on bamboo spears. They were later identified as students at Japan's School for the Deaf.

AFTER MANY HOURS salvaging the Seismology Department's research materials and equipment, Professor Akitsune Imamura finally cycled away from the burning campus of Tokyo Imperial University at 1 A.M. on September 2. Most of Tokyo was still on fire. Two million people crowded every open space in the city: parks, the palace esplanade, burial grounds, temple complexes. Aftershocks broke loose pieces of half-demolished buildings. To the south, the burning ruins of Yokohama glimmered through the darkness, an arc of crimson on the horizon. The conflagration had destroyed everything to the immediate east, north, and south of the Imperial Palace and threatened the western neighborhoods, where Imamura and his family lived. "The flames were swept along the castle moat so that its waters glared like molten lava," Joseph Dahlmann, the Tokyo Imperial University professor, observed. As Imamura cycled through the flaming city toward his home, he encountered a large force of soldiers around the Imperial Palace, axing and dynamiting adjacent houses in an attempt to keep the fires from advancing west. Tokyo's fire department, after early paralysis, was fully deployed as well. The fire brigades were drawing water from the castle moat with two immense hoses, and the roar of the diesel pumps and the hissing of powerful jets of water could be heard above the noise of the fire. For the moment, at least, the water seemed to be getting the upper hand.

Imamura arrived at his house in Ichigaya at two o'clock on Sunday morning. The seismologist found his wife and children safe—but terrified—in the garden. Soldiers had gone from door to door, stirring up fears about the Korean "enemy." "The Koreans are poisoning the wells and setting new fires!" an army captain had warned

Imamura's wife. "Be careful!" While the family slept under the stars, worried about aftershocks and phantom Korean marauders, Imamura made the rounds of Ichigaya. He reassured his frightened neighbors that the worst was over. He wasn't sure it was. To the southeast, he could see fires and smoke. "It is happening just as I expected it would," he thought. "All of Tokyo is burning."

Early on the morning of September 2, Imamura returned to the smoldering campus. The scene devastated him. The library, containing four hundred thousand volumes in European languages and nearly a million in Japanese and Chinese, was a smoking ruin. The buildings of philosophy and literature, the Chinese and Indian studies departments, the lecture halls of law and politics, the large auditorium in the center of the university called the Octagon, the president's home, the chemistry and physics buildings, the Seismology Department, the medical clinic had all burned to the ground. "Everything is gone, an irretrievable loss," wrote Dahlmann, who inspected the campus that morning. "Where I expected to find studious youths immersed in the treasures of literature I found but charred and smouldering remnants of what once was the largest accumulation of occidental science in the Orient."

After midnight, on September 3, Imamura, despondent, left the university and again pedaled toward home. He almost didn't make it. Thirty-six hours after the earthquake, parts of the city were still ablaze; vigilante squads had sprung up across the capital. To protect himself against smoke and ash Imamura had put on a thick alpine jacket and pants and his trademark climbing hat, the same one that he had worn the week before on his expedition up the slopes of Mount Tarumai: a pith helmet covered with burlap, with a low brim that shielded his eyes. It was a sartorial oddity certain to attract attention from the mobs of suspicious and violent young men who ruled the capital during those anarchic hours. Blocks from home, he approached a checkpoint manned by a group of local youths from the neighborhood Self-Defense Committee. They carried the usual arsenal of bamboo spears, knives, pickaxes, and old muskets. A fire burned in a steel drum, casting their faces in an eerie orange glow. They surrounded Imamura. A dozen pairs of eyes peered at him suspiciously, moving from his strange-looking helmet to his thick mountaineering outfit.

"Where are you going?" one man asked him sharply.

"Forty-eight Higashi-Okubo," he replied. Imamura tried to squeeze past the gang. A young man grabbed him by the collar.

"Wait," he ordered. Imamura backed up five steps.

"Take off your hat."

He pulled off the helmet. The gang moved in closer, staring at his face. Then, from the rear, a voice screamed "Yatsukero!" Kill him.

A second voice: "Kill him now!"

"Please," the seismologist said, fumbling for his identification. "My name is Akitsune Imamura. I am a professor of the science department at Tokyo Imperial University." Imamura kept talking, and the men, their suspicions apparently waning, fell silent. The tension seemed to abate.

"Do you want to examine me further?" he asked. The men shook their heads.

"Is it okay that I go?"

"Go!" the leader said, with a dismissive flick of his wrist. Imamura pedaled home, trembling with relief.

FROM A CHAIR perched on the stone steps above Zojoji Temple, Frederick Starr greeted the dawn on Sunday, September 2, with an incongruous realization. "It is my birthday—I am 65 years old," he wrote. "No such disaster has afflicted Yedo since the great earthquake-fire of Ansei. Was it in my birth year? Perhaps." (In fact, the Ansei earthquake occurred three years before his 1858 birth.) He and Maebashi walked down the steps to the priests' quarters, where they shared a breakfast of soldier's bread—a cheap staple made from heavy, dark wheat flour—rice, tea, and bitter herbs. A young priest cleared his table, pulled out a copy of the *National Geographic,* and began to read serenely, while the room filled up with hungry and homeless men, women, and children.

Later that morning Starr toured the burning remains of the city, struck by how close he had come to dying there. In Shiba Park, where Starr and Maebashi had briefly encamped on Saturday evening, the flames had swept in and turned the thick grove of trees that had sheltered them into parched and shriveled skeletons. At the corner of the park, they came upon a rare working outdoor faucet. Soldiers doled out the precious water to a crowd of survivors, who patiently waited in line for their allotment. Tokyo had reverted to a primitive state. "No street cars, no light, little water, no trains, no telephones, no telegraphs—and probable starvation. Kanda, Nihombashi, Asakusa, Tsukiji—all wiped out of existence," Starr noted. "The Imperial Palace is damaged. . . . Many departmental buildings gone. Thousands of dead. The hotel [Kinokuniya] went completely. A crowd taking refuge in the open space before our hotel at Shimbashi Station [was] caught in a trap by changing winds and died there. . . . People pass crying their own names in hope of recognition by some one and news. A can of salmon helps [complement] the rice of Zojoji."

That evening he returned to the temple complex. The priests were laying out piles of corpses—hundreds in all—that people from the surrounding neighborhood had delivered to them for cremation and burial. Rumors of Korean marauders were gathering force. The hysteria consumed everyone: priests, Japanese refugees, even Starr.

It is said the Koreans plan a night attack wherever buildings have escaped [he wrote on the evening of September 2]. Zojoji and the Imperial Hotel are marked for special vengeance. "We had better flee to Aoyama" [the priests told us]. We refused to go, but they sent part of the baggage, including one of my trunks. And when night came, alarms and alarms. . . . "The Koreans come." We were called and led out into an open space before the temple. A crowd of women and children huddle together. We are given two chairs nearby. A dozen young priests and youths wearing headbands with heavy clubs in hand are awaiting the attack. "Do not be afraid; strong men protect you." But nothing happens and at last the little band of non-combatants goes back to the crowded room to sleep.

ON THE AFTERNOON of Monday, September 3, Gertrude Cozad coaxed Hayashi Shotaro into leaving their place of refuge and making their way down from the reservoir to the Bund to catch a steamship out of the devastated port. The gunfire and screams of the previous two nights had subsided, and Cozad believed that the wave of anti-

Korean bloodletting in Yokohama had finally passed. But other horrors awaited them. They skirted Daijingu Temple, where they had
briefly taken refuge on Saturday afternoon. Fire had swept over the
sanctuary minutes after they had left, burning to death the thousand
refugees inside. "I stood and looked up," Cozad recalled, "but
Hayashi-san my Korean boy said, 'Don't get up there. It is too terrible.'" The Korean's red armband warded off suspicion from the
ubiquitous vigilante patrols, and the pair had no difficulty making
their way to the hatoba along a wide street paved with thick concrete
that had broken into pieces. The vista of destruction disoriented
Cozad; all the streets had been obliterated. In every direction, she
could see only roof tiles, chunks of concrete, twisted wire, and ashes.
The smell of burning flesh was ubiquitous, and piles of charred bodies littered the entrances to banks and offices. The situation, Cozad
and Shotaro soon learned, remained volatile. "As we drew near the
sea we saw many men carrying bales of woolen goods [from the] iron
customs godowns. Two fellows had found guns and when the others
saw them they cried, 'Guns! Where did you get them?' And ran as
hard as they could to secure some. One young fellow had tapped a
box of roller skates and had put on a pair and was merrily skating
along a bit of unbroken pavement."

Down at the dock, Cozad and Shotaro came upon a launch that was
ready to sail, and the missionary asked the Japanese crew in her sweetest voice whether they could take the pair to a foreign steamer moored
in the harbor. They were invited aboard, and the boat motored toward
the *André Lebon,* the French liner that had been tied to the hatoba at
the time the earthquake hit, awaiting repairs to her engine. The *André
Lebon,* like the *Empress of Australia,* had been tugged to safety beyond
the breakwater as the fires swept down upon her. Shotaro, still fearful,
attracted suspicion: a member of the crew began to describe the killings
of Koreans in Tokyo, all the while casting a baleful eye on Cozad's
companion. As the launch approached the *André Lebon,* the Japanese
sailors demanded money for having ferried Cozad and Shotaro across
the harbor. Boatmen aboard the French vessel angrily rebuked them
and violently threw back on the launch a young crew member who was
trying to climb aboard. Then they blocked Shotaro as well. Cozad
froze on the lower rungs of the gangway.

"That boy saved my life and I will go back on the launch unless you take him on too," she said. At that point, they took him aboard without objection.

ON SEPTEMBER 5 the Japanese cabinet finally voiced its condemnation of the killing spree with a proclamation signed by Prime Minister Yamamoto: "It is understood that there are some citizens who entertain unpleasant feelings toward Koreans on account of alleged disorderly acts by some Korean malcontents, who took advantage of the recent seismic disaster," the cabinet declared, basing its account of Korean misdeeds strictly on rumor and hearsay. "In case any Koreans are found in the act of menacing performance, notification shall be made to the military or police officers in the district. . . . That the citizens themselves should thoughtlessly persecute Koreans is entirely in contravention of the basic principle of Japanese-Korean assimilation and, further, would bring blemish upon our honor when reported abroad."

It was too little, too late. The killings continued for another week: sixty-five Koreans pulled off the back of a truck north of Tokyo on the night of September 5 and hacked and beaten to death by a mob as they were being transported to a military concentration camp; six Korean passengers thrown from a ferry in Tokyo Bay and drowned. How many Koreans died in the mayhem? Yoshino Sakuzo documented a total of 2,613 Koreans who had been killed in Yokohama and Tokyo between September 1 and September 8. The *Japan Weekly Chronicle,* whose correspondents did perhaps the most authoritative reporting on the Korean massacres, believed that Sakuzo's estimate was far too low. Of a total population of about twelve thousand Koreans in Tokyo and Yokohama before the earthquake, the *Chronicle* reported, the Japanese military interned four thousand in concentration camps for their own protection. Most of the eight thousand who remained at liberty, the *Chronicle* said, were never accounted for. The newspaper claimed that most of those had been killed.

The numbers, as well as the military's role in the killings, remained a source of bitter dispute. In January 1924, writing in the *New York Times,* the foreign correspondent Margaret de Forest Hicks denied that a wholesale massacre of Koreans had taken place and rejected allegations that government forces and their proxies had been involved in any killing. "It is true that in the excitement of the first few days the natural suspicion and antipathy of the Japanese for the Koreans gave vent to mob violence and many were killed," she wrote. "These massacres, however, were committed by ignorant shock-crazed people, and every possible effort was made by the Japanese government and the police to curb their maniacal intentions. Not more than 500 Koreans came to their death in this manner." Ambassador Cyrus E. Woods called the reports about Korean massacres "hysterical and generally untrue." Like many other diplomats and reporters, he accepted without question the allegations that the Koreans were involved in heinous activities in the earthquake's aftermath, even though no evidence was ever proffered to back up such claims. "During the wild excitement there is no doubt that a number of Koreans found engaged in looting the dead were killed, but they [the vigilantes] were only meting out the same punishment as [they did to] Japanese offenders," Woods declared. The *Japan Weekly Chronicle,* which maintained throughout its reporting that the Koreans were innocent victims, responded, "This is about the worst lying on the subject that we have seen. It not only contradicts the reports in the Japanese press and the [Japanese Parliament] which have never been denied, it is even more completely exonerating than the propaganda of the Japanese Embassy in London."

The drumbeat of accusations of anti-Korean pogroms eventually forced the Japanese authorities to take action. One month after the earthquake Woods reported to U.S. Secretary of State Charles Evans Hughes that the Japanese government, concerned about the surge of anti-Japanese feeling in Korea provoked by the killings, had begun an effort at damage control. "[It] is preparing for distribution in Korea films of the earthquake depicting the considerate treatment shown Koreans in establishing them in special [army] camps and providing them with food and shelter as soon as the military authorities assumed control of the situation." The clumsy propaganda campaign placated few Koreans or government critics, who pointed out that the army had allowed the massacres to go on unabated for nearly one week, and that conditions inside the camps had typically been deplorable. The episode was "a national shame that made it impossible for Japan to meet the gaze of the other civilized nations," wrote Yoshino Sakuzo. The massacres represented "an outbreak of national hatred of such an acute nature" that they "are not likely to be forgotten by the Koreans for many years to come," the *Japan Weekly Chronicle* declared presciently in late September, foreseeing generations of resentment and antipathy toward the Japanese by the Koreans. "It is to be feared that any attempts to bring the two peoples into more friendly relations will prove futile."

Despite the efforts of Japan's apologists to present the killings as an aberration provoked by extreme stress, the Korean massacres established a precedent for ethnic targeting and savagery that would worsen over the next two decades. Indeed, some members of the Japanese military seemed to approach the massacres as a dress rehearsal, a practice run for the bloody subjugation of Japan's neighbors that would mark the run-up to World War II and reach full flower during the conflict. The infamous 1937 Rape of Nanking, during which roaming bands of Imperial Japanese troops indiscriminately slaughtered Chinese men, women, and children with truncheons, bayonets, swords, and machine guns, echoed, on a much larger scale, the wanton Korean killings of 1923. "The Japanese Army behaved . . . in [a] fashion reminiscent [of] Attila [and] his Huns," the Japanese foreign minister, Hirota Koki, would report after an inspection trip to Nanking in January 1938, one of the few times that a Japanese high official owned up to the atrocities perpetrated by the army. "[Not] less than three hundred thousand Chinese civilians slaughtered, many cases [in] cold blood." A few years later, the forced enlistment of thousands of Korean women as sex slaves, or "comfort women," for the troops repeated the pattern of dehumanization and contempt with which the Japanese treated the Koreans both in crushing their independence aspirations and in meting out "justice" to alleged well poisoners. And these were only the most infamous of crimes that would be perpetrated by the Japanese against their Asian neighbors in the next two decades, as democracy was snuffed out and the country's right-wing extremists seized control. Historians still debate whether the atrocities of the World War II era can be blamed on the brutalizing effects of conflict, on imperial Japanese policy carried out by blindly obedient soldiers, or even, as some insist, some moral defect in the Japanese character. Whatever the case, they were prefigured by the now all but forgotten wave of Korean killings that followed the earthquake, when fear, bigotry, and official sanction combined to turn ordinary Japanese into murderers.

In the first chaotic days after the earthquake struck, however, the fallout from the ongoing Korean massacres, and the debate over their implications, lay in the distant future. For the moment, as the ashes of Tokyo and Yokohama cooled and the injured wandered the devastated land in search of relief, the dimensions of the catastrophe and the human savagery that had been unleashed by it were still barely understood. With almost all means of communication and transportation destroyed, with newspapers burned down, telegraph towers toppled, the government all but paralyzed, and the stricken zone largely isolated, the world was only gradually coming to know what the 60-second shuddering of the earth had wrought.

9

Spreading the News

A wireless message received at the Taira Radio Station, Iwaki Province, from the *London-maru* in Yokohama, states that since the night of the 1st a red glow reflected in the sky can be seen from the vessel and the disaster ashore appeared terrible. But no news is obtainable owing to the lack of means of communication.

From the *Japan Weekly Chronicle*, September 2, 1923

B Y THE TIME the seismic vibrations reached the mountain resort of Chuzenji, one hundred miles north of Tokyo, where Lyman Cotten and his family rested by the lake, they had weakened to a fraction of their original power. The earthquake unsettled the Cottens, but none of them could have had any appreciation of the temblor's awesome destructiveness. The violent vibrations lasted for about a minute, shattering dishware, toppling furniture, and causing the frightened family to seek protection in the door frame at the cottage's main entrance. They huddled there for several minutes, watching the rain fall in torrents, then cautiously ventured back to various corners of the house. Aftershocks came roughly every twenty minutes for the next few hours; each time, Lyman, Elizabeth, John, Mary Curtis, and their servants rushed back to the shelter of the door frame. The rain ended in the early afternoon, and at that point the Cottens left their house and walked along the lakeshore, encountering fellow expatriates on the path. Everybody was agitated, and everybody had a story to tell. Lieutenant Colonel Francis Piggott, the British military attaché, excitedly told the Cottens that, moments after the earthquake hit, bubbles had risen to the surface of the lake in front of his house, and a wave about three feet high had rolled up on the beach. There was an unsettling sign of disaster: the telephone and telegraph lines to Tokyo were out of commission, and Chuzenji was cut off from the plain below. "If these quakes came from the earth fault off Tokyo Bay I fear Tokyo, Yokohama, etc. suffered severely," Cotten wrote in his diary that evening.

Elizabeth Henderson Cotten shared her husband's trepidation. "There was no real damage here—a few things overturned, tables and books, occasionally a noise of what we suppose to have been stones crashing down the mountain behind the house," she wrote to her mother in Salisbury, North Carolina. "We said, 'if this is not a local disturbance, it must have been terrible in Tokyo.' But of course [we were] utterly unsuspecting of the actual situation."

Tremors shook Chuzenji through the first night, distant echoes of a great tragedy. The family slept little, and Elizabeth counted twenty-four aftershocks by eight o'clock the next morning. The telephone and telegraph lines that reached the mountain resort were still down. Unknown to them, the earthquake and fires had severed or melted all the land lines running out of Tokyo and Yokohama, and fires had burned down many transmission stations. Elizabeth and Curtis innocently set off after breakfast, as scheduled, for a long-planned excursion: two days of touring temples and shrines with a friend, Irene Mann, who lived in Nikko. Lyman and John, who had their own hiking trip planned to Karuizawa, joined them for part of the way. At 11 A.M., in front of the Hotel Chuzenji at the head of the lake, they encountered Hugh Wilson, the chargé d'affaires and counselor of the U.S. Embassy in Tokyo. Wilson, who must have been ashen-faced, hurried up to the family.

"Have you heard the news?" he asked. "The earthquake was very bad in Tokyo—many buildings down." The chargé d'affaires knew little else; he had probably picked up second- and thirdhand reports from people who had talked to refugees fleeing the city. This first indication of a calamity unfolding on the Kanto Plain troubled the Cottens but failed to deter them from their plans. Elizabeth and Curtis continued down the mountain to Nikko; Lyman and John remained at Chuzenji to prepare for their long walk. As they made their descent along the switchback trail, the women noticed signs of geological upheaval: a chunk of mountain above one teahouse had crumbled and fallen into the gorge. Huge stones from a retaining wall had dislodged and lay in the road, making passage along the narrow path difficult.

Clustered at the foot of the mountain leading to Chuzenji, Nikko was an ancient town of winding streets, forested parks, and ornate wooden architecture, most notably the Toshogu, Japan's most opulent Shinto complex, and the mausoleum of Tokugawa Ieyasu, the founder of the Tokugawa shogunate. Rumors of disaster had disrupted the normally serene atmosphere. Anxious foreign residents and tourists were milling around the lobby of the Hotel Nikko on the town's main street when Elizabeth and Curtis walked in. The information they had was sketchy: the earthquake had badly damaged Tokyo; some districts lay in ruins; many people had died. "No details," Elizabeth wrote. "We had luncheon with Miss Mann, all sad and depressed." At half past one o'clock they returned to the Hotel Nikko and "a deluge of horror" poured in. A report had been brought to the emperor and empress at their villa in Nikko, apparently by military airplane, and some details had trickled out to the public. Tokyo was in flames, one "great district" after another destroyed. "This last blooming of 'the flowers of Yedo' eclipsing that of all the other years of its long and tragic history." Elizabeth went on: "On all sides was a story of utter annihilation. We felt turned to stone. Without feeling or comprehension. How is it possible for the mind to grasp it? We thought of our friends—in Tokyo, Yokohama, Kamakura, Zushi, many other places—there was nothing to be heard—of all but Tokyo there was a blank. Ever increasing rumor, which rang in our ears, burned into our brains—that Yokohama was no more . . . Wilson, and Hulings, our assistant naval attaché, took the first available automobile, making an attempt to reach Tokyo, eight hours by motor." The rain fell hard on Nikko on the afternoon of Sunday, September 2, and Elizabeth welcomed it, praying that it would douse the inferno in Tokyo. But the next morning, a car filled with expatriates who had attempted to reach the capital returned to Nikko. They had found it impossible to enter the city. "It was a burning, consuming furnace—five miles away the heat now penetrating," Elizabeth wrote.

The stories that trickled in from the earthquake zone only enhanced the sense of unreality that pervaded Nikko. Except for a few rock slides in the nearby hills and some broken roof tiles lying in the streets, the imperial retreat remained as pristine and beautiful as ever. Tame deer roamed in the Shinto shrines and Buddhist temples that peeked through the forests of maple and birch trees on the town's outskirts; the crisp air, tinged with the first hint of the changing seasons, promised an explosion of autumnal colors in a matter of weeks. For Elizabeth and Curtis, marooned with dozens of others at the Hotel Nikko, the isolation was a source of comfort, but it also allowed their imaginations to wander in torturous directions. The hours crept by. Telephone and telegraph wires remained silent. People drifted through the hallways of the hotel and stopped one another on the streets. How many had died? How bad were the fires? What was the fate of Yokohama? Was there anything left?

Then, on the morning of Monday, September 3, the first eyewitness to the tragedy in Tokyo, a young American, appeared at the hotel in Nikko after a difficult journey on broken roads jammed with refugees. Dozens of people hungry for news swarmed him in the lobby. The mob of foreigners climbed over one another, desperately interrogating the exhausted young man, shouting names, begging him for word about family members, friends, colleagues trapped in the city. For Elizabeth and Curtis, there would be no further talk of the planned temple-touring trip with Miss Mann. "Our friends in Tokyo have miraculously escaped. The American Embassy, with the Chancery, the homes of the Counsellor and Japanese Secretary, burned to the ground. All the people in the compound, trying to save it, were surrounded by a solid sheet of flame, but all were unhurt." The eyewitness also brought the first reports on Yokohama from an acquaintance who had walked, and sometimes crawled, the eighteen miles from the port to the capital. Words resonant with anguish and disbelief, Elizabeth relayed to her mother the news of the city's extinction: "Yokohama is no more. All the sea front, the Bund, the settlement, the business portion, the native city, have vanished from the earth.

The Bluff, the foreign residence quarter is in utter ruin. In the lower city almost all were killed in a moment, in the [blink] of an eye like the day of doom."

A diplomat named Snelling from the Dutch Legation in Tokyo, arriving in Chuzenji after an arduous journey by car, train, and rickshaw, contributed more details later that day. In a conversation by the lake he confirmed to Lyman Cotten that fires had swept over most of the capital and that the U.S. Embassy and neighboring Dutch Legation had burned to the ground on Saturday night. Snelling had left Tokyo on Sunday, with the city still ablaze. Although he hadn't passed through Azabu, the neighborhood near the embassy where the Cottens lived, his graphic account left the naval attaché with little doubt that his house had been destroyed, and all his furniture, clothing, and Japanese art burned with it. "It is reported 20,000 dead in Tokyo and 100,000 dead in Yokohama," Cotten recorded in his diary. Then he added one curious sentence: "I sent [Lieutenant Commander Garnet] Hulings [the deputy naval attaché] down yesterday to see if he can get through . . . and to let me know if I can do anything."

Let me know if I can do anything. Those words, uttered without any trace of self-awareness, would come back to haunt the rest of Cotten's life. At this point, more than forty-eight hours after the earthquake, nobody could deny the scale of the catastrophe. Vivid eyewitness accounts had begun to pour into the lakeside resort. Tokyo and Yokohama lay in ruins and casualties were immense, possibly unprecedented, certainly in the tens of thousands. The expected reaction of any diplomat of Cotten's stature would have been to commandeer a vehicle immediately and head for the capital. Yet Cotten—the man of action who had distinguished himself protecting British ships from German submarines in the English Channel, who had evacuated terrified Americans during the Mexican revolution—remained strangely, inexplicably passive. *Let me know if I can do anything.*

What explains Cotten's paralysis? Perhaps he believed that the reports were exaggerated and opted to wait until he heard the full story from Hulings. It may be that the repeated interruptions of his summer vacation had left him so frustrated that he resolved to remain in Chuzenji no matter what happened. But such a response hardly seems characteristic of a man whose sense of duty and honor had always driven him. Cotten's difficult relationship with U.S. Ambassador Cyrus Woods, who was running relief operations from a temporary embassy in a wing of Tokyo's Imperial Hotel, could well have been a factor. Fatigue, confusion, guilt over the prospect of missing the hiking trip with his son might all have come into play in explaining the apathy that seized America's top naval officer in Japan during one of the worst natural disasters in history.

His diaries and local newspaper articles provide additional clues. The record indicates that Cotten called on Hulings to stand in for him at several important occasions, such as the dedication of the Allied War Memorial in Yokohama in 1922. ("To the Hulings we have become devoted," Cotten wrote in his diary a year earlier about his deputy and his wife. "[They are] natural, wholesome, attractive people.") From time to time Cotten had displayed an obtuseness and a lack of judgment in quite different circumstances that had landed him in trouble. In one of his most embarrassing lapses he appeared at a costume party at the French Embassy in March 1923 dressed as a copy of that morning's *Japan Advertiser*—with a large headline about France's controversial postwar occupation of the Ruhr Valley in Germany emblazoned on his white satin suit. The following day, the outraged French chargé d'affaires had demanded an apology, which Cotten refused to give. "I could not see why such a map should offend the French," Cotten wrote. "They were occupying the Ruhr, said they were doing right, so I could see no impropriety in displaying a map of the occupied region at a fancy dress ball at their embassy. [U.S. Embassy chargé d'affaires] Wilson agreed, and thought this merely another instance of the childishness and insensitivity of the French."

Whatever his motivations, one fact is indisputable: Cotten remained at his summer home in Chuzenji for nearly a week despite a flood of reports of the disaster. Though the diaries aren't clear on the issue, it appears that almost every other diplomat and military officer left Chuzenji a day or two after the earthquake to volunteer his services in Tokyo or Yokohama, leaving Cotten at the lake with several dozen diplomats' wives and their children. Remarkably, Cotten displayed no sense of urgency, no awareness that he might be missed in the disaster zone. In his diary, he wrote:

Tuesday September 4, 1923: Elizabeth and Curtis returned from Nikko. The news continues awful. Yokohama almost totally destroyed by the earthquake. Tokyo two thirds destroyed by the shake and subsequent fires. Total casualties estimated now at half a million. Many reports of sabotage by Koreans and Japanese socialists but nothing definite. Felt several shocks today. Some of the people up here are under such terrible strain. Mme. Claudel, wife of the French Ambassador, with her two younger daughters, and Bette de Bassompierre are here, M. [Paul] Claudel is in Tokyo and Chonette Claudel is in Zushi with the de Bassompierres. Rumor says Zushi is hard hit, but there is no definitive news. Mme. Claudel heard today that the French Embassy had been burned but her husband was saved and left Sunday for Zushi to try and locate Chonette. At least we have only friends and house to worry about.

By the afternoon of Wednesday, September 5, the cumulative weight of eyewitness testimony made further delay impossible. At last Cotten made up his mind to go to Tokyo with relief supplies and report to the American committee that had been set up at the Imperial Hotel. But even at this point he mobilized slowly. He walked down the mountain from Chuzenji to Nikko only on the following morning, Thursday, September 6. He found the town in a state of high excitement. "The rumor has spread that Crown Prince Hirohito had secretly arrived at the Palace in Nikko. Too dangerous for him in Tokyo. . . . I hear numbers of Koreans have been shot by the Japanese who believed the Koreans were rising against the government." Ominous reports filtered in about friends and acquaintances. "Heard today that the Cranes were in Yokohama when the first shock came. Very likely both were killed. Awful! Awful! Such nice people they were." But he also received some hopeful news. "Had a talk with Mr. Oltmans, formerly in our embassy. He was in the Imperial Hotel when the shock came. Oltmans saw my house standing like an oasis in a burnt desert. It seems miraculous." At nine o'clock on Friday morning, September 7—a full six days after the earthquake—Cotten loaded a Ford with food and, with Lieutenant Colonel Francis Piggot, the British military attaché, began his journey to Tokyo.

* * *

BY THE TIME Cotten finally roused himself into action, reports about the disaster had spread throughout the world and set in motion a global rescue effort. The first news had emanated from the death zone in an appropriately dramatic fashion. Early in the afternoon on September 1, Yokohama's police chief, Jiro Morioka, escaped from the burning Prefectural Government Building near the waterfront and led a large group of frightened refugees to Yokohama harbor. Morioka attempted to hail a sampan to take him to one of the steamships moored several hundred yards offshore. But nobody picked him up, and at three o'clock, with the flames at his back, he dove into the water. For more than three hours he floated in a turbulent sea of burning oil slicks. At 6:30 a launch plucked the exhausted policeman from the water and ferried him to the *Korea Maru*. This was one of twelve large ships that, at dusk, had followed the *Philoctetes* past the sunken breakwater to the safety of the outer harbor. Morioka collapsed unconscious on the deck, but he soon revived, and obtained permission from the *Korea Maru*'s captain to use the ship's wireless machine to send out an appeal for help. In a small cabin below the main deck, Morioka tapped a metal telegraph key connected to a coiled antenna strung from bow to stern, and a long-wave electromagnetic signal in Morse code tunneled a path between the ionosphere, an electrically charged particle layer sixty miles above the earth, and the earth's surface. He couldn't have realized that the brief message, in Japanese, that he addressed to the governor of Osaka would be the first to reach the outside world.

> TODAY AT NOON A GREAT EARTHQUAKE OCCURRED AND WAS IMMEDIATELY FOLLOWED BY A CONFLAGRATION WHICH HAS CHANGED THE WHOLE CITY INTO A SEA OF FIRE, CAUSING COUNTLESS CASUALTIES. ALL FACILITIES OF TRAFFIC HAVE BEEN DESTROYED AND COMMUNICATIONS CUT OFF. WE HAVE NEITHER WATER NOR FOOD, FOR GOD'S SAKE SEND RELIEF AT ONCE.

* * *

IN THE FALL of 1923 wireless communication was still a rudimentary, if rapidly evolving, technology. A young German scientist, Heinrich Hertz, had first transmitted electromagnetic energy across a narrow gap without the use of a cable only thirty-five years earlier. Seven years later the Italian inventor Giuseppe Marconi had cobbled together a crude transmitter from a coil, a metal telegraph key, and an antenna and sent radio waves to a receiver that detected the signal and rang a bell. By the turn of the twentieth century the Marconi Company was manufacturing commercial "spark gap" transmitters for both shipboard and land communication that sent dots and dashes through the ether, capable of reception by an antenna more than a thousand miles away. These unwieldy devices consisted of a battery or a generator connected to a transformer, which produced enough voltage to create an electric arc: an intermittent discharge of current, or a spark. Like a hammer ringing a bell, the electric spark caused a large cylindrical coil to resonate, and that energy was fed to an antenna, or transmission wire. During the Russo-Japanese War of 1904–1905, seven spark-gap transmitters, each one weighing hundreds of pounds and packed into wooden crates, had been carried to the front by horses and buggies, and a handful of newspaper correspondents had tapped out short dispatches to their home offices via a series of relay stations. The early wireless sets had transmitted the Morse code as simple bursts of noise; as transmitting techniques improved and the energy became more concentrated at a single frequency, they had become sharp, clear tones. Around the turn of the century wireless pioneers developed continuous-wave radio signals largely free of extraneous noise—and that innovation made voice transmission possible. On Christmas Eve 1905 wireless operators in the Atlantic detected, to their astonishment, a woman's faint voice singing Christmas carols and a symphony orchestra playing between the clatter of dots and dashes.

Wireless's most significant early breakthrough came on the morning of April 15, 1912. The Marconi Station at Cape Grace on the eastern coast of Newfoundland picked up a distress signal fourteen hundred miles away from the SS *Olympic,* the first rescue ship to reach the sinking *Titanic.* The dramatic initial message—"SS *Titanic* ran into iceberg. Sinking fast"—was followed by hourly reports transmitting the names of survivors plucked out of the icy Atlantic. For the next three days, wireless operators at receiving stations in Massachusetts and the eastern tip of Long Island passed on bulletins to the *New York American,* the *New York Times,* and other newspapers. The U.S. Congress soon approved legislation requiring that all oceangoing vessels with the capacity for fifty or more passengers carry wireless transmitters, a law that immediately caused a spike in the Marconi Company's stock price. In 1914 General Electric introduced the Alexanderson alternator, a radio frequency energy generator that enabled transmitters to hurl nearly pure radio signals thousands of miles. At the same time, another innovator, Edwin Armstrong, invented the super-regenerative receiver, a vacuum-tube amplifier that picked up faint wireless signals that earlier receivers had been unable to perceive.

Despite the rapid advances in technology, wireless remained frustratingly unreliable in the early 1920s. Antennas required for the long-distance reception and transmission of long waves, the only method of sending information in the early days, were huge and unwieldy. A one-hundred-kilohertz radio wave, the kind sent by Marconi's spark-gap transmitters, required an antenna thousands of feet long. If strung vertically in towers for better radiation, they could easily collapse in a natural disaster such as a hurricane or earthquake. At the height of the day the sun irradiates the earth and disrupts the particles in the ionosphere, making the medium a poor reflector of radio signals. Short-wave radio signals were more readily reflected by the ionosphere, but they wouldn't be developed for commercial use for another few years. "Wireless enjoys nearly all the boosting nowadays, owing to the adroitness with which it has secured political affiliation, and this distressingly uncertain mode of communications receives more attention than it deserves," declared an editorial in the January 4, 1923, *Japan Weekly Chronicle.* "Of more real interest are the modest announcements made from time to time regarding cable laying."

Even so, on the eve of the Great Kanto Earthquake, a new era of radio communications lay just around the corner. In October 1919 General Electric had purchased the American Marconi Company and created the Radio Corporation of America. Intent on dominating the wireless industry, RCA established wireless links in France, England, Japan, and Germany. On November 8, 1922, the *Japan Weekly*

Chronicle heralded a major advance in the Far Eastern wireless communication network, one that would have great implications for disseminating word of the Japanese disaster: "Mr. Schwerin of the Federal Telegraph Company is . . . about to establish two wireless stations in Shanghai, and one each in Peking, Mukden, and Canton. One of the Shanghai stations will be the biggest in the world. This will keep China in touch with the world's wireless network." In the early 1920s RCA's commercial manager, David Sarnoff, was stringing together stations across America into a rudimentary radio network, and the London Wireless Exhibition in October 1922 revealed the breathtaking possibilities of commercial radio. Sir Henry Norman, described by the *Japan Weekly Chronicle* as a "leading authority on wireless telegraphy," predicted that wireless would be in every home in the United Kingdom within a few years.

On the morning of September 1, Taki Yonemura, the chief engineer at the government wireless station in Iwaki, a small town 152 miles northeast of Tokyo, was monitoring the air waves through his headset in a cluttered room on the ground floor. Topped by a six-hundred-foot tower, Iwaki was the primary receiving station in Japan for wireless transmissions from RCA; the transmitting station lay twenty miles further north at Haranomachi, connected to Iwaki by cable. "At twelve o'clock, we had the most severe shock I have ever felt," recalled Yonemura, the longest-serving communications engineer in the Japanese government. "As soon as it was over I tested the land lines and found the circuit to Haranomachi okay but all the other lines down. I realized at once that the only way we could get anything was from the ether and I kept a close watch for anything that might be sent from a [wireless] station." One can imagine the scene: the operator sitting alone in his receiving room, twisting dials, pressing the earphones against his head, straining to hear the faint dots and dashes above the interference, plucking strands of meaning out of a sea of unintelligibility.

At seven o'clock that night Yonemura picked up a faint staticky signal from the naval station at Choshi trying to send an official message from the chief of police of Yokohama to the governor of Osaka. Huddled in the wireless room below deck on the *Korea Maru*, which was then moored in the harbor, Chief Morioka had narrowly escaped being burned alive in the flaming waters and, summoning all his remaining strength, had tapped out a terse message describing the disaster unfolding around him and begging for help. Corpses bobbed in the oil-slicked harbor, jets of fire from the ruined city pierced the darkness, the air was saturated with the odor of charcoal and burned flesh, and burning sampans continued to float aimlessly on the other side of the breakwater. Morioka wasn't sure whether the governor of Osaka would receive his message, but he assumed that somebody, somewhere, was listening. He was right. Manning his wireless station in distant Iwaki, the telegraph operator pulled down Morioka's plea from the ether and immediately grasped its momentousness. The only employee at his station who spoke English, Yonemura translated the S.O.S. from Japanese and edited it to a nineteen-word bulletin:

CONFLAGRATION SUBSEQUENT TO SEVERE EARTHQUAKE AT YOKOHAMA AT NOON TODAY. WHOLE CITY ABLAZE WITH NUMEROUS CASUALTIES. ALL TRAFFIC STOPPED.

The dots and dashes flickered by wire to Haranomachi, then east by radio across the Pacific to RCA's Honolulu station. Minutes later, a wireless operator in Hawaii forwarded the bulletin to RCA's high-powered receiver in Marshall, California, which, in a replay of the *Titanic* sinking, dispatched the news to its subscriber newspapers and wire services across the United States. And so, early on the morning of September 1, 1923, Pacific Coast time, the Associated Press brought to the world the first sketchy report of the worst natural disaster of the twentieth century. Over the next few hours Yonemura sent a stream of news bulletins to RCA based on transmissions received from naval stations along the coast. "Flames spreading toward Asakusa, Kanda, Hongo. . . . Heavy casualties reported. Rumor afloat that all traffic suspended throughout Tokio," he wirelessed to RCA shortly after midnight, Japan time, on September 2—twelve hours after the earthquake. "Many disastrous accidents have been reported, a number of trains running to Tokio have been wrecked during the quake. It is also reported that a severe tidal wave struck the coast at Yokohama." On the morning of September 2 refugees began arriving by train in Iwaki from Tokyo and Yokohama, carrying eyewitness accounts: the deaths of seven hundred people in the collapse of a twelve-story tower at an amusement park in Asakusa; the escape from harm of Crown Prince Hirohito; the burning of the Imperial Railway Station and the Imperial Theater.

Yonemura's wireless dispatches marked the birth of a new era and revealed just how much the technology had evolved in a few years. Had the Great Kanto Earthquake occurred only half a decade earlier, before governments and private companies such as RCA began investing money heavily in wireless stations both on shore and at sea, it could have taken days, if not weeks, for the enormity of the catastrophe to disseminate widely. But in 1923 powerful transmitters capable of hurling clear signals halfway around the world spanned the globe from Shanghai to San Francisco, and tens of millions of people were able to glean at least some details about the calamity on the day it happened. Yonemura ushered in an age of instant global telecommunications, an era in which disasters were no longer remote events, but tragedies that people around the world could follow in nearly real time, with a powerful sense of immediacy. One important result of those real-time dispatches was the mobilization of huge numbers of people into the first large-scale international relief effort. From the moment the first descriptions of appalling suffering appeared in America's newspapers, the White House, the International Committee of the Red Cross, and the U.S. military began planning a logistical operation of unprecedented reach and complexity. Hundreds of thousands in the earthquake zone were injured and homeless; every moment was critical. Yonemura's dispatches allowed relief teams to begin planning within hours of the disaster and undoubtedly helped to save thousands of lives.

The wireless reports had other reverberations. They demonstrated to the world the reliability of a new technology and sped up the establishment of commercial radio networks: within a year, David Sarnoff's RCA would begin live broadcasts of news, music, and other entertainment from cities across the United States, and the United Kingdom would soon follow. They revealed the power of the media to shape events as much as cover them. Yonemura's vivid dispatches, which reached millions of Americans within a few hours of the events they described, engendered a feeling of solidarity between the United

States and Japan. They established a sense of urgency and helped to draw the nation together in a remarkable—if ephemeral—outpouring of goodwill and material support. They alerted President Calvin Coolidge and the U.S. military to the scope of the disaster and helped to boost Coolidge's political fortunes: he came across as a strong and compassionate commander in chief who took the lead in rushing to the aid of a stricken nation. Yonemura's dispatches prefigured the media's role eighty years later during Hurricane Katrina, when the reporting of Anderson Cooper and other television journalists from New Orleans unified the nation and, unlike in 1923, created an indelible image of government fecklessness. Indeed, the swift global awareness of events that followed the great earthquake makes Lyman Cotten's obtuseness seem all the more incomprehensible. While the armed forces of the United States and Europe were putting together the greatest rescue mission the world had ever seen, while millions were rushing to their newsstands to read the latest accounts of suffering and heroism, the U.S. naval attaché was blithely passing the time in his cottage by the lake, musing in his diary but not lifting a finger to help.

THE IMAGE OF the lone wireless operator forming a fragile link between the suffering cities and the outside world struck an emotional chord in the international press. Even the usually staid *New York Times* became carried away with both the wonder of wireless and the stamina of the man at the telegraph key. The radio man "flashed the [news] across the sea at the speed of sunlight," reported the newspaper, "to tell of tremendous casualties, buildings leveled by fire, towns swept by tidal waves, disorders by rioters, raging fire and wrecked bridges." Operators at Pacific Coast receiving stations said that Yonemura "badly twisted his tenses," the *Times* reported, "and, at times, unable to express himself in English, reverted to Japanese. . . . He ended his dispatches apologetically, 'Please not no more this time.' " Aftershocks shook the facility, once silencing the wireless for four hours until Yonemura and his staff could make repairs. "American operators copying the messages feared . . . that the lofty tower had been shattered to bits," the *Times* reported. "Fortunately it weathered the test, probably because of its exceptional construction, which combines both steel and concrete." The *New York Times* even compared Yonemura to the fleet-footed runner in ancient Greece who raced twenty-six miles from the Plain of Marathon to Athens to convey news of the defeat of the Persians: "It would take the scientific imagination of a Marconi to follow the marvelous run of the Japanese Pheidippides, which brought almost instantly the response of every people on the face of the globe. For he not only carried the message to San Francisco, he carried back to Japan the prompt and helpful answers. He was only an 'obscure' Japanese radio operator, as the report states, but his name ought to be heard and remembered as far as the message he carried has gone."

Yonemura was hardly the only person on the Japanese archipelago whose initial impulse after the earthquake was to get the word out in any way possible. Twelve hours after Yonemura tapped his initial dispatch, after dawn on September 2, Samuel Reber, RCA's representative in Tokyo, found U.S. Ambassador Cyrus Woods "calmly surveying the smoking ruins [of the U.S. Embassy] from which he and his family had with great difficulty escaped with their lives." Woods, disheveled but poised after narrowly avoiding being crushed by the collapsing walls of his office, was consumed, Reber reported, with a single mission: sending messages to Washington, the U.S. Asiatic Fleet, and the governor-general of the Philippine Islands, alerting them about the disaster and requesting immediate aid. Reber told him that the best way would be via the radio station in Funabashi, the Imperial Japanese Navy's facility at the head of Tokyo Bay. Funabashi had a much smaller and less effective antenna than the Iwaki and Haranomachi stations, but it was within a day's walk of Tokyo and would still be able to relay messages to other facilities with more powerful transmitters. Reber recalled, "I said it must be working, and, as it is less than twenty miles from the city, I felt confident that the Navy Department would find some way to get a message through there." Reber and Woods ran to the Navy Department through the smoldering wreckage of the capital. The great Japanese fighting machine that had occupied much of Asia and produced one of the world's most powerful fleets of warships and submarines was barely functioning. "Under a large tree with a plank supported on two barrels," the RCA man recalled, "were several naval officers who were receiving the official messages from the several branches of the Japanese government for transmission by messenger to the Navy radio station at Funabashi." At 10 A.M. on September 2 Woods composed his first emergency radiogram, a note to Secretary of State Charles Evans Hughes: "All embassy buildings totally destroyed but no one in embassy injured," he wrote. "Food situation very acute. Send rations at once from Philippines." A courier ran with the message to Funabashi and urged the naval operators to send it immediately, but the navy men, apparently overwhelmed with official Japanese business, lay the message aside and wouldn't pick it up again for another forty-eight hours. "I continued [trying to raise the station] until the afternoon of the fourth when Funabashi answered and began sending me official messages for the US and Europe," Yonemura recalled. "The first message for the [secretary of state in] Washington was received at 3:30 p.m. September 4 [two days after it was delivered by Woods] and the second at 11:55 a.m. on the fifth. The one addressed to the Commanding General of the Philippine division arrived at 7:34 p.m. of the sixth and was relayed by Pearl Harbor to Camite."

The wireless operators at Funabashi may have been slow to take care of the U.S. ambassador's business, but they wasted no time disseminating accounts of destruction, fire, and mass death brought by refugees from Tokyo. The signals were picked up a few hundred miles away in the naval bases at Sasebo and Nagasaki in western Japan, and also helped to spur the world to action. One brief, vague dispatch made the front page of the *New York Times* on September 2:

People Flee to Boats

NAGASAKI, Japan, Sept. 1—A naval wireless message received at Saseho [*sic*] from Funanash [*sic*] says there have been repeated earthquakes, accompanied by a severe rainstorm, in Tokio today.

Another message reports that fire has broken out in Yokohama and that the inhabitants are seeking refuge in the ships in the harbor.

Faced at first with a dearth of hard knowledge about the earthquake, the world's newspapers didn't miss a beat. In the manner of latter-day cable news presenters who pad their round-the-clock programming with the musings of talking heads, they trotted out every "expert," past resident of Tokyo or Yokohama, and anyone else with a connection to the earthquake whom they could find and filled their pages with speculation. On September 3 the *New York Times* carried a full-page interview with a former Yokohama-based missionary, A. W. A. Austen, that consisted entirely of wild guesses about how the fires had started and what routes they had taken through the port. "Traces Fire's Path through Yokohama," the headline read. "Either of two probable routes would sweep heart of the city." (In fact, Austen's piece turned out to be uncannily accurate.) The *Washington Post* interviewed former residents such as Dr. K. Kayukawa, a student at Georgetown University, who also imagined from afar the shape of the conflagration. "According to Dr. Kayukawa, the beauty of the city lay in its compactness," the *Post* reported, "in the low wooden buildings stretching over much ground, and in the levelness of its territory. These, he says, are the reasons why a fire could spread so rapidly as to wipe from the face of the earth a great city." The first detailed newspaper account of the earthquake appeared on page 1 of the *New York Times* in a later edition on September 3, 1923, under a dramatic headline: "Dead Are in Heaps in Tokio Streets: Path of Destruction Extends for Fifty Miles about the Capital—More Earthshocks Sunday." Datelined Shanghai and pieced together from wireless transmissions relayed from Funabashi, the article accurately reported the destruction of numerous districts in Tokyo, a tsunami on the Izu peninsula, and "[at least] ten thousand casualties" in Yokohama. Wireless messages to Yokosuka had gone unanswered, the article reported, and "it is feared that the entire Naval Department is destroyed." (Those fears proved to be unfounded: Although the earthquake and fire had severely damaged the main naval base at Yokosuka, destroyed battleships, knocked down the transmission tower, and burned 50 million barrels of Batavian oil stored in subterranean reservoirs, most of the fleet remained intact. Thus, despite widespread reports that Japan's military would take decades to recover from the earthquake, the machine would be up and running again, and quietly preparing for its assaults on Asia, in a couple of years.)

Bulletins trickled into the *Times* by wireless throughout the week, such as this dramatic eyewitness account, which appeared on the front page of the newspaper five days after the earthquake:

EYEWITNESS TELLS OF TOKIO CALAMITY

With Dazed Millions He Beheld
City Fall and Then Die in Flames
Saw Appalling Suffering
But People's Patience Was
Marvelous—Strong Carried
the Weak to Safety

Special Cable to THE NEW YORK TIMES

TOKIO, via Nagoya, Sept. 6—By various means have I endeavored to get news out of Tokio, with what success I do not know. By the courtesy of the army authorities, this message is being sent by army airplanes to the nearest working wireless station . . . Yokohama is wiped off the map, and those of the population who are not dead are homeless.

In Tokio 1,500,000 are homeless; 300,000 homes have been demolished by earthquake and fire and it is believed that the casualties in Tokio number 100,000. . . . The sky over the city all night long was scarlet or orange, and vast clouds of gray, black and white smoke rolled up from the earth. Imagination would have failed to conceive such a sight!

A race had begun, meanwhile, among foreign correspondents and Japanese journalists to publish the first detailed, on-scene reports about the earthquake—and bask in the consequent glory. In an era of Thuraya satellite telephones, fiber-optic cables, and high-speed digital technology, it is easy to forget the tenuousness of global communication links available to the press eighty years ago. In normal times, American correspondents sent their dispatches via the Pacific telegraph cable connection from Tokyo to San Francisco via Honolulu. But that cable, as well as all other hard-wire links out of Tokyo, had melted during the fires, and the Central Telegraphic Office remained shut for five days after the earthquake. Communications out of Tokyo

The swift world news coverage of the disaster reflected emerging global communications technology. (© The New York Times)

stayed broken for several days. "All the power stations were burned," Joseph Dahlmann wrote. "Of Tokyo's 80,000 telephones three fourths were destroyed, the others out of commission. The metropolitan belt line as well as the street cars were annihilated. Thus communication with even the nearest suburbs was at a standstill. [For several days] it was impossible for Tokyo to get in touch with the outside world except by roundabout ways." But after three days of paralysis, newspaper editors and correspondents found ways around the obstacles. On September 4 the Japanese daily *Osaka Mainichi* sent a pair of reporters on a biplane to Tokyo; the journalists wandered the streets of the destroyed city for several hours, then returned to Osaka with graphic eyewitness accounts of what they had seen. They repeated the routine each day until reliable communication links from the capital were restored. Several foreign correspondents, having heard that the Great Northern Cable Company might be able to move stories via Vladivostok, set off for distant Nagasaki on Kyushu Island, which had a direct telegraphic link with the Siberian port. On September 4 George Denny of the Associated Press hired couriers to take three of his dispatches to the Iwaki wireless facility, getting the first one into print in the United States on September 6. Probably the most industrious journalist of the pack was a young reporter for the *Asahi Shimbun*, Kenzo Fukuma, who got the jump on his competitors by more than two days. Fukuma set out on foot on the evening of September 1 from Tokyo and walked through the night to the beach resort of Kamakura, forty miles away, his route lit by the glow of fires from the capital and from Yokohama. The reporter hoped to catch a train there to Osaka, but, finding Kamakura paralyzed and the railway line torn up, he hiked another thirty miles along the tracks to the lakeside town of Hakone near Mount Fuji. In some places landslides had blocked the railroad tunnels, and Fukuma was forced to climb over mountains. At last, on the evening of September 3, forty-eight hours after starting his journey, the exhausted journalist reached Fujisuono Station at the foot of Mount Fuji, where he caught a train to Osaka. The next morning, September 4, Fukuma's gripping eyewitness accounts of the calamity made page 1 of the *Osaka Asahi* and were cabled across Siberia to the rest of the world.

The capital restored its links with agonizing slowness. On September 6 Tokyo's Central Telegraph Office finally repaired its cables connecting the capital to the Pacific line. For the first twenty-four hours telegraph operators would send only imperial government telegrams; then the Central Office opened its doors to the public, but the crush of desperate survivors was so great that officials were forced to limit telegrams to fifty words each. The result of the edict was a foreign correspondent's nightmare. Newspaper and wire service reporters converged on the telegraph office, frantically trying to send their dispatches but running up against obstinate telegraph operators and bureaucrats who agreed to transmit only a few sentences and who, to compound the journalists' frustration, often spoke little or no English. Even once the reporters had filed their fifty-word dispatches, they received no guarantees that their cables would reach their intended destination. As Henry Kinney wrote in the *Atlantic Monthly*:

> I sought out my familiars among the foreign press correspondents in Tokyo, but they were an unhappy lot. . . . Each one had . . . made his way through the flames and tremors, to telegraph and cable office, and, later, had tried to give the best possible picture through the maximum of fifty words allowed by the authorities. But they did not know what was going through. They found out later. Even where they had had the ready assistance of the high officials in Tokyo, all the messages had been held up by some petty official at Nagasaki. . . . He held the entire batch, a week's desperate and painstaking efforts of a dozen correspondents, and the first reports of the appalling event came to the rest of the world, mishandled and inaccurate, from Japanese sources in Osaka.

The *New York Tribune* correspondent Philip Kerby, no friend of the Japanese, blamed "crass stupidity and blundering impudence of those in authority" for impeding the flow of information from the earthquake zone. In a scathing account of his experiences covering the earthquake that appeared in late September in the *China Weekly Review*, he wrote:

> I was informed that the Tokyo telegraph station was in a position to accept messages of fifty words in the morning and fifty words in the afternoon, provided that they were not in code and "contained no deleterious statements" to the Japanese government. The correspondents of all the large newspapers and news agencies in the world . . . held a meeting in protest, went to the Ministry of Communications complaining that 100 words a day was manifestly inadequate. . . . The assistant secretary . . . "washed his hands in the

air" several times and remarked "I am veeery sorrow for you—I can do nothing. It is the order." Thus ended the interview. . . . We expostulated [to the secretary] at some length, and tried to explain that every country in the world was doing its utmost to raise large funds for the relief of the stricken population, and that the Japanese were "cutting off their own noses" by not permitting a wider dissemination of news abroad, which would stir up greater giving. The secretary listened patiently for some time, and when at last we had run out of breath, replied, "I am veery sorrow for you."

Much of the initial reporting about the earthquake was inaccurate or wildly exaggerated. A correspondent for a newspaper in Sendai, 120 miles north of the capital, had monitored the crimson sky on the night of September 1 and, believing that billowing magma was causing the phenomenon, reported that Mount Fuji had erupted. An early wireless report claimed that "huge tidal waves" had swept into Tokyo Bay, "fifty or sixty in succession," swamping thousands of homes. "The water rushed up the Sumida, pouring over its banks, destroying or submerging the houses along the river," the *Japan Weekly Chronicle* declared. Another Japanese newspaper reported authoritatively— and mistakenly—that Chichibu Renzan, a volcano northwest of Tokyo, "began to explode on the 30th of August, and reached its peak on the afternoon of the 1st." One of the wildest stories, repeated by newspapers and wire services, maintained that the island of Oshima, near the epicenter of the earthquake, had submerged, Atlantis-like, beneath the sea. On September 8, a full week after the earthquake, the United Press carried the following fantasy by its Tokyo correspondent, Clarence Dubose:

Volcanic Island Gone

Shaken to pieces by a terrific eruption that accompanied the earthquake on Saturday, the volcanic island of Oshima, picturesque site of the city of Mother of Pearl, sank into the sea, all of its inhabitants being killed by spouting lava or drowned.

Dubose went on to report that, as the island disappeared, "great mountains" of water rolled over Yokohama and Tokyo Bay, hurling ships onto beaches and drowning thousands of people. He claimed that Oshima had vanished completely, its quaint teahouses, pearl divers, and shell craftsmen lost at the bottom of the ocean.

In fact, scientists who visited Oshima after the quake reported that it had sustained almost no damage, apparently because the volcanic island had formed out of earthquake-resistant igneous rock. (The earthquake did alter the geology of the region: Japanese naval survey vessels reported in late 1923 that the seabed three miles north of the island of Okinoshima in Sagami Bay had dropped by 1,518 feet during the earthquake; they also discerned a sinkage from 150 to 778 feet in the center of Sagami Bay.) The apocalyptic misreporting carried as far as a village on the Dutch-German border, where a Japanese schoolboy, Nagamasa Kawakita, went to a telegraph office to send a message to his family in Tokyo. "It is impossible," the clerk replied. "Your country is no more."

The Japanese and expatriates living in Japan were often just as much in the dark about the catastrophe as people overseas were. In Karuizawa, the mountain resort near Chuzenji where many Europeans and Americans spent their summers, the seismic vibrations knocked down a few buildings, and a falling beam killed a villager. Benjamin W. Fleisher, the vacationing owner of the *Japan Advertiser,* assumed that the earthquake was a local phenomenon and excitedly filed a dispatch about it to his Tokyo headquarters. He received no reply. Only three days later—following a fifteen-mile, twelve-hour walk from an outlying train station into the heart of Tokyo—did Fleisher learn the full extent of the disaster and discover that his Tokyo office had burned to the ground.

Isolated Japanese officials in the earthquake zone received fragments of information from the Japan Martial Law Authorities in Tokyo through a method that had last been used during the Russo-Japanese War: carrier pigeons. "As soon as the fact was ascertained that all system of communication was broken," the *Japan Times* reported, "and the scorching sky above the blazing city did not allow even aeroplanes to work, an emergency carrier pigeon corps was organized." One thousand birds, selected from a corps of three thousand, flew reports about casualties, military deployments, and relief operations to Hakone near Mount Fuji, to the tsunami-battered towns along Sagami Bay, to Yokohama, and to the emperor and empress in Nikko. (It was the pigeons, and not the military airplanes that Elizabeth Cotten referred to, that first got word about the earthquake to the royal couple.)

The earthquake and fires had destroyed the offices of all but two daily newspapers in the capital, the *Tokyo Nichi Nichi* and *Miyako*. But some resourceful journalists got their presses running even as the fires were still burning. On September 4, Randall Gould, the young news editor of the English-language *Japan Times & Mail*, typed a one-page emergency edition in room 108 at Frank Lloyd Wright's Imperial Hotel. Gould tacked the first issue on the bulletin board outside the hotel, getting the date wrong in his rush to publish the news:

THE JAPAN TIMES AND MAIL
Aug. 4 [sic], 9:45 a.m.

Two general government measures have been taken—establishment of an Earthquake Relief Executive Bureau and proclamation of martial law.

The Japanese squadron of 50 battleships, destroyers, and other vessels is off Chosen [Korea] and will bring food, medical supplies and other articles into Tokyo Bay as soon as possible.

Scientists announce that 300 more shocks will be felt, but none is espected [*sic*] to be of particularly destructive nature.

It is estimated that there are 150,000 casualties in Tokyo of which 80,000 are dead. Two million people are homeless. . . . Communication with the outside world, though of an imperfect nature, was established by the government Sunday night. . . . Water supply will be reestablished in a day or two, Government officials announce. Its failure immediately after the first quake allowed the 22 fires which had started to gain their way.

On September 5 Gould produced a reduced-size "Earthquake Extra" with a distribution of several thousand copies and continued publishing his emergency editions for ten days. It is unclear whether Gould printed his special editions at the damaged *Japan Times* headquarters or, as others claim, installed an offset printing press inside his room at the Imperial Hotel. Whatever the case, his one-page broadsheet, which expanded to four pages a week after the earthquake, served as virtually the only source of reliable news for Tokyo's expatriate population during this chaotic period. (The intrepid Gould would start two English-language newspapers in China, witness the revolution, and return to a distinguished journalism career in the United States after his expulsion by the Chinese Communist leadership in 1949.) Gould brought daily reports of the evacuation of foreigners to Kobe on board steamships, the rising death count, conditions in the countryside, the restoration of electricity and water, the resumption of railway service, the arrival of rice and beans and other relief supplies, and the cabinet's denunciation of anti-Korean rumors, "which are declared ridiculous." Gould had the field to himself. The *Japan Gazette,* the main English-language newspaper in Yokohama, had burned down during the earthquake and never appeared again. Fleisher's *Japan Advertiser,* arguably Tokyo's best English-language paper, was also destroyed. "The Advertiser is gone beyond recall . . . not even private documents are saved, and a life time of work and worry gone with it," Fleisher's wife wrote to her friend Elizabeth Cotten from Karuizawa on September 10. "What any of us are going to do, I don't know, it will be a complete change all around, and a pall over the whole foreign community as well as the Japanese, and we are all waiting to see what is going to happen." Later Lyman Cotten reported to his wife from Tokyo, "Mr. Fleisher seems more depressed than anyone I have seen. Business completely wiped out. Says he does not know where to turn." (Weeks afterward, however, Fleisher wired an order to the United States for new printing presses and made plans to rebuild his shattered operation. "We expect to get out the Japan Advertiser two months hence in a garb richer and more brilliant," the indomitable publisher was quoted as saying by the *Yushin Nippo* in early October 1923. Amazingly, he succeeded.)

FOR A WEEK after the disaster, Tokyo remained a city of fear and death. Like New Orleans in the aftermath of Hurricane Katrina, it was dark, depopulated, and nearly lawless, filled with rumor, wracked by despair. Reverberations of the catastrophe went on for days. Fifty-nine tremors shook the capital on September 3, dislodging half-demolished roofs and broken pillars and crashing wrecked buildings to the ground. Forty-three aftershocks, steadily lessening in intensity but still powerful enough to stoke terror, hit the city on September 4; thirty-four on September 5; twenty-seven on September 6; and twenty-three on September 7. Tens of thousands of refugees clogged the roads leading in and out of the city, some pouring into Tokyo to search for missing relatives, the vast majority evacuating the capital temporarily. Tokyo's population dropped by more than 1 million in the week after the earthquake. Rarely outside the battlefield have human beings died in such numbers. Bodies lay on streets, under buildings, in canals. Corpses carpeted the Sumida and its tributaries, bloating, then bursting in the heat. "It is a fact," wrote Dahlmann, who toured the low-lying districts of the capital on September 2, "that [many of] the dead bodies found there were not the corpses of the drowned but rather of men, women, and children who looked for protection against the flames and were literally cooked to death. The roaring furnace all about had raised the temperature of the water to the boiling point."

As in so many natural disasters, including Hurricane Katrina, destiny was largely determined by geography: the earthquake had spared the affluent, most of whom lived in the higher and more solid terrain in western Tokyo, while killing those who dwelled in the slums constructed on the less desirable, silty ground along the river and by the bay. A police survey conducted two days after the earthquake counted more than two thousand corpses in Asakusa, the densely packed entertainment district on the west bank of the Sumida River. The most horrific scene lay across the river on the grounds of the former Army Clothing Depot, where the police somehow counted a total of 44,315 corpses: 3,720 males, 2,301 females, the rest burned beyond recognition. "The bodies lay, twisted and contorted, naked or with only rags clinging to them, covering acre upon acre," wrote Henry W. Kinney in the *Atlantic Monthly,* who took a walking tour of Tokyo on September 2. "At places the jam had been so congested that they had not been able to fall to the ground. So they stood there, packed, the dead rubbing elbows with the dead." When Dahlmann arrived at the scene that afternoon, he discovered that the police had already begun clearing the area. "Immense piles of charred bones and ashes had been gathered into separate heaps," he wrote. "The black [remains] were surrounded by crowds of people, many of them standing with hands joined in attitudes of prayer. They were visibly moved, they were probably facing the remains of some dear relative. With a shudder of sorrow I turned away." Police encountered a handful of survivors, dazed, often naked, some with severe burns, wandering the grounds of the Army Clothing Depot looking for their families. A heavy rain fell on September 2, and that, combined with the intense heat, hastened the pace of decomposition. "The stench was horrible. Worms were everywhere on the bodies. They were dark with flies," wrote one unflinching Japanese newspaper reporter who surveyed the scene that day.

After mass death came fear of disease. With medical experts warning that the spread of cholera and dysentery was imminent, the Public Health Department dispatched a fleet of trucks on the afternoon of September 2 to begin removing the remains at the Army Clothing Depot. "But eventually they gave up, and they decided to burn them on the spot," a Japanese journalist reported. Desperate for volunteers to dispose of corpses, the police put up signs across Tokyo:

WANTED: WE NEED PEOPLE TO WORK.
WE PAY 5 YEN PER DAY, AND WE
PROVIDE 3 MEALS A DAY.

Not surprisingly, the offer did not get many takers. Eighty-eight people applied for jobs burning bodies at the Army Clothing Depot on September 5. Police trucked in wood and petroleum and turned the grounds into a vast crematorium. The smoke rose in thick clouds over the eastern districts, filling the city, for the second time in four days, with the odor of burning flesh. At the end of what must have been a horrific day, only four of the eighty-eight volunteers remained on the job. "The smell," one Japanese correspondent reported, "was the most difficult part." Police at the main harbor station in Tsukiji had an equally unpleasant task: fishing corpses from the water. Their boats quickly became mired in an impenetrable mass of bodies, luggage, and chunks of burned bridges. On September 9, the logjam broke, and six boats and a staff of fifty got to work, fishing 808 bodies out of the river using metal hooks. More than a thousand more would be retrieved over the next three days.

Periodically, body recovery teams pulled live victims from the wreckage of Tokyo, some of whom had been entombed for a week or more. On September 4 policemen discovered in the pile of corpses and ashes of the Army Clothing Depot a forty-year-old woman, near death, holding a girl of four years old, who was dehydrated but only slightly injured. The girl had been buried beneath a pile of bodies for three days. "We're going to take care of your child, don't worry," the police told the mother. She died moments later; her daughter survived. The recovery effort had a moment or two of comic relief. "There was one foreigner's home from the ruins of which cries of 'Boy, *san*,' were heard," the *Japan Weekly Chronicle* reported. "Rescuers worked strenuously to clear away the debris and succeeded at length in liberating a talking parrot."

NEARLY ONE WEEK after the earthquake, the darkness began to lift. Repeating a pattern seen through the centuries in cities destroyed by natural disasters, from London in the wake of the Great Fire of 1666, to San Francisco after its 1906 earthquake, to New Orleans in 2005, the survivors assessed their losses, mourned their dead, then turned to the business of resurrecting their ruined metropolis. Few cities in history had suffered the kind of devastation experienced by Tokyo, and yet the ashes had barely cooled before the recovery tentatively began. On Friday, September 7, Randall Gould of the *Japan Times* took the measure of the wrecked capital and found numerous reasons for optimism. American battleships, alerted by the wireless dispatches of Yonemura, Woods, and others, were wending their way across the ocean, as were vessels from a half-dozen other nations. They carried food, clothing, and material for shelter. Signs of human resilience in the face of terrible adversity were emerging across the city. Small shacks had sprung up in many quarters. The capital's Martial Law Authorities had already mapped a plan for reconstruction. "The Japan Times can authoritatively announce that rumors of a change in the capital are without foundation," Gould reported. "Such a change was discussed, but this will remain the capital of Japan." From Nikko, the emperor ordered the Imperial Army to cut down thousands of aged and stately cryptomeria to facilitate the rebuilding of the city. The felling of the trees, Gould wrote, was a powerful symbol of the city's determination. "Tokyo," he declared, "is a city that will not die."

IO

Going Home

The Japanese will never forget how, when the first news was received in this country of the dreadful cataclysm . . . a wave of indescribable sympathy swept over the whole of America, which at
once took the form of every sort of relief and assistance. It was a
sympathy of true brotherhood.

F. Cunliffe-Owen in the *New York Times*, September 9, 1923

LYMAN COTTEN began his belated journey to Tokyo at 9 A.M.
on Friday, September 7, six days after the earthquake. Hundreds of pounds of food—bags of rice, canned fish and meat,
biscuits, and other staples—filled the back seat and the trunk of his
British colleague's Ford sedan. Before leaving town Cotten scribbled
a short message to his parents in North Carolina and dropped it at the
telegraph office in Nikko, which had just restored its link to the outside world. "ALL SAFE," he wrote. "INFORM OTHERS." Cotten carried
a police permit—a tissue-thin sheet of white paper listing his name,
rank, and age and affixed with a red official Japanese seal—that would
allow him to move unhindered in Tokyo, still gripped by rumors and
under martial law. "I am awfully tired," he wrote to Elizabeth from a
hotel in Nikko the night before his journey. "What will it be like in
Tokyo?"

The countryside—rolling hills, rice paddies, and wooden houses
with curving roofs—was unscarred for the first thirty miles. Lieu-

tenant Colonel Piggott, at the wheel of the Ford, must have provided lively company. He had first come to Japan in 1884 as a boy with his father, Sir Francis Piggott, who had served as the legal adviser to the Emperor Meiji. The younger Piggot had learned fluent Japanese, fought with distinction for the British Army in France and Egypt, and had been a member of Crown Prince Hirohito's small entourage during the regent's royal visit to England and Scotland in May 1921. Cotten doesn't describe their conversation on the long journey to Tokyo, but one can imagine an animated discussion of Japanese politics, the military, and the economy, and how the catastrophe was likely to affect Japan's thorny relationship with Great Britain and the United States. Before long they focused their attention on the highway: "Suddenly we overtook many carts, autos, trucks, bicycles all loaded and many people on foot trudging along, each with a small pack on his back," Cotten wrote. "Soon the road was most congested. We must have passed fifty thousand people, almost all men, going to Tokyo. I suppose they were people going to look for relatives or friends. Coming from Tokyo was a much smaller stream, chiefly women and children. . . . Then a village little damaged, then one destroyed."

The traffic grew thicker as they reached the outskirts of the city, slowing the Ford to a frustrating crawl. Tram cars stood frozen on the tracks as they had been left when the earthquake hit. Then, without warning, they came on the burned area. "I did not recognize where I was until we reached the foot of Kudan Hill," Cotten wrote. "The British Embassy [was] still standing but badly damaged with its brick walls broken in pieces and tossed about like match-wood. Hibiya Park full of refugees with many little shacks made from sheet iron. The chief police station burned. The Imperial Theater burned. Arrived at Imperial Hotel, where the American Embassy is now located, at 4:30."

STANDING INTACT and nearly alone in a field of ashes and rubble in Hibiya, Frank Lloyd Wright's new hotel had become the hub of the humanitarian relief effort—and the forerunner of other atmospheric oases in more contemporary crisis zones from Sarajevo to Banda Aceh. In the lobby of the mock Aztec fortress, diplomats, military attachés, foreign correspondents, Red Cross officials, Japanese soldiers, and wealthy refugees mingled and exchanged information. Every corner of the hotel, from the Japanese gardens to the kitchen, hummed with urgency. Cotten headed for a block of rooms in the north wing, home of the temporary U.S. Embassy, where he found dozens of staffers and volunteers manning the newly established American Relief Committee. Cyrus Woods had set up the makeshift operation one week earlier, on the afternoon of September 2, at the invitation of the Imperial's manager, Tetsuzo Inumaru, after narrowly escaping death in his embassy office. The new American military attaché, Major Charles Burnett, had yanked Woods out of his chair one second before the ceiling collapsed and buried his desk and chair in debris. "The Embassy buildings and chancery were so badly wrecked by the first shock as to make it exceedingly dangerous for anyone to be in them," Woods later reported to the secretary of state. "The side wall of my private office fell just after I left the room and there was danger of the entire building collapsing." The embassy had burned down that night, nearly taking the ambassador's wife with it. "Mrs. Woods was standing in the garden of the embassy watching the fire, when the wind changed, sweeping the flames upon the embassy structure," the *New York Times* reported. "The Ambassador's wife made her escape from the premises through a barrage of flying sparks, the fire meanwhile spreading to the near-by Dutch legation."

By the time Cotten arrived one week later, the relief committee was running at full speed. It must have been awkward and disconcerting for the naval attaché, after his prolonged stay in the mountains, to walk into a scene of such exigency and frenetic activity. The clatter of typewriters, salvaged by embassy staffers from the destroyed chancery, rose above the murmur of workers who dashed about the large main suite. Piles of stationery and other supplies, donated by the Imperial Hotel and American business houses that had not been damaged, lay in every corner, as did embassy documents recovered from the ruins. "After the Embassy safes and vault had cooled, they were broken open and their contents found intact, including the records," Counselor Hugh R. Wilson reported to Washington. (Oddly, Wilson's report contradicts Woods's own cable to the secretary of state, in which he states definitively that all of the contents inside the safes and vault had been burned to ashes.) In Cotten's absence, Woods had named Bur-

*U.S. Ambassador to Japan Cyrus E. Woods and his wife, Mary Marchand
Woods, barely escaped death during the earthquake.*

nett head of the relief committee, and Burnett greeted the naval attaché coolly upon his arrival. (Woods had dispatched Garnet Hulings,
Cotten's assistant, to Yokohama on September 4 as the American representative there, and he was staying on board a Japanese destroyer in
the harbor.)

All around Cotten, embassy staffers and volunteers were consumed
with the task of making order from chaos. The Information Section
compiled daily lists of American dead, missing, and accounted for;
helped to reunite friends and families; and ran a courier service between Tokyo and Yokohama that carried documents and other important messages between the embassy and the arriving Asiatic Fleet. The
Refugee Section found shelter for refugees at the homes of Americans
in unburned sections of Tokyo, provided cots for others at the Imperial Hotel, and located ship berths for Americans who wanted to leave
Japan. The Transportation Section rounded up a fleet of cars and
trucks to ferry in food supplies and to bring destitute Americans from
Tokyo to the docks of Tsukiji and Yokohama; it also worked with Jap-

anese steamship officials to maintain tug and lighter services and vehicles across Yokohama for passengers and luggage. Two dozen U.S.
Shipping Board vessels in the North Pacific had been diverted to the
port by radio messages to help the evacuation affort. At the American
Relief Committee's request, hotel manager Inumaru had agreed to set
up a branch of the Imperial Hotel on the site of the old British Naval
Hospital in Yokohama to feed and house refugees.

Woods and his staff also tried to deal with the hundreds of requests
and pleas that poured into the embassy each day. "Am safe on *Empress
of Australia*," wrote Otto Robert Kresse, a Yokohama survivor, on
September 4. "Understand I have been reported as killed. Please cor-
rect." Family members begged for news: "Dear sir, can you give me
any information regarding the fate of my brother H. D. Fuller of
Yokohama?" wrote Mrs. G. L. Chamberlain of Schenevus, New York,
on September 6. "As he has been away for 22 years he has lost the
habit of writing to us very often. . . . [Please let us know] if he has escaped the disaster." There were absurd requests: "I escaped from the
falling Grand Hotel and reached the Steamer, *Empress of Australia*,
where now am unable to secure my personal effects in Room 328,"
wrote one survivor on September 5. "There are some papers of irre-
placeable value. . . . I still owe [the hotel] for portion of the week
since their last statement. Can you help?" And poignant ones: "I am
a Russian general of the former Imperial Army," wrote Boris Shelcornicoff aboard the *André Lebon* in Yokohama harbor. "I have twenty
eight years of service, [wounded twice] against the Germans, fought
for three years against the Bolshevists. Now I am a homeless refugee,
with my wife. . . . All my little savings was burnt, and I have now
twelve yen in my pocket. . . . Can not your government sacrifice a
small sum for mine and my wife's transportation [to France]?" (Lieutenant Colonel E. B. Miller on the *André Lebon* counted sixty Russians aboard the docked vessel. "Many of them are absolutely destitute
with no funds and no transportation to another port," he reported to
Woods.) William Jennings Bryan wrote from Hollywood, California,
trying to ascertain the whereabouts of "a Japanese boy whom we ed-
ucated and to whom we are deeply attached. We have had no word
from him for some months and since the earthquake we feel doubly
anxious." Several people queried the embassy about the fate of the

best-known American caught in the disaster. "Will you kindly let me know the safety or otherwise of Dr. Frederick Starr, of formerly Chicago University, who is believed to have been staying at the Kinokuniya, Shimbashi, on September 1," wrote Toshiro Hogetsu of Shizuoka. "If he is safe [please tell me] his present abode and how to communicate with him."

The improvisatory quality of the U.S. Embassy found echoes in every corner of the building. British Ambassador Charles Eliot had re-created his destroyed embassy on a balcony overlooking the Imperial Hotel lobby. The Dutch, who had lost their legation to fire on the night of September 1, had taken a handful of rooms adjacent to the Americans. The French Embassy had burned down on the night of September 2, and the staff had moved to the Imperial as well, but Paul Claudel, the French ambassador, reported to the hotel a full week later. Hours after the earthquake, Claudel had set out with his chauffeur from Tokyo to check on the safety of the French consul, Paul Déjardin, in Yokohama; and of Claudel's daughter, Chonette, who had been vacationing in the Sagami Bay resort town of Zushi. After camping for the night on broken railroad tracks Claudel discovered Déjardin's corpse in the rubble of the French Consulate on the Bluff, "stretched out on a cart, his face blackened, his legs twisted," he would recount in a short memoir about the earthquake. "A looter had stolen his shoes and the sheet with which the sailors from the *André Lebon* had covered him."

Later, in Zushi, Claudel reunited joyfully with Chonette, who had nearly been killed in the tsunami that crashed against the Sagami coast. Chonette's best friend and fellow survivor, Ghislaine de Bassompierre, wrote a dramatic letter to Curtis Henderson about their experience: "Darling—I pray God you are all safe—Here none of our family is hurt—although twice we escaped death by a miracle—we were nearly drowned at bathing when the earthquake began," she wrote. Trapped on a tiny island during the tsunami, de Bassompierre watched cliffs, mountains, and roofs collapse and ships and bridges being swept away by the frothing sea. A skiff carried her and Chonette to safety, and they spent the next two days camped in a bamboo grove while the earth shook and Kamakura, Yokosuka, and Yokohama burned around them. "I thought I was going mad," she wrote. The news of Paul Claudel's appearance on the *André Lebon,* cabled to officials in Paris on September 4, broke four days of silence about the diplomat's whereabouts. "Great relief is caused in France by the reception at the Quai d'Orsay of a cable stating that Paul Claudel . . . is safe aboard the Messageries Maritimes liner *André Lebon,*" the *New York Times* reported on September 5. "The news reached Paris in a message from the Consul at Kobe."

The *Asahi, Mainichi,* and *Yomiuri* newspapers, whose headquarters had burned, had taken over the hotel's banquet hall and the Main Promenade. Hundreds of guests slept in Japanese Army–issue tents pitched in the hotel's gardens and dined on rice, vegetables, and fish trucked in each day from the countryside. Their relative comfort stood in stark contrast to the misery of nearly two hundred thousand Japanese refugees encamped across the street in soggy Hibiya Park; the homeless had chopped down every tree for fuel and shelter and had quickly killed and eaten all of the ducks, geese, and swans in the ponds. Thirty soldiers stood guard in the hotel entrance and on the roof, protecting the hotel against an anticipated attack by Koreans or Bolshevik marauders—and desperate Japanese refugees. "I had an uneasy feeling—all of these refugees outside whom we couldn't feed, and they had nothing," Tetsuzo Inumaru wrote in his diary that week. "Meanwhile we were providing food to the wealthy guests—business executives, embassy people." Particularly bothersome to Inumaru were the "interlopers," foreigners who were not guests at the Imperial who descended on the place in search of handouts. "Some foreigners who lived in Yokohama heard they could get free food at the Imperial Hotel. They walked away with whole hams," Inumaru wrote. He complained to Woods, who assured him that within a week warships would arrive from the United States, carrying plenty of supplies. "He promised to provide as much as possible, and asked me to continue to provide free food to those people," Inumaru wrote.

COTTEN'S DIARY makes no mention of his seeing Woods when the naval attaché stopped by the Imperial Hotel on the afternoon of Friday, September 7. But oblique comments in both his diary and his letters to his wife suggest that he may have picked up rumors that he was in trouble with the ambassador. He left quickly, just after dropping off his load of food, perhaps sensing his colleagues' discomfort, and sailed on the American warship USS *Tracy* from the port of Shinagawa to Yokohama harbor. Here, at least, he was among his own. Admiral Edwin Alexander Anderson, the sixty-three-year-old commander in chief of the Asiatic Fleet, had just arrived from China, and Cotten received a briefing aboard the *Huron* about the early stages of the U.S. relief effort. Six destroyers of the U.S. Navy's Thirty-fifth Division floated in the outer harbor, a heartening sign to Cotten and to the thousands of destitute survivors who were scrounging for nourishment in the port's ruins. "The president of the U.S. has directed Anderson to purchase whatever supplies and make whatever expenditures necessary for relief," Cotten noted. "Surely America is rising as a friend of Japan in her trial." The scope of destruction in Yokohama astonished him. Crevices several feet wide bore silent tribute to the devastating power of the earthquake. All of the landmarks that he had come to know well on his many visits to Yokohama—the Grand Hotel, the Naval Hospital, the United Club—had been reduced to piles of rubble. The breakwater had disappeared from sight, and in places the terrain had sunk several feet. "Everywhere," he wrote, "is desolation."

The U.S. Naval Hospital in Yokohama was leveled by the quake,
killing several patients and staffers.

After the horror of his visit to the port, Cotten received a bit of good news on the return trip to Tokyo the next morning on the *Tracy*. During a conversation with the *Tracy*'s officers about the enormity of the disaster, he remarked that the only real friends he had lost were Captain Mitchell MacDonald, a retired naval officer and major shareholder of the Grand Hotel in Yokohama, killed in the collapse, and "probably" Major and Mrs. Crane. "An officer in the boat said 'the Cranes were saved and Major Crane is on the *Whipple*.' Sure enough when I got to the head of the gangway there he was looking as though nothing had happened to him." He had another burst of euphoria upon his arrival at his house in the Azabu section of Tokyo; the structure was still standing with relatively minor damage: a toppled chimney, a collapsed garden wall, zigzag cracks in the walls, piles of plaster on the floors, and nothing more. "In the middle of our drawing room mantle [had stood] a beautiful and valuable Nakashima vase. It was thrown off but fell on a thick rug and was not even nicked. It was simply too wonderful to believe."

At six that evening Lieutenant Colonel Piggot joined him at the house. With the city in ruins, electricity still out, and water in short supply, the two veteran officers hunkered down together in an urban version of a military bivouac. Cotten found the experience oddly enjoyable, a throwback to his prediplomatic days roughing it in combat zones. They dined in the garden by candlelight, spread sleeping bags and mats on the ground, covered themselves with mosquito nets, and slept side by side with their servants. Every hour volunteer guards with lanterns searched the compound for looters and Korean marauders, who were assumed to be on the loose. Aftershocks rattled the slumbering men during the night. "We are sleeping out in the garden at present," Cotten wrote to Elizabeth on September 9. "It is awfully hot, but if the weather changes I will come inside as there are only a few shakes each day and these not very hard. Lots of food coming in now and no more needed from Nikko. Chief danger now from decomposing bodies. Japanese trying to cremate all of them. . . . See no hope of returning to Chuzenji soon." Living conditions were spartan: Cotten found a leftover box of tea in the house and drew a week's rations from the committee for himself and his servants, including coffee, bacon, sugar, potatoes, and twenty-five pounds of soda biscuits, but "no butter and no jam." A dark note crept in toward the end of the September 9 letter to his wife, a veiled suggestion that he had already heard warnings of trouble ahead with Woods: "Will try to formulate some personal plans."

Then, at 9:30 A.M. on Monday, September 10, Cotten returned to the Imperial Hotel and was summoned to a meeting with Woods. Nine days had passed since the earthquake struck. Did he feel any trepidation as he strode, clad in his white summer uniform, heels clicking on the tile floors, through the crowded hallways toward the north wing? Cotten doesn't mention it. The meeting appears to have been brief, perhaps lasting ten minutes. He describes the fateful encounter in dry, matter-of-fact tones: "Received a personal note from the American ambassador at 9:40 a.m.," he wrote in his diary, "informing me . . . that due to the fact that I arrived late at the embassy after the earthquake I was persona non grata as a member of his staff. I tried to explain the reasons for my delay, but he said the reasons made no difference. The fact that I was not here for the first few days of the crisis was all that he was considering."

Persona non grata. The words must have stung him. Cotten never revealed the details of this painful and potentially career-breaking conversation. But allusions in his diaries and letters indicate that he offered Woods at least one excuse for his failure to show up in a timely manner. The reason he gave was a half-hearted one: He told Woods that he had never received an urgent telegram summoning him to Tokyo that his assistant, Garnet Hulings, had dispatched to Chuzenji from Tokyo on September 3: "AMBASSADOR WANTS YOU TOKYO IMMEDIATELY YOUR HOUSE ALRIGHT ADDRESS EMBASSY IMPERIAL HOTEL." In the confusion that followed the earthquake the telegram had taken a roundabout route—ending up ninety miles west of Tokyo, in the opposite direction from Chuzenji—and hadn't reached the Cotten house until six days after it was sent. By then the naval attaché had already left for the disaster zone with Piggott. Woods, however, considered the wayward telegram a feeble excuse. Writing to Secretary of State Hughes several days later, Woods drew a sharp contrast between Cotten's behavior and that of his colleagues:

I take great pride in reporting that every member of our Embassy staff who was in the city not only remained at his post but reported promptly to me for duty. As for those who were out of the city, only one failed to return promptly, and that was Captain Cotten, Naval Attaché, who was at Chuzenji . . . when the disaster occurred, and failed to report for almost one week. At my request he has been detached from duty at this Embassy. . . . Mr. [Hugh] Wilson and Lieutenant Hulings were also at Chuzenji, but they even walked a considerable distance in order that they might report promptly for duty. . . . All with the single exception of Captain Cotten hastened to report to me, and in order to do this every man had to endure hardship, because the ordinary means of transportation had ceased to function.

Military Attaché Burnett, director of the relief effort at the Imperial Hotel, submitted a report to Woods in mid-September assessing the performance of his staff. In reference to Cotten, he wrote tersely, "The Navy personnel belonging to this Embassy, with the exception of the Naval Attaché, were placed on duty under the Military Attaché on Sept. 10. . . . In every case [but his] they have exhibited, in a time of great stress, those qualities which we are proud to associate with the name of Americans."

Cotten's dismissal from the ambassador's staff was a humiliating rebuke, quite possibly the first real professional setback since his graduation from Annapolis a quarter of a century earlier. Bewildered, ashamed, angry, and worried about an inquiry in Washington and his suddenly cloudy future in the navy, Cotten reacted like a man wronged: he refused to accept blame and accused the ambassador of sabotaging him. It isn't clear how his fellow Naval Intelligence officers viewed the confrontation between Woods and Cotten, though most apparently offered sympathy for the naval attaché, at least within his earshot. "The language officers have learned about the ambassador's action in my case and they are furious," he wrote to Elizabeth on September 13, his pen dripping with indignation. "They all say he has acted like an insane man ever since the earthquake. Too bad I have to be the goat." But even they must have sensed that Cotten had failed in some essential way. The one person who stuck by him as he tried to justify his actions and lashed out at Woods was his devoted wife. On September 13, three days after his dismissal, he wrote to Elizabeth:

> I have read your sweet letter over and over again, and it increases my strength each time. You are a darling wife and a tower of strength and I love you with all my heart. Please don't in any way blame Hulings. He did his very best. It was not his fault that [the telegram] took six days to get to Chuzenji. He then went immediately to Yokohama and did not return until he came back with me on Saturday, the day after I reached Tokyo. He is deeply distressed but is absolutely blameless. . . . Our friends . . . say the ambassador has acted like one demented, not only in my case but in many others. He has often been brutal and cruel to members of his staff who were working for him night and day. Thinks only of himself. Selfish to the extreme. I asked Wilson today what he thought Mr. Woods was going to do further about my case. He said, "nothing." Mr. Woods told him that my detachment would close the matter. I doubt it. Later I think he will write a letter to the State Department justifying his action in his own eyes by saying everything possible that is extreme and putting the wrong construction on everything.

Cotten's letters and diary entries over the next two weeks lay bare a tangle of emotions: embarrassment, defensiveness, rage, bitterness, and regret. Their anguish resonates through the decades, providing a portrait of a man who had let down his colleagues—and himself—during a crisis and would never forget it. Cotten, a proven war hero, was certainly no 1920s version of Michael Brown, the feckless chairman of the Federal Emergency Management Agency during Hurricane Katrina. But his inexplicable lapse in judgment during the days after the Great Kanto Earthquake resembles Brown's own obliviousness while New Orleans filled with water. His behavior, and the consequences, serve as an example of how our actions can remain mysterious even to ourselves, and how a single decision can haunt a person for the rest of his life. "If I had only realized and come down sooner, for even the worst reports gave one no idea of the catastrophe and suffering," he wrote to his parents the day after Woods dismissed

him. "Words cannot describe it." (In fact, his diary after the earthquake clearly shows his awareness of the disaster's epic scale.) Woods
had ordered him to stay out of the relief effort, a humiliation that Cotten tried to play down in a letter to his wife. "I think the Japanese re-
sent all of our assistance, there have been several instances of rudeness
on their part, and I would not be at all surprised to see a real serious
unpleasantness before our Red Cross gets out." Repeatedly he expressed his loathing of his nemesis, accusing him of cowardice, greed,
and two-facedness. "The first time I saw him this morning was in the
large general room [at the Imperial Hotel] that the embassy is using,"
he wrote. "In a very formal and dignified way I said, 'Good morning,
sir.' He waved his hand and said, 'Hello! how are you?' exactly as
though I had been a long lost brother." Cotten's contemptuous descriptions of the ambassador clash so starkly with other accounts of
Woods's behavior after the earthquake—he is portrayed almost everywhere as a hero—that it is hard to interpret them as anything but reflections of Cotten's wounded pride. On September 15, in a typical
dispatch, he wrote to his mother-in-law, Mrs. J. S. Henderson, in Salisbury, North Carolina:

> I am amazed and filled with wondering admiration of the
> courage, unselfishness, and generosity of my fellow man. The one
> exception to this rule is our Ambassador. He is petrified with fear,
> in a tremor over everything and has not a thought for anyone but
> himself and his own comfort. I have blushed for him. The servants
> at the embassy . . . he has turned out without a penny. . . . He says
> truthfully enough that he no longer has any need for them! . . . I
> should be humiliated if his behavior, his callous indifference was
> known by honorable men of other embassys and Legations.

WHILE COTTEN BROODED about his treatment by Woods and ago-
nized over his professional future, other survivors of the earthquake
were picking up the pieces and moving on with their lives. On the afternoon of Sunday, September 2, a massive evacuation of foreigners
from Yokohama began, and Western envoys roamed the hills on the
outskirts of the port to spread the word to those taking refuge there.

The commanders of all functioning passenger vessels in Yokohama harbor—the *Philoctetes,* the *London Maru,* the *Korea Maru,* and a dozen others—volunteered to transport refugees to Kobe, where local officials and leaders of the expatriate community had set up a relief center and field hospital at the Oriental Hotel as soon as they received confirmation of the disaster. Located three hundred seventy miles southwest of Tokyo, the scenic coastal city, with its near-perpendicular hills rising sharply above the Inland Sea, had experienced faint reverberations from the earthquake, powerful enough to cause its citizens to wonder whether a tragedy was unfolding elsewhere on Honshu Island. "The great quake left a strange memory in Kobe, of a slow vibration that kept on until it began to get on the nerves, though not so much as a vase was knocked over," reported the *Japan Weekly Chronicle,* which was based in Kobe. "In the evening it was found that it was impossible to make connection with the north by telephone or telegraph; a serious earthquake was reported; but it was not till next morning that the news was published, picked up from wireless messages, that Yokohama was utterly destroyed. It was incredible, but it turned out to be only too true." On the night of Sunday, September 2, the first refugees arrived in Kobe, a party of foreigners who had been vacationing in the lakeside town of Hakone. Several had been badly injured when their hotel slid down a mountain and fell into the lake, and they brought with them terrifying eyewitness tales of death. On Sunday evening, too, the first ship from Yokohama arrived, the *Philoctetes,* but, because the boat had sailed out of the harbor at the first opportunity on Saturday night, it could only confirm the news of the disaster without offering more details. On Monday evening the first refugees from Yokohama came in, and, day by day, the story grew more horrific.

Eva Downes, the student nurse from Peking, and her friend, Mrs. Macmillan, hiked down from the golf course to one designated gathering point, the ruins of the Grand Hotel on the Bund, on the afternoon of September 2. A small craft picked up the bedraggled pair and took them to the *Dongola,* a steamer belonging to the Pacific & Oriental Line. The vessel had been moored at a buoy in Yokohama's inner harbor at the time of the earthquake and had barely avoided incineration by drifting, burning lighters. "This little ship, which would ordinarily carry about two hundred passengers, took on 600 refugees, and all the officers and members of the crew worked to care for the sick and wounded and feed the able bodied," Downes wrote. The *Dongola* sailed from Yokohama on Monday, September 3, and at noon on Tuesday landed at Kobe. There Downes and Macmillan found shelter with friends at Kobe College for the night and took passage on the *Empress of Canada* for Shanghai the next morning. Moved by her experience over the previous four days, Downes expressed her admiration for the survivors, both Japanese and expatriate, whom she had met along the way: "Even those who had lost members of their families were facing the future with quiet courage. Material loss, if not complete ruin, faced very many of these people, but there was no whining. They had not a moment to steel themselves to face [disaster] calmly or courageously, or to consider the best way of escape for themselves and those who were dear to them. Nevertheless, they reacted . . . like men and women of discipline."

Gertrude Cozad, on the other hand, came away from her ordeal with her optimistic view of human nature shaken. She had witnessed the barbarism of the anti-Korean campaign and had lived for days with the fear that her companion, Hayashi Shotaro, would become one of its victims. But she had also seen acts of generosity and heroism, and she had formed a powerful bond with Shotaro, who had gone from protector to protected in the course of their ordeal. After resting and eating emergency rations aboard the disabled French steamship *André Lebon,* the American missionary was informed late on Monday afternoon, September 3, that she would be taken to the *President Jefferson,* a large American liner that had just arrived from Shanghai, and then would sail on to Kobe. She bade an emotional farewell to Shotaro, who, for reasons that Cozad doesn't explain—though one can assume that Europeans and Americans were given priority in the evacuation from Yokohama—remained aboard the *André Lebon.* As her launch passed beneath the stern of the *Empress of Australia* on her way to the *President Jefferson,* Cozad thought suddenly of her cousin, Ella Brunner, last seen settling into her cabin half an hour before the earthquake. "I said to the officer on board [the *President Jefferson*] 'I would give fifty dollars in gold to be able to call a message to the *Empress,*'" she wrote later to Brunner. "He said their wireless was taxed to the limit but that I could get a message out. I went to the wireless room and asked them to send it. I am also hoping that you saw my name on the list of those who were saved." Brunner never received the message, however, and there is no correspondence that would indicate how long a period elapsed before she learned that her cousin had survived.

Cozad arrived home in Kobe on Tuesday afternoon, September 4, and was joyfully welcomed back by her fellow missionaries and relatives. Two days later, to her surprise and delight, her young Korean friend showed up unexpectedly. Although he hadn't had Cozad's address, he had wandered through the streets of Kobe for hours until he found the missionary's name on her gate post. Shotaro leaned against the gate and burst into tears, and the servants, having heard all about his ordeal with Cozad during the earthquake, rushed into the garden and welcomed him to the house. Cozad committed herself to the improvement of the young Korean with the zeal of an American Pygmalion. She pressed her sister, who was visiting from Seoul, to take Shotaro back with her, and promised to support his education. "He is a fine looking young man, with good features, rather short, and has the finest, white teeth I ever saw," she wrote. "There is something most winning about his personality."

On the evening of September 2 Otis Poole and his father-in-law, the commodore, moored the *Daimyo* in a protected bight, shielded from Yokohama harbor's burning oil slicks. Then they rowed a dinghy through the sunken breakwater to the *Empress of Australia*. On board the crippled liner, packed with nearly two thousand people, they reunited with the rest of the family, who had gone to the *Empress* earlier in the day. "The *Empress* . . . was, of course, still unable to put to sea until divers could be procured to free her propeller," Poole wrote. On Monday morning, hundreds of refugees, including the Campbells and the Pooles, "still as grubby and ragged as ship-wrecked emigrants," were transferred by rowboats to the *Empress of Canada*. The luxury steamer had just arrived in Yokohama after crossing the Pacific Ocean from Vancouver and was ready to sail. The Pooles took with them their children's amah, Miné, "her seamed face as placid as an ivory netsuke." The next morning, September 4, the boat set sail for Kobe. Divers from a Japanese battleship finally freed the *Empress of Australia* from the *Steel Navigator*'s anchor cable the next day. Captain Samuel

Robinson put his ship out to sea at midnight on September 8, taking six hundred Westerners, several hundred Chinese, and a handful of severely wounded Japanese to Kobe.

Unlike Cozad, Brunner, and Poole, Shigeo Tsuchiya and his family would be staying put in Yokohama. For nearly a week the twelve-year-old and other neighborhood boys kept watch in the ashes of their homes, holding burned sticks to ward off the feared Korean marauders who never came. They ate rice kernels and other scraps salvaged from the ruins and drank water that trickled from broken pipes. The first army rice truck appeared on September 4, setting off a near riot. Soon, however, the military restored calm and organized an orderly food distribution system. The corpses of friends and neighbors lay around them for a week, decomposing beneath charred roof tiles, until government body-disposal teams wearing white masks got to work. "They were burning bodies everywhere—and I could smell it all day, a terrible smell, even while we were eating," he recalled. Tsuchiya and his family constructed a crude shelter. "First we put the roof up, and we laid down some half burned boards to make the floor." As it grew chillier at night, they placed burned roofs and trees around their crude barracks to protect them from the wind; clothes and blankets arrived from other areas of Japan to keep them warm. The days passed, they received ration cards, canned food appeared, conditions improved. According to the *Japan Weekly Chronicle,* the relief goods that reached Yokohama's destitute from U.S. warships and Japanese charities a week after the earthquake included "canned beef, salmon, sugar, rice, blankets, kimono, underwear, shirts, sheets, medicine, towels, ironware, matting, cutlery, kettles, cotton yarn, canvas, American corned beef, and shoes," even a few bicycles donated by an Osaka merchant. "My family and I never left this place," Tsuchiya recalled. "Because if we had left it, there would have been no proof that this was our land. We began to build our house again, in exactly the same spot."

WE HAVE, in recent years, witnessed large international relief efforts in response to natural disasters. The U.S. response to the Great Kanto Earthquake was immediate, generous, and not entirely welcome. The

American mission to Japan, which began at 11 A.M. on September 2, 1923, was the largest disaster aid operation in history up to that point. At that hour the Asiatic Fleet commander, Admiral Anderson, was sitting in his cabin aboard the naval yacht in the Chinese seaport of Chefoo, now known as Yantai, located on the northern coast of the Shandong peninsula. Most of his crew had gone ashore, and Anderson was enjoying the unusual quiet of a late summer morning. Then everything changed. A wireless message was received aboard the yacht from a U.S. naval officer in the Chinese port of Dairen: according to a local Japanese-language newspaper, a major earthquake had struck Tokyo and Yokohama. Anderson rounded up his crew, sent out dispatches, and, by 4:15 that afternoon, all U.S. warships in Chefoo, Dairen, and other Chinese ports were raising steam and recalling their men from leave. The secretary of the navy in Washington, Edwin Denby, who had also been alerted by wireless, dispatched a radiogram, by that point redundant, the following morning to Dairen ordering Anderson to send vessels to Yokohama "and to pick up all available equipment and supplies at Chinese ports." Anderson cabled back a terse reply: "ALREADY DONE."

A fleet assembled. The first ship to sail, the USS *Stewart,* set forth from Dairen on the night of September 2, steamed 1,190 miles in sixty-four hours, and reached Yokohama on the morning of September 5. The flagship *Huron,* carrying Anderson, arrived two days later. Anderson was received at the port by Ambassador Woods, his wife, and Mrs. Marchand, Woods's mother-in-law. By September 8 U.S. warships packed with relief supplies purchased in China filled Yokohama harbor. The tonnage delivered to the port was extraordinary. One ship alone, the *Black Hawk,* arrived on September 10 carrying, according to the Information Bureau of the Japanese Foreign Office, "281,000 pounds rice, 95,000 pounds sugar, 215,000 pounds beans, 150,000 pounds flour, 16,000 pounds Japanese miso bean paste, 29,000 pounds Japanese sauce, 250 cases milk, 18,000 pounds salt, 3,000 cans tinned roast beef, 1300 tins mackerel, 32,000 pounds fresh beef, 1100 pounds pork, 40,000 eggs, 30,000 pounds potatoes, 5,000 bushels apples, 3,000 gallons gasoline, 72,000 reed mats for temporary shelter."

John Colbert, an American expatriate physician living in Tsientsin, China, left a vivid account of his role in the Yokohama relief mission,

*Amid the debris at the naval hospital, U.S. sailors attempted to identify
bodies by means of eyeglasses and gold rings.*

the last large-scale incident of Japanese-American cooperation before
the relationship deteriorated into mutual hostility and, ultimately, war.
Colbert's account also provides a look at how Japan's insecurities
nearly derailed the rescue operation before it even got going. On
September 2 Colbert put together a three-man volunteer medical
unit and sailed for Yokohama three days later aboard the U.S. mine
sweeper *Bittern.* They arrived in the ruined Japanese port on September 9, having heard almost nothing about the scope of the destruction. "Amusement was caused by my radio requesting permission to
transfer a patient [with meningitis] upon arrival to the Yokohama
Naval Hospital, for there was nothing left of it," Colbert reported,
"the building on a bluff having collapsed and killed a pharmacist and
his wife, several caretaker [*sic*], and very nearly causing the death of
commander Webb who was in his office when the shock occurred."

Colbert arrived in Yokohama just after an ugly confrontation had
been defused—a clash that provided disturbing insights into Japan's
self-image and interaction with the outside world. As Colbert tells it,
the initial response of some Japanese authorities had been strikingly

similar to that of the Tokugawa shogun when the Black Ships had sailed into Yokohama Bay, and revealed the degree to which the Japanese still viewed foreigners as objects of suspicion. Historians looking back for clues to Japan's psychology prior to World War II might begin here, in this key moment of interaction between the Japanese and their American would be rescuers, when Japan's peculiar pre-conflict combination of pride and insecurity was on full display. Rather than welcome the U.S. ships with open arms, Colbert claimed, the Japanese greeted the American relief effort with hostility. When the *Stewart,* the first U.S. destroyer to reach Tokyo Bay from China, approached Yokohama harbor on September 5, Colbert wrote, the vessel's commander had radioed the Japanese Coast Guard for instructions. The alleged reply, according to Colbert: "We do not need your help." The American captain had then radioed the Japanese that the *Stewart* carried food supplies for the victims; according to Colbert, the captain was informed that "food supplies are not needed" and was told that the ship could not enter Yokohama. The *Stewart*'s commander ignored the Coast Guard, sailed the destroyer into the harbor, and ordered his men to unload supplies on the docks in defiance of the Japanese refusal to accept them. Yokohama authorities, Colbert claimed, continued to sabotage the mission. "Every message that the foreign ships attempted to send from the harbour was jammed by the Japanese until the Admiral was forced to send a destroyer 100 miles out to sea to send the first radios," Colbert claimed. "The Japanese authorities failed utterly to meet this great emergency."

On September 7, two days after the Coast Guard tried to prevent the *Stewart* from landing, Anderson held an emergency meeting on board the *Huron* with the British and American vice consuls in Yokohama, commanding officers of U.S. Shipping Board vessels in the harbor, and members of a newly formed Japan chapter of the American Red Cross, made up of a dozen consular officials and community leaders in Tokyo and Yokohama, headed by John R. Geary, General Electric's representative in Japan. Aware that the Japanese fear of losing face was jeopardizing the relief mission, Anderson urged that the ships follow the *Stewart*'s example: deliver food to the docks, then back off. "[I said that] we were here to do all in our power to help the Japanese," he reported to Washington, "but not here to force any of our ideas on them. It was decided to land stores and turn them over to the Japanese for distribution."

Cyrus Woods had anticipated local resistance to the rescue mission and had independently embraced a similar strategy. "I felt that we had a great opportunity to break down the suspicion and antagonism against the United States existing in the minds of many Japanese," the ambassador wrote to Secretary of State Hughes in his official report about the earthquake and its aftermath on September 24. "In order to avoid the friction which was sure to follow the sending here of relief workers . . . I suggested [to the minister for foreign affairs] that the supplies furnished by us, except for our own nationals, be delivered to the Japanese authorities at the wharf for distribution by the Japanese Relief Bureau. . . . Admiral Anderson, immediately upon [his arrival,] heartily concurred in this policy, and later it was promptly accepted by the American Red Cross."

(Colbert's claim that the Japanese jammed American wireless signals cannot be verified: Anderson's official report mentions that a U.S. naval vessel was stationed outside Yokohama harbor "to act as radio relay," but says nothing of his being forced to dispatch U.S. destroyers one hundred miles beyond Japanese waters.)

The massive American relief mission, carried out decades before the founding of the United Nations and the proliferation of private relief organizations, set an extraordinary precedent. Organized by the U.S. Navy, Army, and Marines with the help of civilian volunteers, the mission established an early model for deployments, from the Bangladesh floods of 1970 to the 1988 Armenian earthquake to the December 2004 tsunami in Southeast Asia. It displayed to the world that America's growing global power could be a force for good, and it cast the U.S. military in a new and highly visible role as humanitarian aid workers, a role that would find distant echoes in such crisis zones as Kosovo and Afghanistan. Though most of the armed forces' effort was aimed at foreigners, Japanese civilians reaped many of the benefits as well. U.S. destroyers of the Asiatic Fleet supplied fresh water to refugees aboard the *André Lebon* and other steamships in the harbor, ferried hundreds of Japanese refugees from Yokohama to other ports on Honshu, and made reconnaissance trips along the coast to retrieve injured and stranded survivors. Navy divers salvaged the sunken U.S. Steel Corporation ship *Selma City* from the bottom of Yokohama harbor. Marine relief teams cleared the debris of the U.S. Consulate and built a temporary camp on the spot; they erected a field hospital on the grounds of the destroyed American Naval Hospital and built a pipeline to supply the facility with fresh water. They canvassed, fed, and treated refugees on Shipping Board vessels; helped the seriously injured ashore; pried open twenty-five safes to recover the valuables of American and foreign businessmen in the city. They scoured the city for foreign dead, recovering the remains of nineteen Americans and Europeans, including some that could not be identified. The teams cremated and buried the remains "with appropriate ceremony" at the Foreign Cemetery on the Bluff. "The ashes of each of the American dead were placed in small metallic caskets covered with mahogany, and marked with name plates," Anderson reported to the navy, "and the debris having been cleared away from the Naval plot of the foreign cemetery, those that were not returned to the United States were interred there."

The U.S. Army dispatched two transport vessels from Manila in mid-September, the USS *Meigs* and the USS *Merritt,* under the command of Brigadier General Frank R. McCoy, assistant to Governor-General Leonard Wood of the Philippines. The army built a tent hospital on the Bluff just below the ruins of the British Naval Hospital and staffed it with fifty-seven male and female nurses and ten Filipino doctors from the Manila chapter of the American Red Cross. "The earth was constantly trembling and seemed almost without foundation," reported Lieutenant Colonel D. W. Hand, Field Artillery. "There were old and new fissures, and the configuration and drainage of the surface was constantly changing. There was at first no water." In keeping with Woods's policy, the army turned over the hospital to Japanese administrators, doctors, and nurses on September 29. A Shanghai Red Cross medical unit consisting of four American surgeons and eleven nurses also assembled in Yokohama; they transferred a few days later to Kobe, where they restricted their activities to treating injured foreigners.

Before sailing to Kobe on September 13 as part of the Shanghai medical team, Dr. Colbert spent several hours inspecting the destroyed city, recording flickerings of life among the ashes. A Japanese sailor picked him up in a Dodge, and the pair drove past thousands of refugees still hunkered down in Yokohama Park, coolies pounding out the twisted frames of their rickshaws, men banging together corrugated iron sheets into flimsy lean-tos. The air was thick with smoke from charcoal cooking fires over which families prepared lunch in huge iron kettles. Many Japanese carried wine bottles filled with drinking water obtained from relief ships; corpses had contaminated all of the city's wells. "The Japanese," Colbert observed, "seemed to be stunned and lying back to catch their breath."

In the ruins of the Russia-Asiatic Bank, Colbert noted the charred remains of a horse on the second floor; the animal had evidently run up the stairs to escape the flames. At the former site of the U.S. Naval Hospital on the Bluff, American sailors had just unearthed a shovel-ful of charred remains and a ring, which was identified as having belonged to the wife of the hospital's chief pharmacist, Lawrence Zembsch. A thieving band of safecrackers appeared and, before the eyes of Japanese soldiers and sailors, pried open the safe of the Grand Hotel. "Unfortunately for the crooks, the paper money they found in the safe was charred and worthless," Colbert noted. "Modern business does not deal in gold coins." No sight moved Colbert more than the pile of charred wood and broken concrete that had once been the Grand: "The Grand Hotel was just another heap of ruins; only the two stone steps at the main entrance, and a broken pillar, remained—and the steps were adorned with a human skull, and spinal column, and thighs without a body. I stood for several minutes in the ruins—in utter amazement—looking around, and recalling many pleasant times I had experienced here—for this had been 'home' to me on my visits to Yokohama. It was hard to realize that this ugly heap of ruins and rubbish was all that was left of one of the finest hotels in the Orient."

HALF A WORLD AWAY, in the United States, the civilian side of the aid effort was also gathering momentum. In an era long before Care, Doctors Without Borders, Oxfam, UNICEF, Catholic Relief Services, and hundreds of other private groups filled the disaster-relief land-

*The solid wall of the domed Yokohama Specie Bank
remained intact amid widespread wreckage.*

scape, competing for money and media attention, one organization
stood nearly alone and unchallenged in the field of international humanitarian assistance: the American Red Cross. At noon on September 4, 1923, from the White House, President Calvin Coolidge—the
fourth president, after Taft, Wilson, and Harding, to serve as the Red
Cross's titular chief executive—issued a proclamation, carried on the
wires and published in most of the nation's newspapers, calling on
Americans to contribute money and supplies to the organization to
aid Japanese earthquake victims. "An overwhelming disaster has overtaken the people of the friendly nation of Japan," he declared. "While

its extent has not as yet been officially reported, enough is known to justify the statement that the cities of Tokyo and Yokohama, and surrounding towns and villages, have been largely if not completely destroyed by earthquake, fire, and flood, with a resultant appalling loss of life and destitution and distress, requiring measures of urgent relief." Coolidge directed Americans to send their contributions either to the chairman of the American National Red Cross in Washington or to local Red Cross chapters, and the Red Cross's formidable grassroots network kicked into high gear.

In the years just after the Great War, the American Red Cross stood at the apex of its power and visibility in American life. The organization had been the brainchild of Clara Barton, a Massachusetts nurse who had followed the Union Army of General George McClellan to Antietam and Fredericksburg and been horrified by the absence of decent medical care on the battlefield. Barton had paid close attention to the First Geneva Convention of 1864: at a conference organized by the Swiss humanitarian Henri Dunant, more than a dozen nations, not including the United States, had agreed to set up committees of volunteer medical personnel to alleviate suffering on the battlefield under international protection and "without regard to nationality." The umbrella group had adopted the name International Red Cross Committee and had taken as its emblem a reverse image of the Swiss flag: a red cross laid against a white field. Barton met with signers of the convention in 1869 and spent a dozen years lobbying three presidents and the Senate to make the United States a signatory. In March 1882, with the prodding of President Chester Alan Arthur and Secretary of State James Blaine, the Senate adopted the treaty by unanimous vote, and Barton's fledgling organization, then called the American Association of the Red Cross, went to work.

Barton's private relief corps of nurses and logisticians made its initial mark raising funds and rushing supplies to victims of Michigan forest fires and Mississippi River floods in 1882 and 1883. In rapid succession the Red Cross provided medical and humanitarian aid during yellow fever epidemics in Florida; the deadly collapse of the South Fork dam in Johnstown, Pennsylvania; famine in central Russia; and Muslim-Christian strife in Armenia. But the organization's expenses had grown enormously; it came under financial pressure, and Barton turned to the federal government for support. In 1905, a new act of Congress reincorporated the Red Cross and turned it into a quasi-public institution, with a headquarters in Washington and the president of the United States as chief executive. The American Red Cross's reputation soared during two epic natural disasters: the 1906 earthquake and fires that destroyed San Francisco and the 1908 earthquake in coastal Calabria and northeastern Sicily that killed an estimated eighty thousand people.

The World War wove the Red Cross indelibly into the fabric of American life. Under the stewardship of President Woodrow Wilson and a powerful executive committee of Wilson appointees (including a future U.S. president, Herbert Hoover), the organization supplied tens of thousands of nurses to the military, set up field and base hospitals in France, and created mobile laboratories for epidemic research. The American Red Cross had begun the war with 107 local chapters; by the conflict's end the number had grown to 3,864 chapters in all forty-eight states. By skillfully reaching out to community leaders and appealing to their sense of patriotism, the organization extended its reach to nearly every city, town, and village in America. By 1918, 30 million out of 105 million Americans were active supporters of the Red Cross, and 8 million served as volunteer production workers, manufacturing blankets and clothes, packing food parcels and medical kits.

"AMERICA TO HELP JAPAN!" proclaimed the *Japan Times & Mail* earthquake edition's headline on September 5, 1923. The Red Cross's Washington Division spearheaded the fund-raising drive. The division set a $2.9 million target for 845 chapters in the District of Columbia and eleven states under its jurisdiction and issued a terse command to chapter leaders by telegram: "Organise as in war drives to raise quotas assigned to you. Unparalleled disaster requires your utmost efforts. Report daily results by night letter during this week." Other regional divisions followed Washington's lead. Young American women wrapped in silk kimonos, their hair tied in Japanese-style buns, paraded through the streets of Chicago, New York, and other American cities; they carried red paper lanterns and displayed Red Cross banners that proclaimed "Japan Needs You: Chip In." Schoolchildren dropped nickels and dimes into designated boxes. Inmates at Maryland State Prison contributed a total of $505. John D. Rockefeller kicked off a $1 million Red Cross fund-raising campaign in New York City by writing a $100,000 check. American expatriates in Rio de Janeiro cabled $300. "States, cities, townships, commercial, industrial and fraternal bodies are organizing to get behind the local Red Cross chapters in raising or exceeding the allotments of the chapters," the Red Cross in Washington proclaimed on September 6. Fourteen ships packed with Red Cross–purchased supplies, including fifteen thousand cases of Alaska salmon, 625 tons of roofing, five portable wooden hospital buildings, hundreds of tons of dishware and Western clothing, and 4,928 kimonos, sailed from the West Coast for Tokyo in September; the first to leave was the *President Taft* on September 6.

That same day Secretary of State Hughes cabled Cyrus Woods in Tokyo and instructed him to set up a committee of a dozen American residents and consular officers "to be known as American Red Cross relief committee Japan chapter . . . acting as liaison with Japan Red Cross." He authorized Woods "to draw from Secretary of State one hundred thousand dollars and pay proceeds to Japanese Red Cross. Draw ten thousand dollars for relief [of] American citizens where needed." Both men agreed that the American outfit should take the same approach as the Asiatic Fleet to avoid offending prickly Japanese sensitivities: "The function of American Red Cross representatives there is . . . solely to turn over supplies and funds to Japanese authorities," Hughes directed. "We do not want hospital or other relief activities in Japan [run by] American Red Cross personnel. If Japanese desire American personnel . . . let them arrange for their service under Japanese auspices."

Woods and Hughes remained in near round-the-clock contact for weeks, micromanaging the shipment and distribution of Red Cross funds and relief supplies. "Following disinfectants purchased and shipped," Hughes telegraphed Woods at the Imperial Hotel on September 28: "Twenty thousand gallons formaldehyde, twenty thousand gallons liquid cresoo, twenty thousand pounds permanganate of potash, two hundred tons chloride of lime. Is quantity sufficient?" In another cable to the embassy he announced, "We are today purchasing one hundred thousand blankets two hundred thousand suits underwear and three hundred thousand pairs socks to be shipped at once from San Francisco." Apparently no detail was too small for him. In October Hughes's personal secretary notified Woods that a Confederate Army veteran from Waco, Texas, had written a small check to the State Department for the benefit of earthquake victims. "You may draw a draft against the Secretary of State for thirty-five dollars ($35), United States Currency, and present it to the Imperial Japanese Relief Bureau, with the compliments of the donor," the secretary advised.

The American relief effort marked a high point in American-Japanese relations in the early part of the twentieth century. President Calvin Coolidge and American Red Cross Chairman John Barton Payne had asked for $10 million in donations; by the time the campaign ended in December 1923, the Red Cross had raised the unprecedented sum of $12 million. Coolidge expressed to the American people his "deep appreciation for this manifestation of their generosity and their willingness at all times to answer the call of suffering humanity." The figure dwarfed the amount raised in fund-raising drives in Great Britain, France, and other European nations. (In early September the Soviet Union, Japan's enemy, dispatched a relief ship, the *Lenin,* to Yokohama, packed with flour, salmon, rice, building material, and medical instruments. But the Japanese navy forced the ship to turn back from the harbor on September 12 "on the suspicion that she was carrying Communistic propaganda," according to the *Japan Weekly Chronicle.* Outraged Soviet authorities dispatched a letter to Viscount Goto Shimpei, minister for home affairs, in which they alleged that "some malicious or foolish people in Japan are twisting this magnanimous, pure, whole-hearted and spontaneous act of the Russian workers and peasants . . . into a weapon of anti-Soviet propaganda.") Silenced, at least temporarily, were the accusations in U.S. newspapers and on Capitol Hill that the Japanese military was planning to invade China or was secretly violating the terms of the 1922 Washington Conference that limited the size of Japan's navy; in traumatized Tokyo, the militarists and imperialists who had regularly exhorted the Japanese to go to war with the West to defend their interests in Asia also went quiet. "The ease and speed with which the request of the American Red Cross for funds has been met is a source of deep satisfaction . . . and is of the best augury for the future relations between Japan and the United States," the *New York Times* declared on September 14.

The *Osaka Mainichi* proclaimed in its "Earthquake Pictorial Edition" in 1923, "The entire American nation rose to the occasion, with the American Red Cross Society as its central moving power, to raise a colossal sum for relief." Reporting to the U.S. Department of the Navy on October 25, 1923, Asiatic Fleet Commander Edwin Anderson wrote that top officials of the Japanese navy and the Foreign Ministry had called on him to express "the heartfelt thanks and grateful appreciation of the Japanese government and Japanese people for the timely and unexpected assistance [by the United States] through the Asiatic Fleet. . . . The Commander in Chief replied that it was a privilege for the American Navy to have served with the Japanese people and that any nation might well be proud of the prompt and effective measures the Japanese people had taken to meet the emergency." Prime Minister Yamamoto sent a personal message of thanks to Coolidge through the Japanese ambassador in Washington: "Such genuine and cordial friendship by the Government and people of the United States . . . will further increase the intimacy of the two countries and strengthen those bonds of concord and peace that exist throughout the world."

The biggest hero of the disaster was Cyrus Woods, who found himself transformed into an icon of Japanese-American solidarity. A cartoon in the usually anti-American *Tokyo Nichi Nichi* in early October 1923 showed a kimono-clad girl pinning a medal of "heartfelt gratitude" on the ambassador, who is surrounded by a horde of flag-waving, ragged survivors. "ALL TOKYO RINGING PRAISES WOODS," U.S. Embassy Counselor Hugh Wilson cabled the American Red Cross in Washington from the Japanese capital. "Ambassador kept embassy functioning summoned speedy relief succored refugees all nationalities while other embassies suspended. Tremendously increased American and American Red Cross prestige. . . . Wife and her octogenarian mother spent week Japanese farmhouse sleeping on floor but Woods neglecting private affairs remained duty." Wrote Samuel Reber of RCA: "His name will be ever linked with that of Perry in all future histories of Japan."

*Little of Yokohama remained standing after the devastation
of the earthquake and subsequent fires.*

Still, tensions and mistrust underlay the Japanese-American relationship. American newspapermen and participants in the aid mission
saw frequent examples of cowardice, passivity, and anti-Western belligerence on the part of the Japanese government and military, though
it is unclear how much of the reporting was based on firsthand observation and how much of it on rumor and prejudice. Japanese authorities, they often claimed, were so suspicious of American intentions
that they ascribed an ulterior motive—espionage, a malevolent plot to
lull the Japanese into passivity—to every act of generosity. These often
inflammatory accounts helped to turn many Americans' opinions
against the Japanese and may have been in part responsible for the
souring of relations that would occur soon after the disaster.

Ten days after the earthquake, the *Chicago Tribune*'s Tokyo correspondent, Roderick Matheson, filed a sensational report that the Japanese military had commandeered Tokyo's Imperial Hotel, "ordering
all foreigners who had taken refuge there to evacuate within a few
hours. These people had absolutely nowhere to go and the American
destroyer *Whipple* was ordered into Tokyo Bay to receive them."
Matheson reported that "emphatic and direct orders were given to

the American commander [of the *Whipple*] that under no circumstances must he pass the fortification lines of [Tokyo] bay. But he did, and sent his launches into the Tokyo canals, taking off all the evicted foreigners. His reply to the Japanese orders was to the point and delivered in the American language, without any of the rough edges trimmed off." The *Japan Weekly Chronicle* claimed that Matheson's version of events was "an absolute falsehood." The forced evacuation of the Imperial Hotel had never occurred, the paper reported. (Many Westerners had left voluntarily after the American destroyers showed up.) And no violent dispute had erupted between Japanese and American naval commanders, only an "amicable" negotiation leading to an agreement to send unarmed American launches, not warships, into Tokyo's "fortified zone." "The alleged incident . . . occurred only in the imagination of people as careless of the truth as Mr. Matheson," the *Chronicle* declared. "[His] romance will make a great hit with some Japanophobe readers in the United States."

Lyman Cotten, who witnessed much of the interaction between the American and Japanese navies, backs up some of Matheson's reporting. Cotten reported that the U.S. Embassy had received a letter from the Japanese Foreign Office on September 15 ordering foreign warships not to sail up Tokyo Bay past Yokohama without special authorization. "We have a destroyer off Shinagawa [the *Whipple*] and run one up from Yokohama twice daily. This has been an enormous help to everybody," he wrote to Elizabeth. "Imagine the spirit such a note shows." The Japanese quickly rescinded the order after the Americans filed a protest, Cotten reported, "but," he added, revealing the bitterness he felt about being cut out of the loop by the ambassador, "I fear some disagreeable incident may take place where junior [officers] have to handle it. I hope the admiral will take our fleet away just as soon as possible for the Japanese want them to go. They are so afraid the world will think the Japanese have not been able to handle the situation."

The most scathing report about Japanese conduct came from the *New York Tribune* correspondent Philip Kerby in a lengthy article he wrote in late September 1923 for the English-language *China Weekly Review* in Shanghai. (Lyman Cotten's personal papers contain a copy of the Kerby report, which suggests that the naval attaché and the journalist had a similar perspective on Japanese behavior.) Kerby's article accused the Japanese government of a litany of offenses, including covering up the scale of its losses at the Yokosuka Naval Base and displaying callous indifference to the lives of earthquake victims. While Yokohama was burning and lifeboats from the *Empress of Australia* and the *André Lebon* were making dozens of trips to shore and taking off as many people as possible, he alleged, the captain of the *Korea Maru* refused to send out boats or throw life preservers to refugees in the water, and even pulled up his ladder to prevent anyone from coming aboard. The captain finally relented at eleven o'clock Sunday morning when he received a wireless message from the Ministry of the Navy officially informing him that an earthquake had taken place and requesting his help in the rescue effort.

> The action of the Captain of the *Korea Maru* was repeated innumerable times by all the officials [Kerby claimed]. Because the central police station burned in Tokyo the substations refused to act on their own authority, to send out details to prevent looting, to assist the sufferers, or to try to establish order. . . . The world mourns for Japan's loss, mourns the death of 147 foreigners [*sic*] killed at Yokohama, some of whom undoubtedly could have been saved if the Captain of the *Korea Maru* played the part of a man instead of a puppet in the navy hierarchy.

Although Kerby's allegations of Japanese incompetence and criminal neglect have never been substantiated, they may contain more than a grain of truth. They are consistent with Thomas Ryan's account of Japanese lighter captains refusing to pick up refugees from the reclaimed ground below the Bluff, and they also square with reports from other survivors that foreigners carried out virtually all of the rescue work during the first twenty-four hours. Whatever the truth, the Japanese press countered such reports with a litany of far-fetched allegations about Western brutality and negligence. Under the heading "Foreign Steamer's Cold Treatment of Japanese Sufferers from Earthquake," the *Yushin Nippon* reported that an unidentified foreign steamer "declined to take Japanese refugees, but only white men. . . . Numberless sufferers, cursing the cold-bloodedness of the so-called rescue boat, threw themselves overboard and were drowned." The *Japan Weekly Chronicle* dismissed the report as a lie inspired by "pure malevolence." In an article headlined "Atrocious British Merchant Ship," the *Tokyo Nichi Nichi* claimed that the crew of the *Empress of Australia* had refused to allow Japanese to take refuge on board following the collapse of the hatoba. "Threatening the Japanese with their pistols, they drove them off, and immediately sailed for their destination," the paper falsely reported. Officials at the U.S. Embassy attacked the article. "[U.S. Military Attaché] Colonel Burnett considers it grossly unjust that these unfounded accusations should be made against the captain, officers, and men of the *Empress of Australia*," the *Japan Times* reported on September 17, "when as a matter of fact they gave their utmost effort to rescuing the refugees."

But it was Philip Kerby's epitaph in the *China Weekly* that would linger long after the disaster and encapsulate the deep ambivalence and mistrust that lay at the heart of the East-West relationship. There had been countless examples of Japanese heroism and generosity during the disaster and its aftermath, but Kerby chose to focus exclusively on the dark side of Japanese behavior. "The [true] story of the Japanese quake will never be told," the *New York Tribune* correspondent concluded in a stinging rebuke of the Japanese authorities, "with the temporary collapse of government, the connivance to the massacre of some 1,500 Koreans, many of whom were tortured and burned in the most fiendish manner possible, before death came at last to relieve them from their sufferings." Kerby claimed to have seen the dismembered corpses of several Koreans on the road between Tokyo and Yokohama. "Perhaps it is just as well that the story of the quake is never told in its entirety," he concluded. "Perhaps the Japanese are right in maintaining their attitude of strict secrecy, since if all the details were known it would make a black bar sinister of the Escutcheon of Nippon, a bar which would preclude her entrance into the family of civilized nations."

ON WEDNESDAY, September 19, nine days after Cyrus Woods dismissed him from his staff, Lyman Cotten received new orders from the navy. An official telegram from Secretary Edwin Denby arrived at his home in Azabu, confirming his detachment from the U.S. Embassy in Tokyo and summoning him to report for duty in the Office of Naval Intelligence in Washington. After a week as a jobless pariah, he received the news as a huge relief. "I went in person and reported this to the ambassador," he wrote before rushing off for Chuzenji to inform his family. "He said he never thought my delay in reporting to the embassy was due to anything except a mistake in judgment. Then he wished me well." Woods's display of bonhomie left the naval attaché unmoved. "I think," Cotten wrote, "that he is the most unscrupulous man that I have ever come in contact with."

Elizabeth Henderson Cotten had spent the past two weeks at the family cottage on Lake Chuzenji, waiting with John, Curtis, and their servants for definitive word about their next move. Aftershocks rattled the mountain retreat for a week; it wasn't until the night of September 8 that the family could sleep with any degree of comfort. Occasional telegrams and notes from Lyman, delivered up the mountainside with great difficulty, constituted almost their only knowledge of life in the earthquake zone. Letters from friends reinforced Elizabeth's sense of isolation. A note arrived in mid-September from Elizabeth's friend Mrs. Kenneth Caldwell, wife of an American diplomat, who had been caught in Karuizawa when the earthquake hit.

> What will you do? Are you going to Tokyo or will you try to stay in Chuzenji or Nikko? I have no idea yet what will be done with us. I have been very busy feeding the refugee trains coming through here, trains covered roof and all with these stricken creatures. All the Karuizawa foreign population has been doing it in shifts, day and night. We made fresh rice balls and wheat tea—gave ice and wet towels and milk for the babies. Their courtesy and thankfulness are most touching. Poor souls—I wonder if their faces will ever lose that look.

She also received periodic letters from relatives in North Carolina, who were starved for news of the family's condition after the catastrophe. In mid-September a letter arrived from her mother-in-law, Sallie, addressed to "Bessie" and dated September 4:

> You cannot realize the relief that we felt today when we read the following telegram from Naval Intelligence Washington D.C.

"Latest report—indicates Capt. Cotten and family are safe." . . . The papers here are literally blazing with accounts of the fire—and we wish to know how Lyman ever got to Tokyo—and if his valuable papers were burned. . . . I have been saving a little money to send you . . . and I wish to know whether to send it now or help pay Lyman Jr.'s school bills with it. [R. R. Cotten, Lyman's father] is meeting some losses—a mule died—a barn of tobacco burned—crop injured by hail—and now the Boll Weevil is bad. But he and I have had too many hard financial blows to meet for such small things to worry us. He is out of debt and able to take care of us—and that makes us very complacent.

The days passed by with agonizing slowness. The weather, and the lake, grew colder, and the first leaves began to turn. Chuzenji was deathly quiet. On September 17 Elizabeth described her own restlessness and anxiety in another note to her mother:

This little colony—so small now—and only women and children—is eating its heart out for news—news of that old world of ours that is no more. Sixteen days since the great disaster—and still we live like poor wrecked souls on a desert island. . . . Chuzenji is peaceful and serene and more beautiful in the early autumn haze than I have ever known it—but sad and still and remote—utterly removed from that tempestuous world below us. . . . No one is quite sure where they will live or can live. . . . Some expect to spend the winter in Nikko. We, I think, will sail for America as soon as possible, even if Lyman can't come with us.

Then, at last, came relief from their anxiety and boredom. On the evening of September 19, after a long journey from Tokyo, Cotten walked through the door of their summer cottage bearing the news of his reassignment. "Oh joy!" Elizabeth wrote to her parents, in her overwrought Victorian style.

Lyman has come. All uncertainty for us is over. He has received his orders to the office of Naval Intelligence at Washington, so as soon as we conveniently can, we will sail for America, good, safe,

Happy America. The house is now in a turmoil! Keshi and Ma Chan and Nebi San, all packing madly. When I think of all the pack horses that brought our numerous belongings up the mountains and realize that they not only have to be gotten down the mountains, but into what is left of Tokyo, my heart stands still. However it must be done.

And so, after one of the worst natural disasters in history, an inexplicable lapse in judgment of the former American war hero, and three weeks of uncertainty, the Cottens' Japanese idyll came to a bittersweet end. Two days later, on Friday, September 21, in the predawn chill, the Cottens woke up, dressed, and prepared to leave Momiji-san for the last time. The house stood nearly empty: the servants had finished packing the family's belongings into thirty-three steamer trunks and would drag them down the mountain on handcarts the next morning. The lake, slate gray, shrouded in mist, lapped gently at the pebble beach below the house. The Cottens' diaries and letters don't linger over the scene, but one can easily imagine it: Elizabeth and Lyman stood together on the verandah, holding hands in the semi-darkness, gazing across the glassy surface toward the silhouettes of the distant mountains. The first birds were singing in the pines and sycamores along the brightening lake shore; a light or two flickered in the homes of other early risers in Chuzenji. Some time before six o'clock, they slipped back inside from the verandah, woke up John and Curtis—they had arranged for the ever-loyal Garnet Hulings to take the young cousins down to Yokohama the following week—and hugged them good-bye. Then, with Elizabeth's maid, Keshi, and Lyman's Irish setter pup, Taisho, they climbed down the mountain by rickshaw to Nikko.

Elizabeth's account of her journey to Tokyo, her first trip there since the earthquake several weeks before, resonates with melancholy and a mounting sense of dread. Hulings's Ford and a Japanese driver were waiting for them at Umagaeshi ("horse go back"), the last stop of the trolley car line, at the foot of the mountain. They climbed into the back and started the next leg of their journey, making a brief stop in Nikko to say good-bye to their friend Irene Mann at her little stone church. Watching the mountains recede through the curved rear window of the Ford, they followed the Imperial Highway, lined for twenty miles by towering cryptomeria trees. From behind the foliage peeked Buddhist temples built to perpetuate the glory of the Tokugawa shogunate and the great daimyos of feudal Japan. Ten miles outside of Tokyo, they passed through a village with every house down, crumbled bamboo, piles of thatch, and red tiles littering the ground. They pushed on through the gathering darkness and a steady rain. After dark, they reached the eastern edge of the capital.

Tokyo by night, three weeks after the earthquake, presented an eerie spectacle. "Complete blackness," Elizabeth wrote. "As though a great knife had cut the terrain in two. The living and the dead city lay side by side." The Ford plunged through a continuing downpour. The car's headlights pierced the lightless night, casting a glare upon the blackened ruins. "Miles of nothingness," Elizabeth wrote. She could see no road signs, no identifiable streets, no landmarks, only heaps of brick and concrete and tiny huts of burned-out sheet iron. In many places she noticed crude wooden boards stuck in the ground, with Japanese characters written on them. The chauffeur, who navigated expertly through the featureless landscape, explained that they identified the remains of houses, put up by the owners to mark what was left of their property. Poor souls, she thought. They crossed a canal. A sickening stench hung in the air; it emanated, she realized, from beneath the mountain of trash that stood in the middle of the road. Junked automobiles and the twisted frames of rickshaws lay side by side. In an open space beside a hill, through the rain and the shadows, she could discern two chimneys and tents pitched atop a mound of wreckage. "There is something strangely familiar," she observed. "I turn to Lyman—yes, it was once the American Embassy. I feel a catchall in the heart, and we make the rest of the drive in silence."

At eight o'clock that evening they arrived in front of their house in the Azabu neighborhood, south of the Imperial Palace, and clambered out of the car onto piles of mud and stones. It was still raining heavily. From outside, the house appeared to be intact, and the leaves of the orange trees shone "green and glossy" in the garden. Morning glory vines covered the outer walls, and the greenness seemed lushly beautiful in a landscape of mud, rock, and broken tiles. Yoshizawa, the caretaker, led them through the house—plaster fallen off the walls, cracks everywhere, the chimney down, a large hole in the ceiling, and several dozen strangers, the staff's homeless friends and relatives, packing the servants' quarters. Late that evening as the rain tapered off, Lyman and Elizabeth left their house and walked through the neighborhood, surveying the destruction. They stood at the top of a steep flight of stone steps that led down from Azabu to the Tora-nomon district. At the base of the steps ran a crooked street that, before the earthquake, had been lined with the stalls of curio dealers, including that of her favorite tradesman, "old Yamamoto," who would kneel and touch his head to the floor in deference to her before opening his silk kerchief and displaying his wares. Elizabeth stared mournfully through a warm drizzle at a scene of desolation. "From the top of the flight of stone steps I can stand and as far as the eye can see, eight miles as the crow flies, there is nothing," she wrote. "The flames have swept everything before them."

Elizabeth exits the Japanese stage with a stark account of her trip on Sunday, September 23, at 5 A.M. to Yokohama, shortly before sailing home to America. It stands as an epitaph for a city—and an era. In the car with her and Lyman on the ninety-minute journey was Kenneth Caldwell, the American diplomat whose wife had corresponded with Elizabeth from her own mountain retreat, Karuizawa.

We drove through deserted streets into a city of the dead—Herculaneum and Pompeii. Today in that great city three buildings stand, and they are gutted by fire. We saw no living thing—neither man nor beast. . . . Along the Bund I search for some landmark. Standard Oil, the Oriental Hotel, the Grand Hotel—where are they? Piles of stones and burned-out iron. . . . There is the Creek. The earth has been flung backward, the bridge has fallen 10 or 20 feet. We . . . climb the bridge, come up on the other side and start up Camp Hill. Complete obliteration. At the top of Camp Hill stood the American Hospital, that splendid institution that has been such a comfort and benefit to our people in the Far East. I look for something that I might take away for sentiment's sake. Only . . . charred brick and mortar. . . . In the valley below lies the great city of Yokohama, an empty blackened plain, without one home left standing. Will Yokohama be a great city again? I think not. And the era of the foreigner in the [life] of the city is gone forever.

EPILOGUE

And after the earthquake a fire, but the Lord was not in the fire: and after the fire a still small voice.

First Book of Kings 19:11–12

ON THE MORNING of September 19, nearly three weeks after the earthquake, Frederick Starr settled into a private cabin aboard the *President Grant*, a luxury steamer of the Admiral-Orient Line moored in Yokohama harbor, and took stock of his situation. He was exhausted, melancholy, and wrenched by his experience. Since leaving Zojoji Temple on the morning of September 3 he had spent two weeks foraging for survival in the ruins of Tokyo. Encamped in a heavily damaged missionary's hostel and, later, a friend's abandoned house, Starr had bided his time, watching, waiting, and absorbing the scale of the devastation. With his loyal young assistant, Takagi, who had returned to his post several days after the earthquake, Starr had traveled by rickshaw across the vast necropolis: "It is awful, nothing like it perhaps in history," he wrote to his mother. "And [everywhere there is] the smell of burned flesh and the worse smell of putrefaction."

Perhaps no other Westerner had lost so many Japanese friends in the disaster. Despite a lack of knowledge of the language, Starr had accumulated a circle of hundreds of people—academics, politicians, Buddhist monks, Shinto priests, mountaineers, booksellers, carpenters, traders—in the course of twenty years of visits to Japan. During the past two weeks he had been methodically searching for them, only to discover that the majority had disappeared, and their houses had burned to the ground. "Most . . . are poor people and common and lived in the districts where the greatest destruction both by earthquake and fire occurred," he wrote. "I cannot expect that many of them escaped." His climbing partner and collaborator on the Fujiyama project, Ikko Sogabe, was missing in Yokohama and presumed dead. (After Starr's departure, Sogabe's remains would be found in the ashes of his home; he had attempted to retrieve his collection of Fuji memorabilia and been caught in the inferno.) Alice Ballantyne Kirjasoff, the U.S. consul's young wife, who had traveled to Japan on the same steamer as Starr in 1919 and held a dinner in his honor soon afterward, had been killed, he learned to his regret, with her husband following the collapse of the U.S. Consulate. Starr's precious research notes, including an account of his Fuji expedition, which he had left behind at the Hotel Kinokuniya on September 1, had been destroyed. He had two yen in his pocket, a black satchel filled with toiletries and notebooks, and two steamer trunks salvaged from the hotel. Still, compared to those around him, Starr felt fortunate. "We have not suffered from hunger," he wrote to his mother from the missionary hostel. "Here we vary [our diet]—breakfast a bowl of rice and stewed dried onion, lunch a bowl of rice and boiled radish, dinner a bowl of rice and a stew of potato and eggplant."

For more than a week after the earthquake, Starr had been determined to remain in Japan. He wanted to help in the rebuilding effort, locate his missing friends and colleagues, resume work on the Fuji project, then embark from Yokohama on a long-anticipated tour of Southeast Asia. But on September 10, after long reflection, he reported to the U.S. Embassy at the Imperial Hotel and put his name on a list of American citizens seeking ships to take them home. His decision to leave Japan had come of necessity, not desire. "I hate to return [to Seattle], but my financial condition was affected by the happenings here and it seems best to get back to where my own hand is on my affairs. . . . I am sorry for my actual losses, financial and others; for the failure to make the hoped for connections in Japan; for the loss of [my planned trips] to Cambodia and Siam. But it is not my fault and I shall weather the storm." On September 15 the first secretary of the embassy told Woods that a berth had been found for him on the *Grant* and that he, like all other American refugees, could reimburse the government later for the cost of the ticket. A launch took Starr to an American destroyer on September 16, where he ate his first good meal in weeks at the officers' mess and spent the night in a comfortable berth. He transferred to the *Grant* the following evening, not sure when he would return to the country that he considered his second home. "According to the *Asahi* [newspaper], he leaves for home with only the clothes he has on," the *Japan Weekly Chronicle* wryly commented. "If he was in his yukata when the earthquake came he will have some trouble in getting ashore the other side, as the kimono is regarded as indecent in America and not allowed in public."

NOT FAR FROM where Starr's vessel lay berthed, the Reverend Eustace M. Strong, chaplain of the Christ Church of Yokohama, was also planning to leave the ruined city. For nearly three weeks, following his escape from the flames of the Oriental Palace Hotel on the Bund, Strong had been leading teams of volunteers through the rubble of the Foreign Settlement and the Bluff on a ghastly search for the dead. Many foreigners had been incinerated, but Strong turned up thirty identifiable bodies and sets of remains. He had presided over funeral after funeral of people whom he had known well. Edwin Wheeler, Yokohama's popular physician, and Tom Abbey, the auctioneer who had led the octogenarian on a desperate flight from the Auction House, only to asphyxiate with him a few hundred feet from the harbor, had been found together in the parking lot of a tea godown between Water and Main Streets. They were buried together on the grounds of the destroyed British Naval Hospital on September 8. "Greater love hath no man than this, that a man lay down his life for his friend," Strong pronounced before gravediggers shoveled earth over the coffins of the two men. The remains of the American Naval Hospital's chief pharmacist, Lawrence Zembsch, and those of his wife—a fistful of ash, several fragments of bone, and the gold wedding band—had been interred in the grounds of the hospital, along with the bodies of several Americans who had died in the collapse of the Cherry Mount and Bluff Hotels. Zembsch had gone to his grave without fully recovering his wits, never revealing what had happened to him on his mysterious journey to the South Sea island of Palau the previous spring. Two Japanese civilians had recovered near the burned-down Customs House the bodies of the American consul, Max Kirjassof, and his pregnant wife, Alice. They were laid to rest at a foreign cemetery in Negishi. U.S. Marines had gathered the ashes of Doris Babbitt, the nineteen-year-old crushed in the Grand Hotel only two days after arriving in Yokohama with her father, the new commercial attaché to the U.S. Embassy, her mother, and older sister. Her grief-stricken family then returned home to the United States, never to return to Japan. "[Babbitt] is in an extremely bad nervous condition and his wife's health is considerably impaired," Secretary of Commerce Herbert Hoover wrote to Cyrus Woods on October 4 from Washington. Babbitt had been forced to borrow $900 from Canadian Pacific Lines to purchase steamship tickets for his wife and surviving daughter and was unable to pay it back; Hoover gently asked Woods to reimburse the steamship company out of American Red Cross emergency funds.

"And so in plots in a foreign land, where the flags of their respective nations have flown for over fifty years," a *Japan Weekly Chronicle* correspondent reported, "the bodies of a few representatives of the British and American communities were committed to Mother Earth by the tender ministrations of their fellow countrymen." Worn out and sick at heart, Reverend Strong planned to leave Yokohama on September 24 for a few days' recuperation in Karuizawa, then travel to Kobe and sail home to America for good in October.

Strong would leave behind a once-vibrant community almost all of whose members had been killed or had fled the city. The American Red Cross and the police department initially identified 173 Westerners who had died in the earthquake and fires in Yokohama, including seventy-eight Americans. But the *Japan Weekly Chronicle* put the figure at eight hundred and noted that the true number might never be known because hotel lists in the city had been destroyed and so many bodies had been burned to ashes. The casualties, the newspaper observed, could have been much higher had many foreigners not still been vacationing at summer resorts or seeing off friends on the *Empress of Australia*. Weeks after the earthquake, according to the *Chronicle*, only two hundred expatriates remained in the city out of a total pre-earthquake population of 4,376. Scattered and isolated, many had been reduced to begging their Japanese neighbors for food and clothing.

Foreign casualties, of course, represented just a small fraction of the total. In late September the Metropolitan Police Board declared that 84,014 people had died in Tokyo, with 200,000 injured, out of a pre-earthquake population of around 2 million. In Yokohama, the police put the casualties at 30,771 dead and 47,908 injured out of a population of 434,170. In December Yokohama police authorities counted 1,831 foreigners killed, including 1,542 Chinese, with 1,007 still missing. The dead and missing included sixty-one British, two hundred Russians, and 167 Americans.

K. Takahashi's *The Story of Japan's Great 1923 Earthquake,* published that year, placed the deaths from the earthquake and fires at 120,345, forty thousand of whom, Takahashi estimated, had died in Yokohama. The Tokyo police put the total at 145,000. The dead, reported the *Tokyo Nishi Nishi,* had far exceeded the 118,000 Japanese soldiers killed during the Russo-Japanese War. Whatever the exact body count, the earthquake and fires would rank as one of the worst natural disasters in history—dwarfing earthquakes of equal intensity in Messina, Italy, in 1908 and Lisbon in 1755, the latter of which had been accompanied by a tsunami. The Great Kanto Earthquake would remain the most terrible calamity of the twentieth century until just before dawn on July 27, 1976, when a massive earthquake measuring 8.0 on the Richter scale struck Tangshan, China, an industrial city built, like Yokohama and Tokyo, on unstable, alluvial soil. Bridges, homes, railroads, and factories collapsed in seconds, and at least 250,000 people—the Chinese government never revealed the exact figure—were killed. That estimated death toll was equaled in this century by the tsunami that swamped the heavily populated coastlines of Southeast Asia on December 26, 2004, drowning and crushing 260,000 people. Hurricane Katrina, for all the ruin and human misery it caused, left just twelve hundred dead. The worst natural disaster of all time is considered to be the January 1556 earthquake that ripped through China's western Chansi province, killing an astonishing 855,000 people.

The scale of the physical destruction of the Great Kanto Earthquake had also been nearly unprecedented. The Metropolitan Police Bureau reported that 440,549 buildings had been destroyed in Tokyo, including 316,087 burned. Of a total population of 2,031,000, the earthquake and fires made 1,357,000, or 67 percent, homeless. In six of the capital's thirteen wards—Kanda, Nihombashi, Kyobashi, Asakusa, Honjo, and Fukugawa—more than 90 percent of the buildings had been razed. As Imamura and other seismologists had predicted, almost all of the destruction had taken place in the low-lying business districts and poor neighborhoods located at the head of Tokyo Bay and spreading over the plain of the Sumida River, where the soft, moist clay and sand that formed the subsoil had greatly intensified the seismic vibrations. "I found marine shells in abundance at depths of three feet to ten feet below the surface," wrote Robert Anderson in the *Bulletin of the Seismological Society of America* after inspecting the earthquake zone the following summer. "The deposits of the plain area are water soaked at shallow depths and thus afford conditions on which the destructivity of the earthquake waves is greatly increased."

The catastrophe had destroyed seventy-five thousand buildings, 92 percent of the total, in Yokohama, leveled dozens of towns and villages on Sagami Bay, and rubbled the great naval port of Yokosuka. A dozen battleships, torpedo boats, and destroyers had been lost. Yokohama's silk trade had been wiped out. Estimated losses to the Japanese economy totaled 3 billion yen ($1.5 billion), or 5 percent of Japan's total wealth. The *Japan Weekly Chronicle* observed that the catastrophe "did enormous damage to Japan's navy, the activities of which were almost paralyzed. It did great damage to Japan's railways and other engineering works which have to be repaired on a scale never before witnessed. . . . Tokyo will be a city of shacks for some years to come." Most experts surveyed believed—wrongly, it turned out—that Japan's imperial ambitions would be curtailed, if not permanently, then at least for a generation. A prominent Japanese industrialist told U.S. Ambassador Woods, "This catastrophe will put Japan in the position of a third-rate power somewhere below Italy. If this had occurred before the Washington Conference, you would have considered that no conference would have been necessary." J. B. Powell, the *Chicago Tribune*'s Shanghai correspondent, wrote in late September 1923, "While most observers of the far eastern situation are assured that Japan will arise from the ashes of her disaster a better country in every way, the belief here is general that it will require at least a quarter of a century for the country fully to recover [its] military and economic strength." That would take Japan to 1948, if accurate. A year later, on the anniversary of the earthquake, the *Japan Weekly Chronicle* attempted to put the catastrophe in perspective:

> One naturally compares the earthquake of a year ago with other great calamities of the sort. Although at the time of the San Francisco earthquake enormous fire losses were incurred, the quake itself was very much milder and the loss of life by comparison trifling. The Lisbon earthquake was a comparable disaster, but that was a long time ago. In recent years the earthquake which leveled the city of Messina—a terror which came by night—was most like the Yokohama earthquake, but the effects were not so widespread—there was no Tokyo to burn—not even an Odawara. Nor was Messina the first port of an Empire with a great trade to disorganize. . . . It is only by evil chance that a great city finds itself in the midst of a seismic disturbance. Yokohama will certainly take rank as one of the most memorable of natural disasters.

AFTER REPEATED DELAYS, Lyman Cotten and his family—Elizabeth, John, and Mary Curtis Henderson—sailed by U.S. naval destroyer from Yokohama to Kobe, and from there left aboard the *President Wilson* on October 9, 1923, bound for San Francisco. All of them were undoubtedly relieved to be putting the horrors of the past six weeks behind them. On November 19, the former naval attaché arrived in Washington and checked into a room at the Army & Navy Club. He offered no account of his emotional state on the Pacific crossing or during the rail trip from San Francisco, but he must have been desperately worried over how his confrontation with Woods would affect his naval career. "Reported to Chief of Operations for duty in [Office of Naval Intelligence]," he wrote in his last diary entry that year. "Secretary [Edwin] Denby was away but I saw Assistant Secretary [Theodore] Roosevelt [son of the U.S. president]. In talking to him about Mr. Woods at Tokyo and his actions after the earthquake

I remarked that Mr. Woods at that time was not a normal man. [Roosevelt] remarked in a very characteristic way, 'No. And he never was.' Everyone seemed very glad to see me and most cordial and friendly."

Despite his warm reception by his colleagues, his failures during the earthquake continued to gnaw at him. In a speech to a packed house at Washington's Algonquin Club on December 2, 1923, on "The Japanese Disaster," Cotten felt compelled to shade the truth about his behavior. "As soon as I learned of the catastrophe in the Yokohama-Tokyo area I left for Tokyo," he disingenuously claimed, skipping over the six days he had remained in the mountains until the evidence had grown too terrible to ignore.

Woods apparently let the matter drop; the State Department inquiry that Cotten had dreaded never took place, and Cotten's career in the navy resumed without further repercussions. As a longtime observer of Japan, he was frequently called on to provide advice and analysis of the Japanese government's ambitions in the Far East and its intentions toward the United States. Cotten sought to dissuade his audiences from believing that a new era of good feeling had arrived. "I have heard the idea frequently advanced since my return to America that the relief measures . . . have fundamentally changed the relations between the two countries. The Japanese, I believe, are very grateful for our assistance, but, of course, the earthquake and fire and our subsequent action did not remove any possible conflict of interests that existed before," he observed in late 1923. "I am afraid the promptness, efficiency, and magnitude of our assistance not only aroused the gratitude of the Japanese, but their envy and jealousy as well. I am pessimist enough to believe that with any people envy and jealousy are apt to remain much longer than gratitude."

As COTTEN HAD FORESEEN, the brief period of goodwill between Japan and the United States collapsed by the end of 1923 into mutual recriminations. But the instigation came from the American side, not the Japanese. Throughout the previous decade, Capitol Hill, western state legislatures, and the opinion pages of western newspapers had resounded with accusations that Japanese immigrants were acquiring much of the best land in the American West and that Japan's territorial ambitions in China and the Pacific Rim threatened U.S. interests in the region. In Washington State, home to thousands of Japanese immigrants, the legislature had already passed tough new laws several years before the earthquake banning further Japanese immigration. In California, where the adult Japanese population had risen from 32,785 in 1910 to 47,557 a decade later, voters in 1920 had passed, by a three-to-one margin, an initiative placed on the ballot barring further Japanese ownership of land. Anti-Japanese groups such as the Japanese Exclusion League, run by retired newspaper publisher V. S. McClatchy and U.S. Senator Hiram Johnson, argued that Japan was "the Germany of Asia" and that the allegiance of Japanese immigrants in the United States "is always to Tokyo." U.S. Senator James Phelan of California, one of the most rabid Japanese baiters, had once declared on the Senate floor that "a Jap is a Jap"; he had warned that the average Japanese was so "clever" that, "unlike a black man or a Mexican," he was "capable of taking the place of the White man."

Two months after the earthquake, anti-Japanese animosity flared anew in both Washington, D.C., and the West Coast. It is unclear how large a part the earthquake played in stirring up the anti-immigration campaign. Without question, allegations that the Japanese had failed to show sufficient appreciation for U.S. postearthquake assistance—accusations whipped up by incendiary, often inaccurate news reports coming out of Tokyo—strengthened the xenophobes' arguments. The Japanese government's strong objections to the anti-immigration campaign brewing in Washington were seen by many as further evidence that the Japanese had failed to behave with proper humility. "It has been impossible since the earthquake for Japan to express anything of her political attitude without our feeling that she shows rank ingratitude [for earthquake assistance]," Frederick Starr wrote for a Seattle labor newspaper several months after his return to the United States. "Almost immediately after my return to this country, there was a public expression by . . . the American Legion in this direction. They said, 'after we so liberally helped her in her need . . . [we consider it] an example of ingratitude that after all we did she should continue to urge her pretensions.' "

In the fall of 1923, James Phelan, now a former senator, denounced what he called a "rising tide of color" before the Senate Immigration

Committee. Leaders of both houses on Capitol Hill called for abrogating the 1907 Gentleman's Agreement, a little publicized arrangement through which the Japanese government had informally agreed to cap Japanese immigration to the United States at several thousand a year. In December 1923—the same month the American Red Cross announced that it had raised a record $12 million for Japanese earthquake victims—Congressman Albert Johnson, chairman of the House Immigration Committee, and Senator Henry Cabot Lodge jointly introduced a bill to cut off almost all Japanese immigration to the United States. (Lodge, a Senate hard-liner, referred to Japan as "the Prussia of the East.") The blandly titled National Origins Act proposed to fix alien quotas at 2 percent of the census figures for individual national and ethnic groups taken in 1890, plus two hundred. (In 1890 the Japanese population, according to the census, was 14,274, which would mean that only 480 Japanese a year would be permitted under the new law.) "New arrivals should be limited to our capacity to absorb them into the ranks of good citizenship," President Coolidge announced in February 1924, appearing to support the draconian new legislation. "America must be kept American."

On the West Coast the anti-Japanese campaign assumed an ugly and sometimes violent tone. Anti-Japanese billboards appeared on California highways: "Japs, don't let the sun set on you here. Keep moving." In early 1924 a mob beat up a Japanese car dealer at his home in Belvedere, a suburb of Los Angeles. Shortly afterward police found two Japanese men murdered in a suburb of San Pedro, apparent victims of a lynch mob. The hate campaign, which was closely covered in the Japanese press, led to an outbreak of anti-American demonstrations in front of the Imperial Hotel, still the site of the U.S. Embassy six months after the earthquake, and a handful of protest suicides.

Ambassador Cyrus Woods, regarded as a hero in Japan because of his role coordinating Red Cross relief efforts after the earthquake, sent a flurry of cables from Tokyo to Secretary of State Charles Evans Hughes, urging him to oppose the bill's passage. In a letter to Johnson and Lodge, according to the *Japan Weekly Chronicle*, Hughes warned, "The bill tends to convert Japanese gratitude for American sympathy and help at the time of the earthquake into high resentment." None of these efforts could stop the anti-Japanese movement. On July 1, 1924, Congress passed by a vote of seventy-six to two the National Origins Act, otherwise known as the Japanese Exclusion Act. A few days later Woods resigned as ambassador to Japan, offering the flimsy cover story that he needed to devote more time to caring for his octogenarian mother-in-law, Mrs. Marchand, who had been lightly injured in the earthquake. The *New York Times* regarded Woods's departure as the tragic—and perhaps ominous—end of an era. "No greater ovation has ever been extended to any foreigner in Japan than was accorded to Ambassador Woods when he left the quake torn districts to return to the United States on a vacation [in November 1923]," observed the paper's State Department correspondent. "Thousands of cheering people crowded into the courtyard of the Imperial Hotel to bid him farewell, while the entire city displayed American and Japanese flags over the ruins. The Japanese public will undoubtedly feel that with the departure of Mr. Woods, another link in the friendship has been severed." The *Osaka Asahi* newspaper claimed that the passage of the legislation "has completely destroyed" the goodwill that had existed between the United States and Japan, that it would fan Japanese hostility toward the West, and that it would strengthen the militarist faction within the government. "To exclude Japanese by law is to stigmatize them legally as an inferior race which is not entitled to the same treatment as is extended to White peoples," declared the *Asahi*. "For this deplorable state of things America must solely be held responsible. Although [the Japanese] keep silent, their blood is boiling within them."

FOR THE JAPANESE GOVERNMENT the resurrection of Tokyo became the top priority on the national agenda, deemed vital not only to Japan's economic revival but also to the country's dignity and honor. "The nations of the world are watching our endeavours for reconstruction, and whether we succeed or fail will prove the test of our national power and ability," Prime Minister Gombei Yamamoto declared on September 16, announcing the formation of the Council for the Reconstruction of the National Capital. "The rebuilding of the capital is therefore, not merely the question of a city; it is an important national undertaking, essential in the promotion of the progress of our empire." Charles A. Beard, former professor of history at Columbia University and a noted urban designer, arrived in Tokyo at the end of September from New York City at the invitation of the new home affairs minister, Viscount Goto Shimpei, an old friend, to help oversee the city's rebirth. Beard set forth a grand vision based on American and European urban models that included digging subway tunnels, dredging Tokyo harbor to accommodate ships of five thousand tons and more, constructing the majority of the city's houses with steel-reinforced concrete, building a radial network of wide avenues spreading like the rays of a sun from the city center, and erecting an arterial highway two hundred yards wide to run on a north-south axis through the heart of the city. He imagined the new metropolis as a cross between Washington, D.C., and Paris, a city of monuments and open spaces, fusing grandiosity and greenery. "In laying out the streets," Beard wrote, "Western ideas undoubtedly will be followed—wide streets on the radial plan, the Government buildings being the center."

The scope and the expense proved too daunting for the Japanese government, however, and the project budget was whittled down from several billion to half a billion yen. The revised plan called for the erection of parks, schools built of reinforced concrete, bridges, canals, markets, employment centers, manual training schools, pawnshops, and day care centers. But, as Edward Seidensticker wrote in *Tokyo Rising*, "The main emphasis in the more modest plans was upon getting roofs over people's heads." This was proceeding even without government direction. A *Chronicle* correspondent reported in February 1924:

> Tokyo has become a city of sheds. One may walk through miles of once familiar streets and see no familiar sight. Everything has been swept away, and in its place are new wooden structures, some a little glorified. But the new wooden camp city, one is constantly reminded, is erected on the ashes of a burnt capital. Every now and then one passes a vast desert of debris or recognizes the burnt shell of some once imposing building. . . . Some [new buildings] are shacks de luxe. A barracks restaurant, for instance, shows many of

the artistic eccentricities of the Imperial Hotel. . . . The "Imperial" style is likely to leave its mark all over the city, for Japanese are great lovers of the grotesque. . . . People [are still] reluctant to live and work [near the Army Clothing Depot]. In the midst is a memorial shrine, rather roughly built of timber. Before it is a large incense burner emitting much smoke. . . . There is a constant stream of people who approach the shrine, stand a moment in prayer, and go their way. Nearly everyone in Tokyo must know somebody who perished there.

Yokohama's recovery proceeded more slowly, hampered in part by its lower priority in the eyes of Japanese officials and by the totality of its destruction. "In Yokohama little seems to have been done towards getting things in order," Lyman Cotten observed in late September. "Very few temporary buildings, streets not cleared. . . . Some human remains have not yet been removed from the ruins. The Japanese look upon Yokohama as a foreign city and their interest is centered in Tokyo." The U.S. government signaled its commitment to the port's revival by opening a new consulate on the grounds of the destroyed one three weeks after the earthquake and appointing a new consul general, Nelson T. Johnson. Johnson worked long, depressing hours repatriating American survivors, retrieving the remains of the dead, and trying to persuade those who had fled to other Japanese cities to return. "This is a great business starting a Consulate in a dead city. A sad odor over us every evening tainted with fumes of sulfur," Johnson reported to Woods on September 24.

I walked down the main street today to examine the bodies of two foreign women. It is pretty bad. I must make some arrangement for locating and identifying the American dead. . . . At four this morning I was ready to quit. At midnight last night I got out in my pajamas and tightened some sixty tent ropes. . . . It began to rain and I had visions of the tents drawing their pegs and coming down upon us. I have no skin on parts of my hands and it is getting blooming cold. Our tails are up though and we trying to make a noise like a consulate. This is being written by the lights of a lantern which will account for errors.

Workmen pulled corpses and skeletons out of the rubble all fall and winter, retrieving the last remains from the wreckage of the Oriental Palace Hotel in late February. Meanwhile, Marshall Martin, a Scottish-born expatriate, silk baron, and former publisher of the *Japan Gazette* who had barely escaped with his life in the collapse of the French Consulate that killed the consul, Paul Déjardin, became the driving force behind the city's revival. One month after the earthquake, Martin returned from Kobe to serve as chief adviser to the rehabilitation committee set up by Yokohama's mayor, Ariyoshi Chuichi. Martin tracked down hundreds of leaseholders, many of whom had fled back to Europe and America, and persuaded them to grant permission for the replanning of town lots. He also oversaw the creation of a memorial park built on reclaimed land in the harbor, using bricks of collapsed buildings on the Bund, the stones of the One Hundred Steps, and earth carved from a shattered spur of the Bluff.

The moribund city received a significant shot in the arm that winter, when American, British, and Indian silk merchants trickled back from Kobe, lured by tax incentives and the rehabilitation commission's offer to build them new facilities at the city's expense. Sturdy new wood-frame constructions, lined with fireproof asbestos, appeared along the Bund. On the site of the Grand Hotel a tent city sprang up that winter, housing expatriates who had returned. "[It is] warmer than any of the shacks constructed, according to those who have stayed there," the *Japan Weekly Chronicle* reported. "Each [tent] is erected over a low wall, which runs round the room and serves to shut out draughts, inundations and other inconveniences. A coal stove in the center keeps it warm. And there is no danger of anything falling on your head."

AKITSUNE IMAMURA'S VINDICATION in the wake of the great earthquake made him a popular figure in Japan. Effusive articles about the "heroic seismologist" who had "predicted" the catastrophe on the Kanto Plain filled Japanese newspapers and magazines for months after the earthquake. He advised Tokyo's Rehabilitation Commission on reconstructing the city. His lectures were widely broadcast on the new medium of radio. He traveled the country, advising municipalities on fire and earthquake mitigation methods. As a result of the earthquake Tokyo Imperial University expanded the Seismology Department— and for the first time paid Imamura a salary. Imamura came away from the earthquake more confident than ever of his abilities to forecast seismic upheavals. "My [prediction] has stood the test of fact and Dr. Omori's view has fallen to the ground," he all but gloated in an interview with Tokyo's *Mainichi* newspaper in the fall of 1923.

On October 4, 1923, the *Tenyo Maru,* a steamship of the Nippon Yusei Kaisha Line, arrived in the ruins of Yokohama from Melbourne, Australia. On board, sick and weary, shadowed by an air of defeat, was Imamura's longtime rival and occasional nemesis, Fusakichi Omori. During the scientific conference that had caused him to miss the seismological event of the century, he had suffered from intense headaches, and by the time he arrived in Japan, his health had sharply deteriorated. The *Japan Weekly Chronicle* reported, "Dr. Omori is now very ill, and the doctors think that he can never recover his mental health, some disease effecting his brain having made great inroads." On board the *Tenyo Maru,* Omori gave a speech before the passengers and crew in which he insisted that he had foreseen the catastrophe that destroyed Tokyo and Yokohama. "It would appear that Dr. Omori's illness had caused him to imagine things," the paper commented. "It would surely have been remembered if he had prophesied the earthquake, for his words were always promises of security." Days after this report, Omori learned that he was dying of a brain tumor. In late October Imamura visited him at a Tokyo hospital, where he found him in intense physical pain and tortured by guilt. No longer claiming that he had predicted the seismic disaster all along, the great seismologist blamed himself for instilling a fatal complacency in government officials and the public. "It was all my fault," Omori told his underling. Imamura tried to comfort him, and the two men toasted the Seismology Department's postearthquake prestige over glasses of sake. On November 8, 1923, two months after the quake, Omori died. He was fifty-five.

THE *PRESIDENT GRANT* docked in Seattle harbor on October 4, 1923, returning Frederick Starr to a celebrity far greater than the fame he had enjoyed before leaving for Japan in late July. Initial newspaper reports in the United States had erroneously claimed that Starr had been climbing Mount Fuji at the time the earthquake struck, and he was widely feared to have been killed. But in late September the *New York Times* excerpted a note from him to his mother in Auburn, New York, and set the record straight. Letters poured into his home in Seattle from friends around the world. "We were very much worried about you until we found in the newspapers and later by your post-card, that you were all right and in this country," Clarence Darrow wrote to him in October. "As long as you got away without serious injury, it must have been a wonderful experience." In a sly reference to their Chicago debate over human prospects in 1920, Darrow added, "Although I am a pessimist, I am glad you got out all right and your many friends feel the same." A colleague at the University of Chicago wrote on October 24, 1923, "You can imagine that the Tokyo death list was scanned daily by scores of us here until word came that you had escaped the quake. What an experience you had!!! If only you could reproduce in speech the rocking, upsetting sensa-tions of those few minutes, you'd have no end of engagements. Like the loss of the *Titanic* the disaster is too big to take in."

Starr took his colleague's advice and ventured onto the lecture circuit after his return to America, recounting his frightful nights in Zojoji Temple and offering his thoughts on the future of Japanese-American relations. In Seattle Starr contributed an article to the *Union Record*, a labor newspaper, warning of "grave consequences" if Congress passed the anti-immigration legislation brewing in Wash-ington. His experiences had heightened his admiration for Japan's self-discipline, rapid modernization, and imperial ambitions, and he became convinced that the world would be a better place if Japan expanded its military and economic control over the East. His out-spoken celebration of Japan's virtues became increasingly shrill and controversial. "The only hope of China lies in Japan," he pronounced, to widespread criticism, a few years before Japan invaded Manchuria and set the stage for World War II. "China can never pull herself to-gether alone."

* * *

ANOTHER SURVIVOR of the earthquake, Frank Lloyd Wright's newly
built Imperial Hotel, also profited from the catastrophe. The Imperial had escaped with only minor damage. And, thanks in part to
Wright's genius for self-promotion, much of the American public
came away convinced that the hotel was one of the few buildings in
Tokyo to survive the cataclysm. "This pile of stones, this wild dream
of an American architect, had met the test and stood better than any
other building of its size in Tokyo," proclaimed an article in the
American Contractor magazine in December 1923. Architect Louis
Sullivan wrote that month that "the emergence, unharmed, of the
Imperial Hotel, from the heartrending horror of the Tokyo disaster,
takes on . . . momentous importance . . . as a triumph of the living
and the real over the credulous, the fantastic, and the insane." Wright
was "a poet," Sullivan declared, who had resolved "never to relax his
grip on the basic fact of earthquake as a menace."

The reality was less flattering to Wright. Dozens of other Western-
style buildings in Tokyo, including the main train station, had also
withstood both the seismic vibrations and fire as well as, if not better
than, the Imperial Hotel. The Tokyo Building Inspection Department listed as "undamaged" 19 percent of the city's brick buildings
and 20 percent of its steel and reinforced concrete buildings, and
placed the Imperial in the second category of structures that had received "some" damage. In later years many architectural critics would
reassess Wright's "earthquake-proof" design and attribute the hotel's
survival far more to General Manager Tetsuzo Inumaru's fast reponse
to fires than to Wright's technical ingenuity. But the Imperial's reputed indestructibility, as well as its flamboyant architecture, became
a part of its mythology, and over the decades the hotel attracted a
stream of celebrities ranging from Babe Ruth to Will Rogers, from
Albert Einstein to the honeymooning Marilyn Monroe and Joe
DiMaggio.

SEVERAL MONTHS AFTER the calamity the Radio Corporation of
America presented a 500 yen reward ($250) to the Iwaki telegraph
operator Taki Yonemura for transmitting the first reports about the
earthquake and for helping to initiate the global relief effort. The dis-

patches that Yonemura sent, RCA Tokyo representative Samuel Reber declared in an unabashed bit of flackery for his own company, were "the most striking example of the superiority of radio communication in times of emergency. . . . What would have been our plight if we had not had this newest and best handmaiden of communication?"

Thomas John Ryan Jr., the New Orleans sailor who had pulled Mrs. Slack from the wreckage of the Grand Hotel, was dispatched to Kamakura on rescue duty immediately after the earthquake, where he again performed heroically: he rounded up marooned Japanese and Americans, and other foreigners, "many in immediate need of medical attention," according to a U.S. Embassy citation, and helped them board rescue ships anchored in Sagami Bay. He received the Congressional Medal of Honor from President Coolidge in March 1924, partly on the strength of Lyman Cotten's recommendation.

For his dramatic rescue of the *Empress of Australia* and its passengers in Yokohama harbor, Captain Samuel Robinson became a Knight Commander of the British Empire in December 1923 and received commendations from around the world. The emperor of Japan decorated him, the king of Siam awarded him the Order of the Elephant, and the Canadian Pacific Line soon gave him the command of its fastest ship, the *Empress of Canada*. (The next year, 1924, Robinson inaugurated an annual around-the-world tour aboard the *Empress of Canada*, sailing the vessel from Vancouver to New York via the Panama Canal, then across the Atlantic, through the Suez Canal to India, the Philippines, China, Japan, and Hawaii, and finally back to Vancouver.) Modest and uncomfortable with his celebrity, he portrayed his actions as part of a group effort. "One of the most gratifying things, and the dominant factor in the whole proceedings," he wrote in his report to Canadian Pacific after the earthquake, "is the way that everyone with whom we have had to deal on board has worked together without friction, disagreement, or complaint during this terrible catastrophe . . . some of the hardest workers having lost families or homes or business possessions, and in some cases all of these."

* * *

IN THE FALL of 1925 Lyman Cotten at last realized one of his life's ambitions: the command of a U.S. warship. Secretary of the Navy Edwin Denby appointed Cotten, then working for the Office of Naval Intelligence in the bowels of the Navy Department in Washington, the captaincy of the USS *Richmond,* a seven-thousand-ton Omaha-class light cruiser that had been commissioned two years earlier. For the career naval officer, the appointment must have represented a definitive vindication, a sign that any questions about his role during the earthquake had been buried for good. On January 6, 1926, the *Richmond* sailed out of New York harbor toward Norfolk, Virginia, on its first voyage with Cotten at the helm. One can imagine the pride, exhilaration, and maybe even relief that Cotten felt as he returned to the sea, his self-doubt banished, the passivity he had displayed two and a half years earlier a fading memory. Perhaps he felt an irresistible urge to push himself that day, and perhaps his eagerness to display his courage was at least partly responsible for the tragedy that followed.

"A terrific gale was blowing with snow and sleet," according to the *Chapel Hill Weekly.* "[Cotten] was ill at the time but went to the bridge and took his ship safely through the channel out to sea. The next day in Norfolk he was taken to the Naval Hospital with pneumonia. He died there on Tuesday, January 12 at the age of 51 . . . as real a casualty as if he died in action." Cut down in early middle age, at the very time when his career appeared to be regaining its momentum, Cotten never really had a chance to redeem himself in the field after the earthquake embarrassment. After his burial at Arlington National Cemetery, the *Raleigh News & Observer* declared that Cotten would be remembered as "one of the ablest officers in the American Navy."

OTIS MANCHESTER POOLE lived for nearly two years in Kobe with his family, trying to resurrect Dodwell & Co. He reassembled his Yokohama employees, reconstructed records that had been incinerated, and sought—without success—to claim both personal and business losses from his insurance company. Only after the disaster did he and thousands of other expatriates in Yokohama read the fine print on their policies and learn that they excluded compensation for damages sustained by "fire from earthquake." Wiped out by the disaster, the Pooles departed Kobe for Vancouver, British Columbia, on the *Empress of India* of the Canadian Pacific Line on July 7, 1925, twenty-two months after the earthquake, for what was intended to be three months' recuperative leave. But he never went back to Japan. Poole took over Dodwell & Co.'s New York office and later became the company's director in the United States and Canada.

From North America, he kept an eye on Yokohama's gradual rebirth in the late 1920s and early 1930s: the construction of a new Grand Hotel on the site of the old, a landscaped park built on top of Foreign Settlement debris that had been dumped offshore, the rise of a modest colony of foreigners' homes on the hills surrounding the Negishi Race Course, and, to his chagrin, the reclamation and development of many acres of tidal flats. "In the old days it was a lovely sight when the fishing fleet of forty or fifty sea-going sampans came gliding up the bay on a summer evening, their lofty oblong sails gleaming pink in the rays of the setting sun," he wrote. But the "curse of reclamation" had converted the flats into "geometric patterns of ochre-coloured building sites covered with drab industrial structures." Years after leaving Yokohama, Poole looked back lovingly on his days growing up in the pre-earthquake port. "The Yokohama I still see in my mind's eye is the old one created by the pioneers, with its open bays and virgin hills I roamed in as a boy," he wrote. "Thoughts of those scenes of the community I knew so well bring on a nostalgia that is like the scent of incense in a temple grove. In this I know that I am not alone."

THE DESTRUCTION of Yokohama and the dispersal of the port's American and European population slammed shut a window into Western society that had inspired a generation of artists, writers, intellectuals, and other liberal-minded Japanese. As Lyman Cotten had accurately predicted in December 1923, "Yokohama will . . . never again be the big foreign settlement that it was before. It will merely be a big shipping port with modern harbor conveniences, shipping offices, warehouses and incidental businesses." Followed by the racist, anti-Japanese legislation that the United States enacted in July 1924, the catastrophe, many historians argue, hastened Japan's rejection of the West. Militarism, fascism, and xenophobia—always present in Japan but balanced before the earthquake by tentative movements toward democracy and liberalism—quickly gained the upper hand. Japanese imperialists had just begun to retreat from their policy of unbridled expansion; in October 1922 the War Office had withdrawn its troops from Siberia and from Chinese ports and railway lines. Soon after the earthquake, however, Japanese right-wingers again claimed that economic and military control of Asia was imperative. "For the next few years Japan will be laboring under a severe handicap, and therefore all the more in need of seizing an advantage real or fancied," Cotten observed in his speech at the Algonquin Club in Washington in December 1923.

The declaration of martial law gave an already aggressive military new power and stature in Japanese society. Many of the officers who rose to positions of authority in the earthquake's aftermath would play prominent roles in the radical antidemocratic groups that formed in the late 1920s and early 1930s, the same groups that would lead the country to war. The impunity that followed the killing of Koreans and a handful of other perceived enemies of the state—including Japanese Socialist and Communist Party leaders believed to be working for Japan's enemy, the Bolshevik government of Russia—emboldened the militarists further. In December 1923 Morita Kichiemon, a leader of the Self-Defense Committees who had butchered Korean civilians, received a punishment of eighteen months in prison, with a suspension of his sentence for three years; a proviso allowed him to avoid jail altogether if he committed no further crimes during that period. "He goes scot free," the *Japan Weekly Chronicle* declared. That same month 105 Japanese defendants, charged with the murder of 150 Koreans in Saitama Prefecture, got one- to three-year sentences; many were let out on probation. The most notorious killer, military police captain Masahiko Amakasu, had strangled a charismatic socialist leader, Sakae Osugi; his wife, Ito Noe, a feminist and literary critic; and her seven-year-old nephew with a cord in a jail cell at his headquarters in Tokyo on September 15. He went on trial before a military tribunal in October 1923; sentenced to ten years in prison, he would be released after serving only twenty-four months.

For Japan, the disaster inflicted a trauma unmatched in its history, until the firestorms and atomic bombs of the Second World War. The near total destruction of its two most important cities, the loss of 4 percent of the country's population, was an unthinkable calamity, even in a country used to once-a-decade seismic disasters. It was as if New York City and Washington, D.C., had been burned to the ground, leaving hundreds of thousands dead and injured. The disaster created among many Japanese a sense of fatalism, a tendency to retreat inward, a desire to cling to ancient traditions and symbols of strength and absolute authority, such as the emperor and the army. The earthquake marked a decisive break from the period of optimism, prosperity, and freedom that had been best symbolized by the cosmopolitan port of Yokohama.

The era of Taisho democracy, named after the mentally enfeebled emperor who ruled Japan from 1912 until his death in 1926, lingered for a few years after the disaster. Although most power still rested in the hands of Japan's elites, the period saw the emergence of the parliamentary system, civilian cabinets, and liberalized election laws. Four years after the earthquake, however, the reformist movement unraveled. The government began arresting, torturing, and murdering members of the Japanese Communist Party, which it had legalized in 1923, and their sympathizers. China's continued domination by weak and feuding warlords provided an opportunity for Japanese expansionism. In 1931 the Japanese army occupied the Manchurian port of Mukden and moved into southern Manchuria; the next year came the Shanghai incident, in which Japan sent troops to the Chinese port to "protect" Japanese residents and the navy bombed the city. In 1932 the autonomous Japanese Kwangtung Army established the puppet state of Manchukuo in Manchuria, and young army officers assassinated Japan's prime minister, who had opposed the army's intervention. Three years later Japan abrogated the Washington Naval Treaty. The rise of militarism climaxed on February 26, 1936, when the Army First Division seized Tokyo's police headquarters, the War Ministry, and the Diet Building and killed top politicians and government and military leaders. Loyal government troops put down the rebellion after three days, but the attempted coup marked the point of no return on the road to global war.

AFTER SURPRISING Calvin Coolidge by resigning his ambassador's post in protest, Cyrus Woods left the U.S. State Department, returned to his native Pittsburgh, and became active in Pennsylvania politics. Appointed the state's attorney general in 1928, he retired just two years later. One of Japan's strongest defenders, Woods spent the next decade watching in consternation as Japan repudiated democracy and the West and brutally extended its dominion over much of Asia. When he died in 1938 in Philadelphia of Bright's disease at the age of seventy-seven, eulogies hailed him as a gallant figure from a bygone era. Woods, the *New York Times* obituary remarked, "made diplomatic history when, refusing to seek personal safety in flight, he took charge of American Red Cross relief and reconstruction activities and directed them with such efficiency that he became, to the Japanese, one of the outstanding heroes of the disaster."

Like Woods, Frederick Starr never lived to see the final rupture of the American-Japanese relationship. He died of bronchial pneumonia during a research trip to Tokyo in 1933, at the age of seventy-four, still claiming that Japan was a positive force in Asia. Starr's unapologetic defense of the country in the face of growing international criticism, and his continued championing of its religion and culture, had won him a slew of Japanese admirers, though his idiosyncracies attracted suspicion as well. Friends and acquaintances paid tribute to him in a crowded memorial service in Tokyo. "Professor Starr was often taken for a monozuki—an eccentric man who acts merely on the dictates of his pleasures or impulses," remarked Takashi Oda, chairman of Japan's Department of Railways. "So far as I know, nothing was further from the truth. A man of strong will, Dr. Starr was very earnest in doing everything, and once he had determined to do a thing he would have it done at all hazards." In the United States, newspapers and colleagues praised him for his courage and his boundless curiosity, even if some were troubled by his extravagant praise for a country that, by the early 1930s, was showing its aggressive bent. His strong will failed him only at the end, the *New York Times* noted in its lengthy obituary of Starr: "The adventurous scientist, whose research took him into the dark corners of the earth to live for months with savage tribesmen, had [said that] he would live to be 120."

Lieutenant Ellis M. Zacharias became an increasingly important player in the U.S. Far Eastern policy apparatus as countries marched to war. The Florida-born navy man left Tokyo in 1925 to become the head of the Far Eastern Division of the Office of Naval Intelligence in Washington, where he distinguished himself as a leading practitioner of psychological warfare and perhaps America's most astute observer of the growing Japanese threat. Zacharias later testified that he had warned Admiral Husband E. Kimmel, commander of the Pacific Fleet, that the Japanese would attack Pearl Harbor on December 7, 1941, a claim that Kimmel denied. (The admiral retorted, according to the *New York Times,* that Zacharias "had earlier warned him that the Japanese would attack the fleet off Long Beach, Calif., from an airfield in Mexico.") At the time of the U.S. entry into World War II, Zacharias was commanding the cruiser *Salt Lake City,* which avoided destruction at Pearl Harbor, and he participated in the first U.S. counterattacks against the Japanese at the Marshall Islands and Wake Island—the same heavily fortified atolls that Colonel Earl Hancock Ellis had set out to explore on his ill-fated 1923 spy mission from Yokohama. (When the United States occupied Truk, Jaluit, Palau, and other South Sea atolls, they discovered antiquated defenses, old guns, and primitive landing strips, not the heavy fortifications that U.S. Navy Intelligence had led them to expect. Weakness, not strength, was what the Japanese had been trying to conceal from Ellis, Lawrence Zembsch, and other Western spies, Zacharias noted in his memoir.) In the summer of 1945 Zacharias, who spoke fluent Japanese, made a series of broadcasts to civilian and military leaders in Japan urging them to surrender and accept "peace with honor." The broadcasts were ignored, and atomic bombs exploded over Hiroshima and Nagasaki weeks later. Zacharias died, a retired rear admiral, at his summer house in West Springfield, New Hampshire, in 1961 at the age of seventy-one.

Shigeo Tsuchiya, who experienced the disaster as a twelve-year-old schoolboy, lived to see Yokohama rise—and burn—and rise again. Three months after the earthquake, his parents, to relieve financial pressure on the family, sent him to school in the town of Shizuoka on the Izu Peninsula, where he remained until he was a teenager. As a young man he found a job with the Yokohama Shipping Company, a trading firm, and entered the navy at the height of the war in 1944. Tsuchiya was waiting on the island of Kyushu for the U.S. invasion when, he recalled, "I heard that there had been a bomb." He returned home at the end of August 1945 to a destroyed city: U.S. firebombing in May had razed Yokohama for the second time in two decades. "When I arrived at the old Yokohama Station, it was just like the Great Kanto Earthquake—everything was burned. My house again was destroyed. My family was again living in barracks. But this was a better barracks than during the earthquake time. Again, everybody had taken refuge in the Kuboyama Cemetery, and no one in my family had been hurt." Tsuchiya got married, had three sons, one daughter, and six grandchildren, and as of this writing in 2005, lives at the same address where he was born, a few blocks from the Yokohama waterfront. Today, at ninety-five, he is a small, wizened figure with large ears and liver spots on his elfin face. Slightly hard of hearing, he otherwise seems improbably youthful as he dashes through the hallway of a Yokohama ward office, a handler at his side, to talk to a group of retirees about the port's history. He gives several such speeches a week at elementary schools, retirement homes, and community centers and serves as an adviser on senior citizens' affairs to Yokohama city government.

WRIGHT'S IMPERIAL HOTEL suffered damage again in the 1945 aerial bombardment of Tokyo, although "U.S. reporters who visited the hotel last week found that it had stood up remarkably well," *Time* magazine reported weeks after the Japanese surrender. "Some 400 incendiaries had gutted the south wing, burning out 150 bedrooms. Also destroyed was the Imperial's fancy Peacock Hall. The rest of the building was rubble-littered and damaged but usable, and already put to housing U.S. brass hats. Outside, red and white lilies bloomed in the pool. Last week the hotel's management begged Wright . . . to come back and rebuild the gutted wing. Said Wright: let the Japs do it themselves."

In the 1950s the structure began to sink into the loamy soil, a phenomenon that structural engineers blamed partly on the eight-inch-long "pincushion" foundations that Wright had designed to "float" the building on a bed of mud. Cracks appeared in the walls and ceilings, and Tokyo's astringent pollution ate away at the soft green lava rock used by Wright for the building's unique facade. In 1966 the novelist Anthony West proclaimed that the Imperial had become "hideous, inconvenient, inadequate and a depressing eyesore." The following year Tetsuzo Inumaru, now eighty, who had become the hotel's owner and president, announced that the old Imperial would be demolished and a modern eighteen-story hotel would rise in its place. Protests poured in from around the world. The influential architect Kiyoshi Higuchi called the old Imperial "a swan afloat on a lake." Young Japanese architects formed a society to save the hotel as "a symbol of courage and originality." Wright's widow, Olgivanna, then in her seventies, flew in from Taliesin, Wisconsin, in an attempt to persuade Japanese officials to save the "spiritual presence of my husband." The hotel was dismantled in 1969, but its facade was moved to the Meiji Village near Nagoya, a theme park containing remnants of early twentieth-century Japanese architecture. It remains there today, a testament to both Wright's architectural genius and Inumaru's efforts to save the hotel. Called by the *Japan Times* the country's "preeminent hotelier," Inumaru died soon after the dismantling of the old Imperial, and his son became president of its high-rise replacement.

ELIZABETH HENDERSON COTTEN never remarried following the premature death of her husband. She went home to North Carolina and resumed the working life that she had given up for Lyman after the World War. Long after she left Japan, Elizabeth would be recalled with affection by members of the foreign community that had flourished there during the brief golden age between the end of the World War and the earthquake. One fellow expatriate called her "the most admired and beloved American woman who has ever lived in Tokyo." Her marriage to Lyman Cotten, whom she first met in 1895 at a social gathering at R. R. Cotten's plantation in Pitt County, when Lyman was a young Annapolis graduate, was also an object of admiration. A reminiscence from an anonymous friend, contained in Lyman Cotten's papers, captured Cotten's love for the woman whom he often addressed in his correspondence as "Sunshine." "Captain Cotten spoke feelingly of her influence upon him: 'all that is best in me is because of her—the worst is in spite of her. I would be nothing without her.' " She was present at the ceremony in October 1942 in Norfolk, Virginia, when U.S. Secretary of the Navy Frank Knox granted her late husband a small touch of immortality, naming a destroyer in his honor. The navy secretary cited Cotten's record of "serving with honor, bravery and courage" during times of both war and peace.

After a long career as the curator of the Southern Historical Collection at the University of North Carolina, Elizabeth died in February 1975, shortly before her one hundredth birthday. Her gregarious niece, Mary Curtis Henderson, married a North Carolina businessman, Claude C. Ramsey, while in her early twenties and settled down to a domestic life in Salisbury, the Hendersons' hometown. Lyman A. Cotten Jr., who had just arrived at Woodberry Forest boarding school in North Carolina when the catastrophe struck Japan, graduated from the University of North Carolina at Chapel Hill, received a doctorate at Yale University, and went on to a thirty-four-year career as a popular professor of English literature at the University of North Carolina. He died in 1991 at the age of eighty-two. His younger brother, John Cotten, had, like his father, a distinguished naval career and died, age sixty-nine, in 1982.

Thomas J. Ryan rose to the rank of rear admiral and died at the age of sixty-eight in 1969; he was buried at Arlington National Cemetery. When Captain Samuel Robinson retired in March 1932, after forty-eight years at sea and thirty-five years of service in the Pacific Ocean, company officials gave him an elaborate sendoff aboard the *Empress of Canada* in Yokohama. He died in 1958, at the age of eighty-eight. The luxury steamer that made him famous, the *Empress of Australia,* was rebuilt in the mid-1920s into a faster, more economically viable vessel and spent a decade taking wealthy tourists on round-the-world cruises before her refitting at Southampton, England, as a troop transport ship in September 1939. She survived two hazardous voyages to Norway during the German invasion, ferried soldiers to Iceland, Murmansk, and Hong Kong, and was nearly sunk in a German U-boat attack on a convoy in the North Atlantic in 1943 that claimed her sister ship, the *Empress of Asia*. In 1952, forty years after the laying of her keel in Stettin, Germany, the aging ship was sold for scrap.

Other survivors of the Yokohama disaster—Gertrude Cozad, Eva Downes, Ella Brunner, Hayashi Shotaro—disappear into history. No record exists of what they did after the castastrophe, or of the circumstances of their deaths. Their lives, as we know them, are bounded within their memoirs and letters or their appearances in the diaries of others.

In 1934 AKITSUNE IMAMURA, who succeeded Omori as chairman of the Seismology Department at Tokyo Imperial University, left the university and founded his own earthquake and tsunami research facility in the town of Wakayama on the Honshu seacoast. In the 1930s Imamura calculated that Japan's next major temblor would occur in a fault zone west of Osaka and urged the government to upgrade building codes there and to teach earthquake safety methods in schools; again, he was largely ignored. When the Nankai earthquake struck on December 7, 1944, in the area that Imamura had pinpointed, building, road, and bridge collapses killed thirteen hundred people. "All my years of work were in vain," Imamura lamented. He had more success in persuading prefectural authorities to construct a seawall of his own design near the beach town of Wakayama, an innovation widely credited with reducing casualties when a tsunami struck the coast in 1946. Imamura died in 1948 of pneumonia at his home in Seiji Setagaya, a neighborhood of Tokyo, eight years after his retirement. He never gave up his quest for a predictive formula. Until his death at the age of seventy-eight, the *New York Times* reported in its short obituary, "Dr. Imamura had conducted research into the possibility of forecasting earthquakes."

Imamura's primary legacy was that the Japanese government poured vast amounts of money into earthquake prediction research in the following decades. Scientists at several Japanese universities received tens of millions of yen to support projects ranging from constructing logarithmic formulas based on historical models of seismic upheavals, to placing sophisticated measuring devices in active faults across the archipelago, to investigating whether catfish and eels display "unusual movements," such as tail twitching or whisker wiggling, in advance of earthquakes. China and the United States lavished funds on similar research. Predicting earthquakes, however, remained a hit-or-miss proposition, often a matter of luck, and a subject of intense debate within the seismological community. In 1969 the Chinese government under Mao Zedong established a state-of-the-art research facility that tracked a variety of possible earthquake precursors, ranging from ultra-low seismicity to gas emissions to weird animal behavior. "Earthquake prediction was established and advertised as a national policy of the highest priority," seismologist C. B. Raleigh wrote in *Eos* magazine in 1977. After minor earthquakes struck northeast of the city of Haicheng on December 22, 1974, and again on February 3, 1975, accompanied by odd groundwater activity and animal behavior, seismologists at the research facility reportedly issued a warning at 2 P.M. on February 4 that Haicheng itself would be hit within two days. According to Chinese news reports, the Provincial Revolutionary Committee immediately evacuated the city's one hundred thousand residents, and few people were said to have died when a massive temblor, registering 7.4 on the Richter scale, struck Haicheng the same evening. The facility was showered with commendations. "There may well have been a great deal of luck involved in the amazing accuracy of the prediction," wrote Carl Kisslinger, chairman of the American Geophysical Union. "This does not reduce the significance of the first real success achieved anywhere in predicting a destructive earthquake." *Time* magazine published an enthusiastic cover story on earthquake prediction on September 1, 1975, and declared, "Buoyed by their rapid progress in forecasting, scientists are already talking about an even more exciting possibility: actually taming the more destructive convulsions of the earth."

But skeptics dimissed the story of the prediction and the mass evacuation of Haicheng as propaganda, and an authoritative 1988 report stated that nearly twenty thousand people had in fact been killed or injured by the Haicheng earthquake. One year later an 8.0 magnitude earthquake leveled the northern Chinese city of Tangshan, killing 250,000 people, one of the deadliest temblors in history. Not a single one of the indicators that had preceded the Haicheng earthquake had been present before the 1976 catastrophe—a damaging blow to the credibility of would-be earthquake predictors. After two decades of major funding and research, many American seismologists concluded by the mid-1990s that trying to pinpoint the time and place of earthquakes was an impossible task. Although seismologists could estimate, with reasonable accuracy, the number of earthquakes that would strike a given region over a thousand years, "earthquake prediction research has been conducted for over 100 years with no obvious successes," Tokyo University seismologist Robert J. Geller, a longtime critic of such work, wrote in 1997. "Extensive searches have failed to find reliable precursors. . . . Reliable issuing of alarms of imminent earthquakes appears to be effectively impossible." But most Japanese seismologists take a different view, insisting, as Imamura did, that their research is bringing humanity ever closer to the day when earthquakes will be forecast like typhoons and thunderstorms.

EIGHTY-TWO YEARS after the Great Kanto Earthquake, few remnants of the cataclysm remain in either Tokyo or Yokohama. A second wave of destruction—the aerial bombardments of 1944 and 1945— obliterated almost everything that had survived the 1923 disaster. In Tokyo, the musty Earthquake Memorial Hall on the site of the Army Clothing Depot near the Sumida River, an adjacent Buddhist temple filled with lurid oil paintings of the catastrophe, and a few stone bridge trestles over the Sumida River that date back to the Taisho era, are virtually the only reference points that still exist. In Yokohama today, a prosperous industrial metropolis of 3.3 million people, the pier where the *Empress of Australia* once lay berthed, Main and Water Streets, a rebuilt Chinatown, and the Creek, a cement-lined canal leading to Yokohama harbor, faintly trace the outlines of the Taisho-era port. Above the city a handful of reconstructed Victorian villas rise on the Bluff, and officials have kept the shattered foundations of one American family's mansion—the wife was crushed to death in the kitchen— as a testament to the earthquake's power. A visitor can walk to the edge of the precipice overlooking Yokohama harbor and imagine Otis Poole's frightening descent with fire at his back. But only at the Yokohama Foreign Cemetery, sprawling across a nearby hillside, can one really lose oneself in the city that was.

The cemetery is built on an intricate series of terraces, connected by flagstone footpaths that wind through dense groves of birch, maple, and elderberry. A few towering palm trees sway over the cluster of vegetation, fronds withering and browning in the summer heat. Moss grows on 150-year-old retaining walls, and the foliage abounds with the songs of nightingales and the cries of ravens. Weathered tombstones scattered haphazardly across the terraces trace the city's transformation from a Pacific Ocean frontier hamlet to the City of Raw Silk.

At the base of the hill, in the oldest part of the cemetery, one can find the tomb of Charles Richardson, a vacationing Shanghai merchant who was stabbed by samurai on the Tokaido while out for a horseback ride with friends in September 1862. "Native of Shanghai," the inscription reads, "cruelly assassinated by the Japanese." On a terrace above rests a U.S. soldier, Sergeant John Smith, who died of undisclosed causes in Yokohama in August 1871, one of scores of military men buried in this Far Eastern graveyard thousands of miles from their native countries. The epitaph reads: "Far from his home and under here / lies a loving husband and father dear / His career through life none could excel / And as a soldier did his duty well." A small section of gravestones with lettering in Hebrew and English recalls the panicked flight of thousands of White Russians, including many Jews, from Siberia following the withdrawal of Japanese troops in October 1922. One inscription reads: "Jacob L. Kurlyandsky, born in Nikolaevsk-on-Amur, Siberia 1890, died Kanagawa, 1978." And scattered throughout the graveyard, in no apparent order, lie victims of the earthquake.

Names call up images, inscriptions evoke the fire and the terror, the pain and the prayers. On a tiny square block: "Jennie M. Kuyper, April 3, 1872–September 1, 1923. 'Thy Will Be Done.' " A sloping red granite slab in the shape of a scroll reads: "In Memory of a Beloved Daughter, Minnie R. Robinson of Yokohama, who died on the 4th of September on Board the S.S. Dongola from wounds received in the great earthquake." Not far away a white marble column stands above a mass grave: "To the memory of unidentified members of the Yokohama United Club. Killed in the earthquake of September 1, 1923. Erected by their fellow members." In the torpid heat of the Japanese summer a gentle breeze blows from Tokyo Bay and rustles the pines and the palm trees. Soft rays of sunlight filter through the tangle of branches that enclose the cemetery and cast a luminous glow on 150-year-old markers whose epitaphs long ago faded into illegibility. It is possible to shut out the modern world for a few moments here and imagine Yokohama on a glistening Saturday morning, serene and confident, before the earth trembled.

NOTES

Prologue: September 1, 1923

The entire description of Shigeo Tsuchiya's childhood and his activities on the day of the earthquake is taken from two two-hour-long interviews that I conducted with him in Yokohama in July 2004.

1: City of Silk

I assembled the portrait of the early foreign settlement of Yokohama from a number of sources, most of which I found at the Yokohama Historical Archive, which contains a trove of information about the nineteenth-century port. Besides the sources mentioned below, I gathered useful detail from "Reminiscences of Yokohama," John P. Mollison's lecture delivered in 1909 at the Yokohama United Club, found in the Don Brown Collection at the Yokohama Historical Archive; the diaries of Townsend Harris, 1856–1858, which I found in the Manuscripts Collection at the Library of Congress; *Yokohama Yarns*, a collection of short stories about the port published by Kelly & Walsh Ltd. of Hong Kong in 1905; Douglas Sladen's *The Club Hotel Guide: How to Spend a Month in Tokyo and Yokohama* (Yokohama: R. Meiklejohn, 1890); *Murder on the Bluff: The Carew Poisoning Case*, by Molly Whittington-Egan (Glasgow, Scotland: Neil Wilson Publishing, 1996); and *The Social Directory of Tokyo and Yokohama 1914*, compiled and published by Ava J. Hamilton Seabrook and James Branner Melton in Yokohama.

Details of the Earl Hancock Ellis espionage case came from several sources, including Ellis M. Zacharias's 1946 memoir, *Secret Missions: The Story of an Intelligence Officer,* published by G. P. Putnam's Sons; *A Marine Corps Son: Col. Earl Hancock Ellis, the Prophecy of War and a Mysterious Death,* a booklet by Justin H. Libby of Purdue University; the 1922 and 1923 diary entries of Lyman Atkinson Cotten, contained in the Southern Historical Collection at the University of North Carolina at Chapel Hill; and *Pete Ellis: An Am-*

phibious Warfare Prophet, 1880–1923 by Dirk Anthony Ballendorf and Merrill Lewis Bartlett (Annapolis, Md.: Naval Institute Press, 1996).

5   *"California adventurers, Portuguese desperadoes":* Neil Pedlar, *The Imported Pioneers* (Tokyo: Japan Library, 1990), p. 61.

6   *"dwellers from Mesopotamia":* Bell's Life in Yokohama, September 21, 1878, p. 2.

6   *"Nowhere is there a greater influx":* Harold S. Williams, *Tales of the Foreign Settlements* (Tokyo: Charles E. Tuttle Company, 1958), "History of Yokohama" chapter.

6   *"carelessness on the part of the natives":* from the unsigned article "A Night with Japanese Firemen" in Charles Dickens's *All the Year Round* magazine, December 1, 1877.

6   *"In moving [to Yokohama]":* Japan Times Overland Mail, March 19, 1869, cited in Williams, *Tales of the Foreign Settlements.*

7   *"A deplorable scene of demoralization":* Ibid.

7   *"Two officers showed":* Pedlar, *The Imported Pioneers.*

8   *"gave me a blow or push":* Samuel Eliot Morison, *Old Bruin: Commodore Matthew C. Perry: The American Naval Officer Who Helped Found Liberia, Hunted Pirates in the West Indies, Practised Diplomacy with the Sultan of Turkey and the King of the Two Sicilies: Commanded the Gulf Squadron in the Mexican War, Promoted the Steam Navy and the Shell Gun, and Conducted the Naval Expedition Which Opened Japan* (Boston: Little Brown and Company, 1967).

8   *"conformed to the conventional Japanese manner":* Ibid.

8   *"He was a blunt, yet dignified man":* Quoted in William Elliot Griffis, *Matthew Calbraith Perry: A Typical American Naval Officer* (Boston: Cupples and Hurd, 1887).

8   *"In my former commands upon the coasts of Africa":* Quoted in Morison, *Old Bruin.*

9   *"People in the town made such a fuss":* Ibid.

10   *"The dwellings indicated little thrift":* Williams, *Tales of the Foreign Settlements.*

10   *"establish firm, lasting and sincere friendship":* M. Nakada, *The City of Yokohama Past and Present* (Yokohama: Yokohama Publishing Office, 1908).

10   *"long straggling town":* John R. Black, *Young Japan: Yokohama and Edo* (London: Trubner & Co., 1880–1881).

10   *"the largest ship may ride":* Joseph Heco, quoted in Nakada, *The City of Yokohama.*

10   *"We turned down the main street":* Alcock, quoted in Williams, *Tales of the Foreign Settlements.*

14   *"the best mixed drinks"* in town: Japan Gazette, September 10, 1874.

14   *"the most colossal combination troupe":* Ibid.

16   *"Vermilion paper":* Scidmore, cited in Burritt Sabin, *A Historical Guide to Yokohama; Sketches of the Twice Risen Phoenix* (Yokohama: Yurindo Co., 2002).

17   *"evil smells":* Katherine Baxter, quoted in Sabin, *A Historical Guide.*

17   *"exciting drunk":* Jack London, quoted in Williams, *Tales of the Foreign Settlements.*

17   *"completely free of tradition":* Heiner Fruehauf, Urban Exoticism and Its Sino-Japanese Scenery 1910–1923," *Asian and African Studies* 6 (1997), 140.

17   *"I have grown tired":* Ibid., p. 138.

17   *"a timeworn playhouse":* Tanizaki, quoted in Sabin, *A Historical Guide.*

17   *"I want to breathe in":* Kaoru, quoted in Sabin, *A Historical Guide.*

18   *"a riot of loud Western colors":* Tanizaki, quoted in Sabin, *A Historical Guide.*

18 *"To the traveler"*: Frederick S. Starr, *Fujiyama* (Chicago: Covici-McGree Company, 1924), chapter 1.

19 *"may be found everywhere"*: Quoted in Nakada, *The City of Yokohama*.

19 " *'Hold tight'* ": quoted in Pedlar, *The Imported Pioneers*, p. 78.

21 *"Silkworm-raising peasants"*: J. Ellis Barker, *The Rural Industries of Japan* (Yokohama: Yokohama Seishi Bunsha, 1906).

21 *"The City of Raw Silk"*: *A Short Story of Raw Silk* (Yokohama: Central Raw Silk Association of Japan, 1933), p. 2.

22 *"The Prince motored"*: *Japan Gazette*, April 23, 1922.

22 *"Everyone is congratulating themselves"*: *Japan Gazette*, April 29, 1922.

23 *"Those who have lived for years"*: Ibid.

24 *"find out what the hell"*: Ellis M. Zacharias, *Secret Missions: The Story of an Intelligence Officer* (New York: G. P. Putnam's Sons, 1946), chapter 5.

24 *"We could never understand"*: Ibid.

24 *"He was unshaved, unkempt"*: Ibid.

2: The Morning Before

I obtained details about the landscape and history of the mountain resort of Chuzenji during a visit to the lake on July 6, 2004. A small museum on the lakeshore, on the grounds of the former Italian summer consulate, offers a variety of historical displays and photographs as well as a short video about the expatriate community before World War II. The reconstruction of Lyman Cotten's morning at the lake came from his diaries and letters to family members in the United States and Elizabeth Henderson Cotten's letters. I also culled biographical information about Cotten and his naval career from newspaper articles contained in the Cotten Collection. For the political background of Japan between the wars and American-Japanese relations, I consulted a variety of sources, including Ellis M. Zacharias's *Secret Missions*; Cotten's diaries; issues of the *Japan Weekly Chronicle* from 1920 to 1923 in the Yokohama Historical Archive; interviews with Justin Libby, Purdue University professor of Japanese history and the author of the short work on Earl Hancock Ellis; the definitive work about post–Great War Japanese society and politics, *Japan under Taisho Tenno*, by Arthur Morgan Young (London: Allen & Unwin, 1928); and *Society and the State in Interwar Japan*, an anthology of articles published by Routledge in 1997 and edited by Elise K. Tipton.

I consulted numerous sources to piece together the life of the anthropologist Frederick Starr. Those not sourced below include a transcript of the 1920 Darrow-Starr debate "Is the Human Race Getting Anywhere?" archived at the Harvard Law School Library (Chicago: Maclaskey & Maclaskey Shorthand Reporters, 1920); Adam Hochschild's *King Leopold's Ghost: A Story of Greed, Terror, and Heroism in Colonial Africa* (New York: Warner Books, 1999); and "Shinto: The Native Religion of Japan, an address given at Abraham Lincoln Centre by Frederick Starr on Sunday, March 28, 1915" (reprinted from *Unity,* April 22, 1915). Background about the formation of the new cabinet and Crown Prince Hirohito's movements on the day of the earthquake came from articles in the *Japan Weekly Chronicle* ("Yamamoto as Premier: A Second Term" in the September 6, 1923, issue), the *Japan Advertiser* ("Japan Press Comment on Topics of the Day," August 31, 1923), and the *Japan Times.* For foreshadowings of the Great Kanto Earthquake in the months before the temblor I consulted a *New York Times* article of September 9, 1923, "Series of Shocks All Over Pacific: Widespread Death and Ruin Began Last November in Chile"; articles in the *Japan Weekly Chronicle;* as well as a booklet I found in the Diet Library in Tokyo: *The Japanese Disaster or The World's Greatest Earthquake: Together with Missionary Travels and Experiences by Evangelist B. S. Moore and Wife. Ten Years in Japan* (New York: Pentecostal Searchlight, 1923).

Details about the planned opening-day banquet at the Imperial Hotel came from Noel F. Busch's *Two Minutes to Noon* (New York: Simon & Schuster, 1962) and background about Frank Lloyd Wright's project came from many sources. These included *The Imperial at 100,* a booklet published by the hotel on the centennial of the original Imperial's construction in 1890; *An Autobiography* by Frank Lloyd Wright (New York: Horizon Press, 1972); "In the Cause of Architecture: The New Imperial Hotel, Tokio, Frank Lloyd Wright, Architect" by Frank Lloyd Wright, *Western Architect* magazine, April 1923; "The Seismic Legend of the Imperial Hotel," *AIA Journal,* June 1980; "Imperial Hotel Tokyo Japan" by Julius Floto in *Architectural Record,* February 1924; and two articles by Louis H. Sullivan in *Architectural Record,* "Concerning the Imperial Hotel" in April 1923 and "Reflections on the Tokyo Disaster" in February 1924.

27 *"I often miss the years of work":* Letter of Elizabeth Henderson Cotten to her sister Mary, December 12, 1922, Lyman A. Cotten papers, Southern Historical Collection, University of North Carolina at Chapel Hill.

28 *"John is swimming":* Letter from Lyman A. Cotten to his son, Lyman Jr., in the United States, August 14, 1923, Lyman A. Cotten papers, University of North Carolina.

30 *"The army quartermaster":* Letter from Lyman A. Cotten to Elizabeth Henderson Cotten, July 15, 1923, Lyman A. Cotten papers, University of North Carolina.

30 worried that *"radicals":* Letter from Lyman A. Cotten to his parents, Mr. and Mrs. R. R. Cotten, August 14, 1923, Lyman A. Cotten papers, University of North Carolina.

31 *"We ran into a terrific thunder storm":* Letter from Elizabeth Cotten to her parents, August 15, 1923, Lyman A. Cotten papers, University of North Carolina.

31 *"Kato was a man of splendid character"*: Lyman A. Cotten diary entry, August 25, 1923, volume 25, diaries 1923–24, Lyman A. Cotten papers, University of North Carolina.

32 *"Lyman has been ordered"*: Letter from Elizabeth Henderson Cotten to her mother, January 3, 1922, Lyman A. Cotten papers, University of North Carolina.

33 *"There were cliques and cabals"*: Zacharias, *Secret Missions*, chapter 5.

34 *"Japan was never really an ally"*: Quoted in "Warns of Japan as Peril to World," *New York Times*, December 18, 1922, p. 17.

35 *"If all possibilities"*: "Prepare for War with America," *Tokyo Nichi Nichi*, cited in "The Prelude to the Washington Conference for Arms Reduction," *Japan Weekly Chronicle*, August 4, 1921.

35 *"Perhaps the most important duty"*: Article in Bruce, North Carolina, weekly newspaper, February 12, 1922, Lyman A. Cotten Papers, University of North Carolina.

36 *"One has to have the training"*: Lyman A. Cotten diary entry, October 18, 1922, volume 23, private notes 1922–23, Lyman A. Cotten papers, University of North Carolina.

37 *"I should say"*: Letter from Lyman A. Cotten to Elizabeth Henderson Cotten, July 16, 1923, Lyman A. Cotten papers, University of North Carolina.

37 *"He has the reputation"*: Letter from Lyman A. Cotten to Robert and Sallie Cotten, August 14, 1923, Lyman A. Cotten papers, University of North Carolina.

37 *"I believe that [Woods] is jealous"*: Letter from Capt. Luke McNamee, U.S. Naval Intelligence, Washington, to Lyman A. Cotten, May 21, 1923, Lyman A. Cotten papers, University of North Carolina.

37 *"You may be sure"*: Letter from Lyman A. Cotten to U.S. Naval Intelligence officer Capt. Luke McNamee, June 22, 1923, Lyman A. Cotten papers, University of North Carolina.

38 *"the awfully depressing weather"*: Lyman A. Cotten diary entry, July 29, 1923, volume 25, 1923–24, Lyman A. Cotten papers, University of North Carolina.

39 with *"graying hair"*: Frederick S. Starr, *The Ainu Group at the Saint Louis Exhibition* (Chicago: Open Court Publishing Company, 1904).

40 *"We white men"*: Ibid.

40 *"It is doubtful whether the Congo native"*: Frederick S. Starr, *The Truth about the Congo* (Chicago: Forbes & Co., 1907).

40 *"It is true that there are floggings"*: Ibid.

41 the *"splendid cone"*: Starr, *Fujiyama*, chapter 1.

41 *"I am glad to see him"*: Letter from Frederick Starr to his mother, August 14, 1923, personal correspondence 1876–1930, Frederick Starr papers, University of Chicago Library, Department of Special Collections.

42 *"We looked down"*: Starr, *Fujiyama*, chapter 1.

42 *"I presume except for mountain summit cold"*: Frederick Starr, diary entry, August 27, 1923, Frederick Starr papers, University of Chicago.

43 *"a fine cassava"*: Frederick Starr, diary entry, September 1, 1923, Frederick Starr papers, University of Chicago.

43 *"Takagi talked of"*: Frederick Starr, diary entry, August 31, 1923, Frederick Starr papers, University of Chicago.

43 *"I shall be a prisoner"*: Ibid.

44 *"His face displayed"*: Lyman A. Cotten diary entry, May 3, 1922, volume 23, private notes 1922–23, Lyman A. Cotten papers, University of North Carolina.

45 *"links in the chain"*: T. J. See, quoted in "Pressure of Undersea Disturbances in Abyss Five Miles Deep Caused Earthquake; Submarine Range a Factor," *New York Times*, September 9, 1923.

45 a *"great free spirit"*: Louis H. Sullivan, "Concerning the Imperial Hotel Tokyo, Japan," *Architectural Record*, April 1923, p. 334.

46 the *"last resource"*: Frank Lloyd Wright, *An Autobiography* (New York: Horizon Press, 1972), p. 243.

46 *"As I lay there"*: Ibid., p. 244.

48 *"There is something peculiar"*: Kakue Washio, in *Collection of Survival Stories from the Great Kanto Earthquake (Kanto Daishinsai Taiken Kirokushuu)* (Tokyo: Sumida Ward local government printing office, 1985); passage translated by Taeko Kawamura.

3: On the Waterfront

For my portrait of Yokohama on the morning of the earthquake I consulted articles in the *Japan Gazette*, Yokohama's English daily; the *Japan Weekly Chronicle;* the *Japan Advertiser;* and *The City of Yokohama, Past and Present*. The reconstruction of Lois Crane's morning came from letters of Lyman and Elizabeth Cotten found in the Lyman A. Cotten Collection. I obtained details about the *Empress of Australia* from *The Pacific Empresses: An Illustrated History of Canadian Pacific Railway's Empress Liners on the Pacific Ocean* by Robert D. Turner (Sono Nis Press, Victoria, British Columbia, 1981); information about the ship's movements in the hours before the earthquake came from articles in the *Japan Gazette* on August 30 and 31, 1923. Gertrude Cozad's story came from her unpublished manuscript about the catastrophe, *Account of the experiences of Miss Gertrude Cozad in the earthquake at Yokohama, Japan September 1 to September 4 1923*, which I found in the Manuscripts Room at the Boston Athenaeum Library, unopened since it was donated in 1924. The story of Akio Hatano's and Takeo Arishima's double suicide was taken from articles in the *New York Times* and the *Japan Advertiser* in the summer of 1923.

The portrait of the Grand Hotel was pieced together from several sources, including *A Historical Guide to Yokohama: Sketches of the Twice-Risen Phoenix* by Burritt Sabin; *Guide Book for Yokohama*, by Nobushige Amenomori, published by the Grand Hotel, Yokohama, 1898; *Yokohama Guide* (F. R. Wetmore & Co., Yokohama, 1874); *The City of Yokohama Past and Present* compiled by M. Nakada; the diaries of Lyman Cotten; *Hotels in the Orient, Africa, Mexico and Canada*, a guidebook published in 1927; and articles in the *Japan Gazette, Japan Advertiser*, and *Japan Weekly Chronicle*.

The arrival in Yokohama of the Babbitt family is detailed in Mrs. Douglas Adam's lengthy article for the September 20, 1923, issue of the *Chronicle*, "Yokohama Survivors: Tragedies and Escapes." The *Japan Gazette* provided further information about the Babbitts. Ensign Thomas J. Ryan gave an account of that morning and afternoon in a letter he sent to the Cotten family a week after the earthquake; I found it in the Lyman A. Cotten Collection at the University of North Carolina. For the headlines of September 1, I consulted the pages of the *Chicago Tribune*, the *New York Times*, and the *Washington Post*. Shigeo Tsuchiya provided me with a thorough account of that morning in two interviews I conducted with him in Yokohama in July 2004. The snapshot of the movements of other residents of Yokohama just before the earthquake came from several sources, including *The Death of Old Yokohama in the Great Japanese Earthquake of 1923* by Otis Manchester Poole (George Allen and Unwin Ltd., London, 1968); articles in the *Japan Weekly Chronicle* and the *Japan Gazette; A Memorial: Miss Jennie M. Kuyper, Principal of Ferris Seminary, Yokohama, Japan, who lost her life in the earthquake, September 1, 1923*, a pamphlet published that year by the Women's Board of Foreign Missions, Reformed Church of America, in New York, and found at the Columbia University Library; *The Pacific Empresses* by Robert T. Turner; and a letter from Eva Downes of Peking Union Medical College that I found in the Roger Sherman Greene Papers at Harvard University's Lamont Library.

53 *"in good season"*: "An Account of the Experiences of Miss Gertrude Cozad in the earthquake at Yokohama, Japan September 1 to September 4 1923," unpublished manuscript, Boston Athenaeum Library.
54 *"I . . . said my goodbye"*: Ibid.
54 *"The Company can safely challenge"*: Nobushige Amenomori, *Guide Book for Yokohama, Grand Hotel* (Yokohama: Grand Hotel, 1898), p. 1.
55 *"The fish, entrees"*: Dresser, quoted in Shunro Kusama, "The Beginnings of Western Food Culture in Yokohama: Food, and Wines and Spirits in Hotels and Restaurants," online publication (Yokohama: Yokohama Association for International Communications and Exchanges, 2000).
56 *"veranda that affords its occupants"*: Amenomori, *Guide Book for Yokohama.*
57 *"Seven years ago"*: *Japan Weekly Chronicle*, August 19, 1923.
58 *"they will go to China"*: *Japan Gazette*, August 31, 1923.
58 a *"beautiful romance"*: *Japan Gazette*, August 29, 1923.
58 *"joke of the day"*: *Japan Gazette*, August 31, 1923.
59 *"foreigners cannot be allowed"*: *Japan Advertiser*, August 25, 1923, p. 15.
60 *"For the last few days"*: Lyman A. Cotten, diary entry, August 28, 1923, volume 25, Lyman A. Cotten papers, University of North Carolina.
61 *"The weather had cleared"*: Unpublished letter by Eva Downes and Mrs. Macmillan of the Peking Union Medical College, Roger Sherman Greene Papers, Houghton Library, Harvard University, Cambridge, MA.

4: The Catfish and the Keystone

Background on the mythology of Japanese earthquakes came from *Two Minutes to Noon: The Story of the Great Tokyo Earthquake and Fire* by Noel E. Busch; "Histoires de Poissons-Chats: Les Images du grand seisme de 1855 a Edo" by Jean-Michel Butel and Pascal Griolet, contained in a 1999 special Japanese earthquake edition of *Ebisu (Etudes Japonaises)* published by the Maison Franco-Japonaise in Tokyo; "The Relationship between Catfish and Earthquakes," published on the Internet by the Tokai University Seismology Department; and a lengthy interview that I conducted on July 11, 2004, with Tsuguo Hagiwara, the head Shinto priest at the Kashima Shrine in Ibaraki Prefecture, Japan. Hagiwara presented me with a book in Japanese, *The Catfish Pictures Collection,* an anthology of *namazue* inspired by the 1855 Ansei earthquake; several of the originals are on display in the Department of Seismology at Tokyo University. My description of the shrine comes from my day-long visit there in July 2004. I found J. J. Rein's quote about the 1855 earthquake in *The Great Tokyo Earthquake: September 1, 1923: Experiences and Impressions of an Eye-Witness* by Joseph Dahlmann, translated and adapted from the German by Victor F. Gettleman, published by the America Press in New York City in 1924. Information about Japan's long history of seismic disasters came primarily from *The Great Earthquake in Japan: October 28, 1891, Being a full description of the disasters resulting from the recent terrible catastrophe, taken from the accounts in the Hyogo News by its Special Correspondent and from other sources,* published by Hyogo News in Kobe in 1892. The account of the December 1854 earthquake and tsunami in Shimoda, Japan, came from the second volume of *Narrative of the Expedition of an American Squadron to the China Seas and Japan Performed in the Years 1852, 1853, and 1854 Under the Command of Commodore MC Perry USN by order of the government of the United States.*

  John Milne: Father of Modern Seismology by L. K. Herbert-Gustar and P. A. Nott (Paul Norbury Publications, Tenterden, Kent, United Kingdom, 1980) is a thorough account of the life of the pioneering seismologist, the atmosphere at Tokyo Imperial University, and the state of seismological research in the nineteenth century. I also consulted *Transactions of the Seismological Society of Japan* 10 (1887), published in Yokohama at the office of the *Japan Mail,* for material about the scientific investigations into earthquakes that were going on at the time. I drew the account of the discovery of the Tuscarora Deep in 1874 from Captain George E. Belknap's *Deep Sea Soundings in the North Pacific Ocean Obtained in the United States Steamer Tuscarora,* published by the U.S. Government Printing Office in 1874; and in "Something about Deep-Sea Sounding," also by Belknap, contained in the *United*

Service Almanac of 1879. (Both of these were found in the Louis Agassiz Library at the Harvard Museum of Comparative Zoology.) My writing about the state of seismology at the time of the Great Kanto Earthquake is based on a *New York Times* article from September 9, 1923, "Pressure of Under Sea Disturbances in Abyss Five Miles Deep Caused Earthquake; Submarine Range a Factor." Edgar W. Woolard's essay "The Japanese Earthquake" appeared in the *Review of Reviews* 68, no. 4, published in New York in October 1923.

I summarized the theory of plate tectonics based on several sources, including one of the most popular textbooks on the subject, *Earthquakes* by Bruce A. Bolt (W.H. Freeman, New York, 2002); *The Earth: An Introduction to Physical Geology,* 4th ed., by E. J. Tarbuck and F. K. Lutgens (Macmillan, New York, 1993); and interviews and e-mail exchanges with Dr. Robert Geller, professor of seismology at Tokyo University; Paul Somerville, a former professor at California Institute of Technology and a geophysicist with the URS Corporation in Pasadena, California; and Phillip Hogan, a marine geologist with URS.

Several biographies and newspaper articles in Japanese provided rich detail about the life of Akitsune Imamura and his feud with Fusakichi Omori. These include "The Self Believer: Pioneer of Earthquake Prediction Imamura Akitsune" by Makoto Sakae, an April 19, 2004, retrospective article in the *Sankei* newspaper; *The Life of Akitsune Imamura* by Fumiko Yamashita (Seijisha Press, Tokyo, 1989); and *Japanese Seismology (Nippon no Jishingaku)* by Yoichiro Fujii (Kinokuniya Publishers, Tokyo, 1967). For a description of Imamura's birthplace, Kagoshima, and of Mount Sakurajima, I drew on "Sakurajima, Japan's Greatest Volcanic Earthquake," by T. A. Jaggar, director of the Hawaiian Volcano Observatory, in *National Geographic,* April 1924.

The summary of Imamura's theories about earthquakes I drew largely from the aforementioned works as well as from *Theoretical and Applied Seismology* by Imamura, published in Tokyo by Maruzen Co. in 1937. Imamura's description of the physical characteristics of seismologists I took from *The Control of Earthquakes (Jishin no Seifuku)* by Imamura. The police blotter of 1909 and the description of the Kanda fire of 1913 were found in *The Nightside of Japan* by T. Fujimoto (T. Werner Laurie Ltd., London, 1914), part of the Don Brown Collection at the Yokohama Historical Archive. Imamura's analysis of the San Francisco earthquake and fires is part of his *Theoretical and Applied Seismology.*

Imamura talks about his trip to climb volcanoes in northern Japan in his two-page "A Diary of the Great Earthquake," and I found more detail about the journey in "The Self Believer: Pioneer of Earthquake Prediction Imamura Akitsune" by Makoto Sakae. For a description of Mount Tarumai and the surrounding landscape I drew on *Unbeaten Tracks in Japan: An account of travels in the interior including visits to the aborigines of Yezo and the shrine of Nikko* by Isabella L. Bird, published by John Murray in 1911. The account of Imamura's activities that morning and during the Hokkaido trip comes from a variety of sources, including "The Self Believer: Pioneer of Earthquake Prediction Imamura Akitsune"; *The Life of Akitsune Imamura* by Fumiko Yamashita (Seijisha Press, Tokyo, 1989); and Imamura's two-page "A Diary of the Great Earthquake."

64 *torrent of "hail"*: Eyewitness, quoted in Starr, *Fujiyama*, chapter 1.
64 *According to the great Japanese seismologist:* Charles Davidson, "Fusakichi Omori and His Work on Earthquakes," *Bulletin of the Seismological Society of America,* July 1923.
64 *"the secret place of God"*: Interview with Tsuguo Hagiwara, head Shinto priest at Kashima Shrine, Ibaraki Prefecture, Japan, July 11, 2004.
64 *"Yedo was turned into a rubbish heap"*: J. J. Rein, quoted in *The Great Earthquake in Japan: October 28, 1891. Being a Full Description of the Disasters Resulting from the Terrible Catastrophe, taken from the accounts in the Hyogo News by its Special Correspondent and from other sources* (Kobe: Hyogo News Publishers, 1892).
65 *"While I was absent"*: *The Catfish Pictures Collection,* an anthology of *namazue,* translated by Taeko Kawamura.
65 *"Every house and building"*: H. A. Adams, quoted in *Narrative of the Expedition of An American Squadron to the China Seas and Japan Performed in the Year 1852, 1853, 1854 under the Command of Commodore M. C. Perry USN by order of the government of the United States, volume 2* (Washington: U.S. Government Printing Office, 1856).
66 *"What the public imagine"*: John Milne, quoted in Robert J. Geller, "Earthquake Prediction: A Critical Review," *Geophysical Journal International,* no. 131 (1997):425.
67 *"pheasants scream"*: L. K. Herbert-Gustar and P. A. Nott, *John Milne: Father of Modern Seismology* (Kent, UK: Paul Norbury Publications Ltd., 1980), pp. 85–86.
67 *"Perhaps no problem"*: Capt. George E. Belknap, "Something about Deep-Sea Sounding," *United Service Almanac* #1, no. 2 (April 1879): 161.
68 *"rope, cod-line"*: Ibid., p. 162.
68 *"wire spooling machine"*: Ibid., p. 181.
68 *"the Thomson machine"*: Capt. George E. Belknap, "Something about Deep-Sea Sounding," *United Service Almanac* 1, no. 4 (July 1879): 355.
68 *Departing Yokohama on July 9, 1874:* Ibid., p. 362.
69 *"These deep casts"*: Ibid.
69 *"Several soundings"*: Quoted in ibid. p. 363.
70 *"It is not necessary"*: T. J. See, quoted in "Pressure of Undersea Disturbances in Abyss Five Miles Deep Caused Earthquake; Submarine Range a Factor," *New York Times,* September 9, 1923.
70 *"slowly tilting"*: Henry S. Washington, quoted in "Disaster Originated in Depths of Ocean," *New York Times,* September 9, 1923, p. 21.

70 *"The rocks are held":* Edgard W. Woolard, "The Japanese Earthquake," *The Review of Reviews* 68, no. 4 (October 1923).

71 *"Destructive earthquakes":* "Position of Australia Just Outside Earthquake Zone," *The Age* (Australia), September 4, 1923.

75 *"Light stones were blown out":* T. A. Jaggar, "Sakurajima, Japan's Greatest Volcanic Earthquake," *National Geographic,* April 1924.

78 *"foremost living authority":* Makoto Sake, "The Self-Believer."

78 *"act of foolishness":* Ibid.

78 *"At the time when":* Quoted in Fumiyo Yamashita, *The Life of Akitsune Imamura* (Tokyo: Seijisha Press, 1989), translated by Taeko Kawamura.

78 *"the biggest shame":* Ibid.

79 *"Should inflammable liquids":* Akitsune Imamura, *Theoretical and Applied Seismology* (Tokyo: Maruzen Co., 1937), p. 336.

80 *"That should do it":* "The Self-Believer: Pioneer of Earthquake Prediction Imamura Akitsune," *Sankei,* April 19, 2004, translated by Taeko Kawamura.

80 *"sweating profusely":* Yamashita, *The Life of Akitsune Imamura.*

82 *"a sea of fire":* T. Fujimoto, *The Nightside of Japan* (London: T. Werner Laurie Ltd., 1917).

81 *"Owing to breakage of the mains":* Imamura, *Theoretical and Applied Seismology,* p. 331.

81 *"The fire departments of large [Japanes] cities:"* Imamura, *Theoretical and Applied Seismology,* pp. 333–334.

82 *Based on his studies:* "Position of Australia," *The Age;* Sake, "The Self-Believer."

83 *"With bare gray top":* Isabella L. Bird, *Unbeaten Tracks in Japan* (Palo Alto: Traveler's Tales Guides, 2000), letter 39.

84 *"Beautiful day":* Akitsune Imamura, journal of August 24, 1923, quoted in Yamashita, *The Life of Akitsune Imamura.*

84 *"a great city that is a gigantic village":* Wright, *An Autobiography,* p. 229.

85 *"To have lived through":* Basil Hall Chamberlain, *Things Japanese: Being Notes on Various Subjects Connected with Japan for the Use of Travelers* (London: J. Murray, 1898).

5: Inferno

The description of the fault zone slippage beneath Sagami Bay and the seismic waves' journey from the focal point near Oshima to Yokohama was drawn from interviews with Professors Geller and Somerville and Phillip Hogan, as well as from Akitsune Imamura's diary. I pieced together the account of the collapse of the Yokohama pier from disparate sources. These included Ellis Zacharias's *Secret Missions;* the letter of Eva Downes; and the testament of a passenger on board the SS *Philoctetes* that appeared in the September 6, 1923 issue of the *Japan Weekly Chronicle,* entitled "Destruction of Yokohama; Experiences of Eye-Witness. Graphic Account of Scene from Harbour." I also relied on the "Official Report of Captain S. Robinson, R.N.R., Commander of the Canadian Pacific S.S. Empress of Australia, on the Japanese Earthquake, the Fire, and Subsequent Relief Operations," on file at Harvard's Widener Library; and

"Diary from September 1st, 1923 to time of sailing from Yokohama on the 'Empress of Australia,' September 12th, at 8 P.M." by John W. Doty and W. W. Johnston, found at the Library of Congress in Washington.

Thomas Ryan's graphic account of the earthquake was drawn from the letter he wrote to Lyman and Elizabeth Cotten, in the University of North Carolina's Southern Historical Collection. Lois Crane's survival story is taken secondhand from letters written by Elizabeth Henderson Cotten and Lyman Cotten; Gertrude Cozad's account can be found in her letter in the Boston Athenaeum collection; and Shigeo Tsuchiya provided his tale of escape in our two interviews in Yokohama. The descriptions of the collapse of the Yokohama United Club and the French, British, and U.S. Consulates are taken from eyewitness accounts that appeared in the *Japan Weekly Chronicle* on September 6, 13, and 20, 1923. Ulysses Webb, chief administrator of the American Naval Hospital, told his dramatic story in a report to the secretary of the navy filed aboard the USS *Huron* in Yokohama on September 11, 1923, and kept on file at the Library of Congress. Poole's narrative comes from *The Death of Old Yokohama*. The interview with the survivor who watched Yokohama collapse, and the account of the resident who tried to free the doomed Mrs. Komor from the wreckage of her antiques shop, are taken from Henry W. Kinney's excellent *Atlantic Monthly* article "Earthquake Days," published in January 1924.

88   *"The smiles vanished"*: Zacharias, *Secret Missions*, chapter 7.

88   *A "tremendous jolt"*: Eva Downes, unpublished letter, Roger Sherman Greene Papers, Houghton Library, Harvard University.

88   *"The huge pier"*: Zacharias, *Secret Missions*, chapter 7.

88   *jolts "similar to"*: "Destruction in Yokohama: Experiences of Eye-Witness. Graphic Accounts of Scene from Harbour," *Japan Weekly Chronicle*, September 6, 1923, p. 339.

89   *"Another quake like that"*: Noel F. Busch, *Two Minutes to Noon: The Story of the Great Tokyo Earthquake and Fire* (New York: Simon & Schuster, 1962), p. 65.

89   *"For a moment"*: "Official Report of Captain S. Robinson, R.N.R., Commander of the Canadian Pacific S.S. Empress of Australia, on the Japanese Earthquake, the Fire, and Subsequent Relief Operations," p. 1.

91   *"A merciful death"*: Cozad, "An Account."

92   *"Children, get out of the house"*: Interview with Shigeo Tsuchiya, Yokohama Ward Office, July 9, 2004.

93   *"What's that?"*: "The Death of the French Consul," *Japan Weekly Chronicle*, September 13, 1923, p. 375.

94   *"a great and most painful pressure"*: "Report of Disaster by Ulysses Webb, Commanding Officer, U.S. Naval Hospital, Yokohama, Japan, aboard the U.S. Huron, September 11, 1923," addressed to the secretary of the navy, Library of Congress, Manuscripts Division, p. 2.

94   *For "half a minute"*: Otis Manchester Poole, *The Death of Old Yokohama in the*

Great Japanese Earthquake of 1923 (London: George Allen and Unwin Ltd., 1968), p. 31.

95 *"It was here that the full measure"*: Ibid., p. 35.

97 *"I was right in the entrance"*: Henry W. Kinney, "Earthquake Days," *Atlantic Monthly*, January 1924.

97 *"By standing or sitting in the water"*: Downes, letter.

98 *"If we dug out around the leg"*: Unpublished memo written by Ensign Thomas J. Ryan for Lt. Garnet Hulings, U.S. Navy, September 12, 1923, Lyman A. Cotten papers, University of North Carolina.

98 *"It was either leave her in there"*: Ibid.

99 *"The leg which had been buried"*: Ibid.

99 *"in others only pillars"*: Lois Crane, quoted in Lyman A. Cotten diary entry, September 7, 1923, University of North Carolina.

100 *"All was silent"*: Poole, *Death of Old Yokohama*, p. 39.

101 *"In the few minutes"*: Ibid.

101 *"Approaching the warehouses"*: Zacharias, *Secret Missions*, chapter 7.

101 *"Thick black columns"*: "Destruction in Yokohama," *Japan Chronicle*, p. 339.

102 *"All over were people one knew"*: Kinney, "Earthquake Days."

104 *"There were many"*: "Destruction in Yokohama" *Japan Chronicle*, p. 340.

104 *"struck down and pinned to the earth"*: Webb, "Report of Disaster."

105 *"it was too late"*: Diary entry of Dr. John W. Colbert aboard the USS *Bittern*, Yokohama, Japan, September 11, 1923, Library of Congress, Manuscripts Division.

105 *"God's will be done"*: "A Memorial: Miss Jennie M. Kuyper, Principal of Ferris Seminary, Yokohama, Japan, who lost her life in the earthquake, September 1, 1923," pamphlet published in 1923 by the Women's Board of Foreign Missions, Reformed Church of America, in New York, and found at the Columbia University Library.

105 *"We must go to an open area"*: Interview with Shigeo Tsuchiya, July 12, 2004.

106 *"Everyone to the hills"*: Cozad, "An Account."

107 sunk *"like a hammock"*: Poole, *Death of Old Yokohama*, p. 42.

107 *"Although only an hour"*: Ibid., p. 46.

108 *"like a flight of steps"*: Ibid., p. 47.

108 *"heave up anchors"*: Robinson, "Official Report," p. 4.

109 *"taking the risk"*: Ibid., p. 5.

109 *"As our stern passed"*: Ibid., p. 5.

110 many would sink: Downes, letter.

6: Tokyo Burning

Kinney's *Atlantic Monthly* piece provides a vivid account of the damage wreaked by the seismic waves as they wended their way north from Yokohama to Tokyo. Frederick Starr's diaries at the University of Chicago recounted his experience from the near collapse of the Hotel Kinokuniya to his climb to the top of the Zojoji Temple. I pieced together the description of the train wreck at Nebukawa from both Noel Busch's *Two Minutes to Noon* and from *The Great Earthquake of 1923 in Tokyo* by Takashi Takagi, published in Japanese by Hara Shobo in 1983. The description of the tidal wave at Kamakura came from Busch's *Two Minutes to Noon* and Kinney's "Earthquake Days."

For accounts of the great Tokyo fire I relied on many sources, the most important being *The Great Tokyo Earthquake: September 1, 1923: Experiences and Impressions of an Eye-Witness* by Joseph Dahlmann. I also drew on K. Takahashi's "The Story of Japan's Great 1923 Earthquake," published by the *Japan Times;* articles in the *Japan Weekly Chronicle;* and the diaries of Frederick Starr. Tetsuzo Inumaru's recollections are drawn from one diary in *One Hundred Years of the Imperial Hotel (Teikoku Hoteru no Hyaku Nen),* published by the Imperial Hotel in Tokyo, and another excerpted in Busch's *Two Minutes to Noon;* I found Enod San's description of the earthquake quoted in "Imperial Hotel Tokyo Japan" by Julius Floto in the *Architectural Record,* February 1924. The scene in Yoshiwara was pieced together from two sources: *The Nightside of Japan* by T. Fujimoto (Philadelphia: Lippincott, 1914) and Takashi Takagi's *The Great Earthquake of 1923 in Tokyo.* The survivors' tales from the Army Clothing Depot come from three main sources: *Collection of Survival Stories from the Great Kanto Earthquake,* compiled by Sumida Ward in Tokyo; *The Great Kanto Earthquake (Kanto no Daishinsai),* compiled by the Research Group of the Pacific War and published by Fukuro no Hon in Tokyo; and *Great Kanto Earthquake (Kanto Daishinsai)* by Akira Yoshimura, published in 1977 by Tokyo's Bungei Shunju Company. Additional details of the catastrophe were culled from Noel Busch's *Two Minutes to Noon.* For the account of the burning bridges over the Sumida River I relied on both the Yoshimura book and K. Takahashi's "The Story of Japan's Great 1923 Earthquake."

112   *"It did not slide"*: Kinney, "Earthquake Days."
112   *"[The room] shook"*: Frederick Starr, diary entry, September 1, 1923, Frederick Starr papers, University of Chicago.
112   *"Terror was on every face"*: Ibid.
114   *"The Nebukawa, a swift mountain stream"*: Professor D. B. Langford, quoted in T. A. Jaggar, "The Yokohama-Tokyo Earthquake of September 1, 1923," *Bulletin of the Seismological Society* 13 (December 1923): 136.
114   *The sea receded:* Ibid., p. 135.
116   *the earthquake brought the house down:* Kinney, "Earthquake Days."
116   *"From every fire tower"*: Joseph Dahlmann, *The Great Tokyo Earthquake: September 1, 1923: Experiences and Impressions of an Eye-Witness,* translated and adapted from the German by Victor F. Gettleman (New York: American Press, 1924), p. 16.
116   *"Dark masses of smoke"*: Ibid., p. 24.
117   *"strong breezes"*: Ibid., p. 26.

117 *"The Manager of the Imperial Hotel"*: M. W. Pett, quoted in *Japan Weekly Chronicle*.

118 *"I urged Takagi"*: Starr, diary entry, September 1, 1923.

118 *"it was sheer folly"*: Ibid.

119 *"rivers of fire"*: Dahlmann, *Great Tokyo Earthquake*, p. 43.

119 *"Everything in the street"*: Starr, diary entry, September 1, 1923.

119 *"The building was shaking"*: Tetsuzo Inumaru in *One Hundred Years of the Imperial Hotel (Teikoku Hoteru no Hyaku Nen)* (Tokyo: Imperial Hotel, 1990), translated by Taeko Kawamura.

120 *"First came the shock"*: Extract of a report by Enod San, assistant to Frank Lloyd Wright, dated September 8, 1923, and reprinted in Julius Floto, "Imperial Hotel, Tokyo Japan," *Architectural Record*, February 1924, p. 119.

120 *"Since there is no water"*: Inumaru, *Imperial Hotel*.

122 *"For years I had believed"*: Akitsune Imamura, "A Diary on the Great Earthquake," *Bulletin of the Seismological Society of America*, March 1924, p. 2.

122 *"Some of the Japanese journalists"*: Imamura, "A Diary of the Great Earthquake," p. 3.

123 *"When I [made my prediction]"*: Interview with Imamura in *Mainichi Shimbun*, translated in *Japan Weekly Chronicle*, September 20, 1923, p. 412.

123 *"There was even an eminent scientist"*: A. Imamura, "Preliminary Note on the Great Earthquake of Southeastern Japan on September 1, 1923," *Bulletin of the Seismological Society of America*, November 1923, p. 136.

123 *"Contrary to Professor Omori"*: Ibid., p. 137.

124 *"The sight," Imamura wrote*: Imamura, "A Diary of the Great Earthquake," p. 4.

125 *"As she walked"*: Deaconess Knapp, quoted in a letter from Elizabeth Henderson Cotten to her mother, September 9, 1923, Lyman A. Cotten collection, University of North Carolina.

125 *"HAS DEACONESS KNAPP SURVIVED"*: Original telegram, files of the American Embassy, Tokyo, September–October 1923, volume 16, National Archives, College Park, MD.

125 *"show rooms"*: Fujimoto, *Nightside of Japan*.

126 *"Some people brought"*: Akira Yoshimura, *The Great Kanto Earthquake of 1923* (Tokyo: Bungei Shunju Publishing Company, 1977), translated by Taeko Kawamura.

127 *"People were rushing"*: quoted in ibid.

128 *"He grabbed my arm"*: Testimony of Shin Nakamura, in *Collection of Survival Stories from the Great Kanto Earthquake (Kanto Daishinsai Taiken Kirokushuu)* (Tokyo: Sumida Ward local government printing office, 1985), translated by Taeko Kawamura.

129 *"just a lone hound dog"*: Testimony of Saburo Hasebe, in ibid.

130 *"Suddenly the fire"*: Dahlmann, *Great Tokyo Earthquake*, p. 30.

130 *"The flames were singeing people"*: K. Takahashi, *The Story of Japan's Great 1923 Earthquake: With Details of the Tremendous Conflagrations Which Swept Tokyo and Yokohama in Consequence, Japan Times & Mail*, September 25–30, 1923, chapter 7, p. 5.

130 *"[People] saw a large"*: Peter Pernin, "The Great Peshtigo Fire: An Eyewitness Account," *Wisconsin Magazine of History* 54 (summer 1971): 246–272.

131 *"It was 100 to 200 [yards] high"*: Quoted in Busch, *Two Minutes to Noon*, p. 95.
132 *"People panicked"*: Nakamura, in *Survival Stories*.
132 *"People, horses, tin roofs"*: Testimony of Masao Murakami, in *Survival Stories*.
133 *"Everybody was totally motionless"*: Nakamura, in *Survival Stories*.
133 *"But many people convulsed"*: Washio, in *Survival Stories*.
134 *"Lanterns, awnings"*: Starr, diary entry, September 2, 1923.
134 *"The glow from [the north]"*: Ibid.
135 *"He was an old friend"*: Ibid.
135 *"Secret place" of refuge*: Ibid.
135 *"We sat there"*: Ibid.

7: Rescue

The story of Yokohama's final hours was assembled from Otis Manchester Poole's *Death of Old Yokohama;* a lengthy interview with the Reverend Eustace Strong in the *Japan Weekly Chronicle*'s edition of October 4, 1923, "The Evacuation of Yokohama: System in the Midst of Chaos"; Ulysses R. Webb's official report to the U.S. secretary of the navy; Gertrude Cozad's unpublished manuscript; and Henry Kinney's "Earthquake Days" in the *Atlantic Monthly*. I pieced together a mosaic of the rescue effort from Zacharias's *Secret Missions*, Poole's memoir, Robinson's report, Thomas Ryan's letter, the *Japan Weekly Chronicle* article on Strong, the *Philoctetes* passenger's story in the September 6 *Japan Weekly Chronicle*, Lois Crane's account of her escape as told to Elizabeth and Lyman Cotten, Eva Downes' letter, Cozad's manuscript, and the interview with Shigeo Tsuchiya.

137 *"Some were disheveled"*: Poole, *Death of Old Yokohama*, p. 54.
138 *"By ropes and by clinging"*: Webb, "Report of Disaster," p. 2.
139 *"Hold tight"*: Poole, *Death of Old Yokohama*, p. 57.
139 *"The cliff face"*: Ibid., p. 58.
139 *"Red-flushed billows"*: Ibid., p. 60.
140 *"with my pillow"*: Cozad, "An Account."
141 *"Still, I could not"*: Ibid.
141 *"He would go on"*: Ibid.
142 *"Had we waited"*: Ibid.
142 *"Against the glare"*: Ibid.
143 *"We came to a point"*: Kinney, "Earthquake Days."
143 *"one thousand prisoners"*: Robinson, "Official Report," p. 6.
144 *"A couple of thousand"*: Poole, *Death of Old Yokohama*, p. 61.
144 *"They were steaming around"*: Ryan, unpublished memo, Lyman A. Cotten papers.
145 *"All the Europeans"*: Robinson, "Official Report," p. 6.
145 *"It took a half hour"*: Ryan, unpublished memo.
145 *"From this point hardly anything"*: "Destruction of Yokohama," *Japan Chronicle*, September 6, 1923, p. 341.
146 *"At the suggestion of"*: Robinson, "Official Report," p. 6.

146 *"In the enveloping"*: Poole, *Death of Old Yokohama*, p. 76.
147 *"Wherever we looked"*: Downes, unpublished letter.
147 *"Yokohama, the proudest city"*: "Destruction of Yokohama," *Japan Chronicle*, p. 341.

8: Massacres

For background on Japanese-Korean relations I consulted the *Japan Weekly Chronicle*'s extensive coverage of the March 1, 1919, uprising in Seoul and of the massacres in its editions of September and October 1923; and *Korea's Fight for Freedom* by Fred Arthur McKenzie (1920; Seoul: Yonsei University Press, 1969). I also consulted Yoshino Sakuzo's "The Korean Massacre Affair," reprinted in the 1999 special earthquake issue of *Ebisu*, published by the Maison Franco-Japonaise. I conducted an extensive interview in Tokyo with Kan Dokusan, a retired professor of Korean studies at Hitotsubashi University and Shiga University in Japan and one of the world's experts on the Korean massacres.

150 *"It was," Zacharias wrote*: Zacharias, *Secret Missions*, chapter 7.
151 *"Just as the work was begun"*: Ibid.
151 *"sometimes rolling up"*: Robinson, "Official Report," p. 7.
151 *"We tried the engines again"*: Ibid., p. 8.
152 *"As the water shoaled"*: Poole, *Death of Old Yokohama*, p. 94.
153 *"three Koreans"*: "Korean Massacres," *Japan Weekly Chronicle*, November 1, 1923.
153 *"Koreans who had escaped"*: Cozad, "An Account."
153 *"It is said that three hundred Koreans"*: Document provided and translated by Kan Dokusan, retired professor of Korean studies, Hitotsubashi University, Tokyo, interviewed July 11, 2004.
153 *"knew he was a Korean"*: Cozad, "An Account."
154 *"The Japanese viewed the Koreans"*: "Korean Massacres," *Japan Weekly Chronicle*, November 1, 1923.
154 *"Two hundred Korean students"*: Article in *Tokyo Jiji*, quoted in *Japan Weekly Chronicle*, March 27, 1919.
155 *"Troops, as well as"*: *Japan Weekly Chronicle*, March 27, 1919.
155 *"but nothing more was heard of it"*: "Koreans in the Earthquake," *Japan Weekly Chronicle*, October 25, 1923.
156 *"dangerous to national security"*: "The Imperial Decree Concerning the State of Siege," files of the American Embassy, Tokyo, volume 15.
156 *"When the fatal story"*: *Japan Weekly Chronicle*, October 25, 1923.
157 *Jews "were led"*: John Kelly, *The Great Mortality: An Intimate History of the Black Death, the Most Devastating Plague of All Time* (New York: HarperCollins, 2005), p. 176.
158 *"Hedstrom vouches for"*: "Protests to Hughes on Killing Koreans," *New York Times*, November 23, 1923, p. 4.
159 *"During this ride"*: John W. Doty and W. W. Johnston, "Diary: From Saturday September 1st, 1923 to time of sailing from Yokohama on the 'Empress of Aus-

tralia,' September 12th at 8 P.M.," booklet, Collections of the Manuscripts Division, Library of Congress, p. 21.

160 *"Keep quiet":* So Insung, "A Night of Terror," reprinted in *Ebisu: Etudes Japonaises,* "Le Japon des Seismes," special issue 21 (Tokyo: Maison Franco-Japonaise, 1999), p. 84.

160 *"A black fog":* Ibid., p. 86.

161 *"Most Korean residents": Japan Weekly Chronicle,* September 27, 1923.

161 *"On the second night":* Yoshino Sakuzo, "The Korean Massacre Affair," reprinted in *Ebisu: Etudes Japonaises,* special issue 21 (1999), p. 68.

161 *"Koreans, organizing themselves":* Ibid.

162 *"The flames were swept along":* Dahlmann, *Great Tokyo Earthquake,* p. 56.

163 *"It is happening just":* Yamashita, *Akitsune Imamura.*

163 *"Everything is gone":* Dahlmann, *Great Tokyo Earthquake,* p. 79.

164 *"Where are you going?":* Yamashita, *Akitsune Imamura.*

164 *"It is my birthday":* Starr, diary entry, September 2, 1923.

165 *"No street cars":* Ibid.

165 *"It is said":* Ibid.

166 *"I stood and looked up":* Cozad, "An Account."

167 *"That boy saved my life":* Cozad, op. cit.

167 *"It is understood":* Yamamoto, quoted in *Japan Weekly Chronicle,* September 27, 1923.

168 *"It is true that":* Margaret de Forest Hicks, "After the Earthquake in Japan," *New York Times,* quoted in *Japan Weekly Chronicle,* January 10, 1924.

168 *"hysterical and generally untrue":* Quoted in *Japan Weekly Chronicle,* January 10, 1924.

168 *"This is about the worst lying":* "The Vigilantes," editorial, *Japan Weekly Chronicle,* November 1, 1923.

168 *"[It] is preparing for distribution":* Ambassador Cyrus E. Woods, cable to Secretary of State Charles Evans Hughes, Files of the American Embassy Tokyo, volume 16.

169 *"a national shame":* "The Korean Massacre Affair," p. 68.

169 *"an outbreak of national hatred": Japan Weekly Chronicle,* editorial, November 1, 1923.

169 *"The Japanese army behaved":* Quoted in David M. Kennedy's review of Iris Chang's "The Rape of Nanking," *Atlantic Monthly,* April 1998.

9: Spreading the News

Kenneth Bilby's *The General: David Sarnoff and the Rise of the Communications Industry* (New York: Harper and Row, 1986) provided valuable detail about the early days of wireless telegraphy. To grasp the basic principles of the technology I also consulted *Wireless Course in Twenty Lessons: A Treatise of Instruction and Reference Covering Radio Telegraphy and Telephony* by S. Gernback, A. Lescarboura, and H. W. Secor (New York: Experimeter Publishing Co., 1923); articles in the *Japan Weekly Chronicle,* including "Wireless in Every Home Shortly, Prophesies Sir Henry Norman" from October 1922; and

I interviewed Mitchell Cotter, a physicist and engineer whose career has included development work for Alcatel and Solitron. The odyssey of the *Asahi* journalist Kenzu Fukuma came from *Two Minutes to Noon*, as did the stories of Jiri Morioka and of the Japanese boy on the Swiss-German border. George Denny's activities were related in Samuel Reber, "How Iwaki Told the World," in the U.S. Embassy files. I found original copies of the *Japan Times's* "Earthquake Edition" from September 4 to 9, 1923, in Lyman Cotten's papers and got more information about Randall Gould's efforts from an interview with Yutaka Mataebara, editor in chief and managing director of the *Japan Times*.

172   *"If these quakes"*: Lyman A. Cotten, diary entry, September 1, 1923, volume 25, Lyman A. Cotten papers, University of North Carolina.
172   *"There was no real damage"*: Letter from Elizabeth Cotten to her mother, September 8, 1923, Lyman A. Cotten papers, University of North Carolina.
172   *"Have you heard"*: Ibid.
173   *"No details"*: Ibid.
173   *"On all sides"*: Ibid.
174   *"Our friends in Tokyo"*: Ibid.
175   *"It is reported 20,000 dead"*: Lyman Cotten, diary entry, September 3, 1923.
176   *"To the Hulings"*: Lyman Cotten, diary entry, September 16, 1922.
176   *"I could not see why"*: Lyman Cotten, diary entry, March 12, 1923.
177   *"Tuesday September 4"*: Lyman Cotten, diary entry, September 4, 1923.
177   *"The rumor has spread"*: Lyman Cotten, diary entry, September 6, 1923.
180   *"Wireless enjoys"*: *Japan Weekly Chronicle*, January 4, 1923.
181   *"Mr. Schwerin"*: Ibid.
181   *"At twelve o'clock"*: Samuel Reber, "How Iwaki Told the World," unpublished interview with Taki Yonemura, files of the American Embassy, Tokyo, September–October 1923, volume 17, National Archives, College Park, MD.
182   *"CONFLAGRATION SUBSEQUENT TO SEVERE EARTHQUAKE"*: Quoted in Busch, *Two Minutes to Noon*.
182   *"Flames spreading toward Asakusa"*: Ibid.
184   *"flashed the [news]"*: "Radio Brought the News of the Disaster," *New York Times*, September 9, 1923, p. X10.
185   Woods *"calmly surveying"*: Reber, "How Iwaki Told the World."
186   *"All embassy buildings totally destroyed"*: Original telegram of Cyrus Woods, files of the American Embassy, Tokyo, September–October 1923, volume 17.
186   *"I continued [trying]"*: Reber, "How Iwaki Told the World."
187   *"According to Dr. Kayukawa"*: "Says Yokohama's Beauty Cause of Its Destruction," *Washington Post*, September 2, 1923, p. 2.
189   *"All the power stations"*: Dahlmann, *Great Tokyo Earthquake* p. 48.
191   *"I sought out my familiars"*: Kinney, "Earthquake Days."
191   *"crass stupidity"*: Philip Kerby, "The Crash of 'Superefficiency,' " *China Weekly Review*, September 29, 1923.
191   *"I was informed"*: Ibid.
192   *"huge tidal waves"*: *Japan Weekly Chronicle*, September 6, 1923, p. 338.
192   *"began to explode"*: Yoshimura, *Great Kanto Earthquake*.

192 *"Volcanic Island Gone"*: Clarence Dubose, "Volcanic Island Gone," *Chicago Tribune*, September 9, 1923, p. 2.

193 *"It is impossible"*: Quoted in Busch, *Two Minutes to Noon*, p. 129.

193 *"As soon as the fact"*: "Carrier Pigeons Take News of Disaster: Wing Their Way from the Flaming City," *Japan Times & Mail*, September 19, 1923, p. 1.

195 *"which are declared ridiculous"*: *Japan Times & Mail, Earthquake Edition*, September 6, 1923, p. 1.

195 *"The Advertiser is gone"*: Letter from Mrs. Benjamin Fleisher, sent from Karuizawa, Japan, to Elizabeth Cotten, September 10, 1923, Lyman A. Cotten papers, University of North Carolina.

195 *"Mr. Fleisher seems"*: Letter from Lyman A. Cotten to Elizabeth Cotten, September 13, 1923, 4:30 P.M., Lyman A. Cotten papers, University of North Carolina.

195 *"We expect to get out"*: *Yushin Nippon* quoted in Benjamin Fleisher, *Japan Weekly Chronicle*, October 4, 1923, p. 471.

196 *"It is a fact"*: Dahlmann, *Great Tokyo Earthquake*, p. 91.

196 *"The bodies lay"*: Kinney, "Earthquake Days."

197 *"Immense piles"*: Dahlmann, *Great Tokyo Earthquake*, p. 91.

197 *"The stench was horrible"*: Japanese reporter, quoted in Yoshimura, *Great Kanto Earthquake*.

197 *"But eventually they gave up"*: Ibid.

197 *"WANTED"*: Ibid.

197 *"The smell"*: Ibid.

198 *"We're going to take care"*: Ibid.

198 *"There was one foreigner's home"*: *Japan Weekly Chronicle*, September 20, 1923.

198 *"The Japan Times can authoritatively announce"*: "Tokyo Will Live!," *Japan Times & Mail*, September 7, 1923, p. 1.

10: Going Home

Much of this chapter, including the account of Lyman Cotten's belated journey to Tokyo from Chuzenji, his confrontation with Woods, and the family's last days in Japan, came from diaries and letters in the Cotten Collection at the University of North Carolina. I obtained background on Francis Piggott from an article that ran in the June 9, 1921, issue of the *Japan Weekly Chronicle*. I re-created the atmosphere at the Imperial Hotel after the earthquake using several sources, including the letters of Lyman Cotten, the diaries of Imperial General Manager Tetsuzo Inumaru, Noel Busch's *Two Minutes to Noon*, and articles in the *Japan Weekly Chronicle* and the *New York Times*. For a description of the activities of the American Relief Committee I relied on the files of the American Embassy in Tokyo, September–October 1923, volumes 16, 17, and 18 at the National Archives in College Park, Maryland. For information on the relief effort in Yokohama led by the U.S. Navy, I drew on "With the Shanghai Unit, the American Red Cross in Japan" by Warwick M. Tompkins, a member of the expedition; "The Forgotten Earthquake," an unpublished manuscript that John W. Colbert wrote in 1963; and several dispatches that Colbert filed while aboard the USS *Bittern,* including "One Hour's Shore Leave in Desolate Yokohama: Sept. 12, 1923." I also consulted Dr. Ulysses Webb's official report from the *Huron* on September 11, 1923, and the report from Commander in Chief Edwin Anderson to the chief of Naval Operations. I found all of these in the Manuscripts Collection at the Library of Congress. The early history of the American Red Cross was drawn from *Under the Red Cross Flag at Home and Abroad* by Mabel T. Boardman (Philadelphia: J. B. Lippincott, 1915); *The Life of Clara Barton* by Percy Epler (New York: Macmillan, 1915); *Pioneering with the Red Cross: Recollections of an Old Red Crosser* by Ernest P. Bicknell (New York: Macmillan, 1935); and *The Great Influenza* by John M. Barry (New York: Viking, 2004).

200   *"ALL SAFE":* Original telegram received September 8, 1923, in Salisbury, NC; Lyman A. Cotten papers, University of North Carolina.

200   *"I am awfully tired":* Letter from Lyman A. Cotten at the Nikko Hotel to Elizabeth Cotten, September 6, 1923, 6 P.M., Lyman A. Cotten papers.

201   *"Suddenly we overtook":* Letter from Lyman A. Cotten to Elizabeth Cotten, September 8, 1923, 5 P.M., Lyman A. Cotten papers.

201   *"I did not recognize":* Ibid.

202   *"The Embassy buildings and chancery":* letter to U.S. secretary of state, U.S. Embassy files, 1923–24, National Archives.

202   *"Mrs. Woods was standing":* "Woods Barely Escaped Injury in Earthquake: Military Attaché in Tokyo Dragged Ambassador from Under a Falling Ceiling," *New York Times,* September 12, 1923, p. 1.

202   *"After the Embassy safes":* Wilson letter to Department of State, Washington, files of the American Embassy, Tokyo, volume 17.

204   *"Am safe on* Empress*":* Letter from Otto Robert Kresse, files of the American Embassy, Tokyo, volume 15.

204   *"Dear sir, can you give me":* Letter from Mrs. G. L. Chamberlain, files of the American Embassy, Tokyo, volume 15.

204   *"I escaped from":* Letter, files of the American Embassy, Tokyo, volume 15.

204   *"I am a Russian general":* Letter from Boris Shelcornicoff, files of the American Embassy, Tokyo, volume 15.

204   *"Many of them are absolutely destitute":* Report from E. B. Miller to Ambassador Cyrus Woods, files of the American Embassy, Tokyo, volume 15.

204   *Whereabouts of "a Japanese boy":* Letter from William Jennings Bryan, files of the American Embassy, Tokyo, volume 15.

205   *"Will you kindly":* Letter from Toshiro Hogetsu, files of the American Embassy, Tokyo, volume 15.

205   *"stretched out on a cart":* Paul Claudel, "Across the Cities in Flames," reprinted in *Ebisu,* special issue 21 (1999): 44.

205   *"Darling—I pray God":* Letter from Ghislaine de Bassompierre, quoted by Elizabeth Henderson Cotten in letter to her mother, September 9, 1923, Lyman A. Cotten papers.

206 *"Great relief"*: "French Envoy Escapes," *New York Times*, September 6, 1923, p. 2.

206 *"I had an uneasy feeling"*: Inumaru, *Imperial Hotel.*

207 *"The president of the U.S."*: Lyman A. Cotten, diary entry, September 7, 1923.

208 *"An officer in the boat said"*: Lyman A. Cotten, diary entry, September 8, 1923.

208 *"We are sleeping"*: Letter from Lyman A. Cotten to Elizabeth Cotten, September 9, 1923.

209 *"Received a personal note"*: Lyman A. Cotten, diary entry, September 10, 1923.

209 *"AMBASSADOR WANTS YOU"*: Original telegram, Lyman A. Cotten papers.

210 *"I take great pride"*: Cyrus Woods, report to Secretary of State Charles Evans Hughes, files of the American Embassy, Tokyo, volume 17.

210 *"The Navy personnel"*: Charles Burnett, report to the U.S. State Department, Washington, files of the American Embassy, Tokyo, volume 17.

210 *"The language officers"*: Letter from Lyman A. Cotten to Elizabeth Henderson Cotten, September 13, 1923, 4:30 P.M., Lyman A. Cotten papers, University of North Carolina.

211 *"I have read your sweet letter"*: Letter from Lyman A. Cotten to Elizabeth Henderson Cotten, September 14, 1923, Lyman A. Cotten papers, University of North Carolina.

211 *"If I had only realized"*: Ibid.

212 *"The first time I saw him"*: Letter from Lyman A. Cotten to Elizabeth Henderson Cotten, September 12, 1923, 3:30 P.M., Lyman A. Cotten papers.

212 *"I am amazed"*: Op. cit.

212 *"The great quake left"*: "Anniversary of a Disaster," *Japan Weekly Chronicle*, September 4, 1924.

213 *"This little ship"*: Downes, unpublished letter.

214 *"I said to the officer"*: Cozad, "An Account."

215 *"He is a fine looking"*: Ibid.

215 *"The Empress . . . was"*: Poole, *Death of Old Yokohama*, p. 106.

215 *"her seamed face"*: Ibid., p. 107.

216 *"They were burning bodies"*: Interview with Shigeo Tsuchiya, July 12, 2004.

216 *"canned beef, salmon"*: *Japan Weekly Chronicle*, January 10, 1924.

216 *"My family and I never left"*: Interview with Shigeo Tsuchiya, Yokohama Ward Office, July 13, 2004.

217 *"and to pick up all"*: John W. Colbert, "The Forgotten Earthquake," unpublished manuscript, 1963, Library of Congress, Manuscripts Division, p. 15.

217 *"281,000 pounds rice"*: Bureau of Japanese Foreign Affairs, file of the American Embassy, Tokyo, September–October 1923, volume 17.

218 *"Amusement was caused"*: Diary entry of Dr. John W. Colbert aboard the USS *Bittern*, Yokohama, September 11, 1923, Library of Congress, Manuscripts Division, p. 1.

219 *"We do not need"*: "The Catastrophe in Japan," address by Dr. John W. Colbert to the Rotarians in Tsientsin, China, October 6, 1923, reprinted in *Peking & Tsientsin Times*.

219 *"[I said that] we were here"*: Admiral Edwin A. Anderson, "Operations of the U.S. Asiatic Fleet in connection with the earthquake and fire at Yokohama and Tokyo, Japan, 2 September to 21 September 1923," p. 9.

220 *"I felt that we had"*: Cyrus Woods, cable to Secretary of State Charles Evans

Hughes, files of the American Embassy, Tokyo, September–October 1923, volume 17.

220 *"to act as radio relay"*: Anderson, "Operations," p. 6.

221 *"The ashes of each"*: Ibid.

221 *"The earth was constantly trembling"*: Lieutenant Colonel D. W. Hand, "Final Report on the Medical and Hospital Activities Pertaining to the Japan Relief Mission, October 12, 1923," files of the American Embassy, Tokyo, volume 17.

222 *"The Japanese seemed to be stunned"*: Colbert, diary entry, September 11, 1923, p. 2.

222 *"Unfortunately for the crooks"*: Ibid.

222 *"The Grand Hotel was"*: Colbert, "The Forgotten Earthquake," p. 11.

223 *"An overwhelming disaster"*: President Calvin Coolidge, quoted in *New York Times*, September 4, 1923, p. 1, and in John A. Dougherty, "Japanese Disaster Relief," unpublished manuscript, Washington Division, American Red Cross, Library of Congress, Manuscript Collection, p. 2.

225 *"Organise as in war"*: Dougherty, "Japanese Disaster Relief," p. 3.

226 *"States, cities, townships"*: Ibid., p. 4.

226 *officers "to be known as"*: Cable from Secretary of State Charles Evans Hughes to Ambassador Cyrus Woods, files of the American Embassy, Tokyo, volume 17.

226 *"Following disinfectants purchased"*: Ibid.

226 *"We are today purchasing"*: Ibid.

227 *"You may draw a draft"*: Ibid.

227 his *"deep appreciation"*: "Japan Relief Fund Gratifies Coolidge," *New York Times*, September 17, 1923, p. 2.

227 *"on the suspicion that"*: "Russian Relief Ship: Expulsion from Yokohama; Questions to Viscount Goto [Shimpei]," *Japan Weekly Chronicle*, September 27, 1923, p. 451.

227 *"The ease and speed"*: *New York Times*, September 14, 1923, p. 1.

228 *"The entire American nation"*: *Osaka Mainichi "Pictorial Edition,"* November 1923 (Osaka: Osaka Mainichi Publications, 1923).

228 *"the heartfelt thanks"*: Anderson, "Operations," p. 10.

228 *"Such genuine"*: "Premier Yamamoto Thanks America," *Japan Times*, September 8, 1923, p. 1.

228 *"heartfelt gratitude"*: Woods, files of the American Embassy, Tokyo, volume 17.

228 *"ALL TOKYO RINGING"*: Cable of Counselor Hugh Wilson, files of the American Embassy, Tokyo, volume 17.

229 *"ordering all foreigners"*: Roderick Matheson, *Chicago Tribune*, quoted in *Japan Weekly Chronicle*, December 13, 1923.

230 *"an absolute falsehood"*: "More Slanders: Thrusting Japanese Off Foreign Ships," *Japan Weekly Chronicle*, September 27, 1923.

230 *"We have a destroyer"*: Letter from Lyman A. Cotten to Elizabeth Henderson Cotten, September 15, 1923.

231 *"The action of the Captain"*: Kerby, "The Crash."

231 *"declined to take Japanese"*: *Yushin Nippon*, quoted in "More Slanders."

232 *"pure malevolence"*: "More Slanders," *Japan Weekly Chronicle*, September 20, 1923, p. 422.

232 *"Threatening the Japanese"*: *Tokyo Nichi Nichi*, quoted in "More Slanders:

'Thrusting Japanese off Foreign Ships,' " *Japan Weekly Chronicle*, September 27, 1923, p. 441.

232   *"[U.S. Military Attaché] Colonel Burnett"*: Quoted in *Japan Times*, September 17, 1923.

232   *"The [true] story"*: Kerby, "The Crash."

233   *"I went in person"*: Lyman A. Cotten, diary entry, September 17, 1923.

233   *"What will you do?"*: Letter from Mrs. J. Kenneth Caldwell to Elizabeth Cotten, September 11, 1923, Lyman A. Cotten papers, University of North Carolina.

233   *"You cannot realize"*: Letter from Mrs. R. R. Cotten to Elizabeth Cotten, September 4, 1923, Lyman A Cotten papers, University of North Carolina.

234   *"This little colony"*: Letter from Elizabeth Henderson Cotten to her mother, September 16, 1923, Lyman A. Cotten papers, University of North Carolina.

234   *"Oh joy!"*: Letter from Elizabeth Henderson Cotten to her mother, September 19, 1923, Lyman A. Cotten papers.

236   *"Complete blackness"*: Elizabeth Cotten, letter to her mother, September 24, 1923, Lyman A. Cotten papers.

237   *"We drove through"*: Ibid.

Epilogue

The account of Frederick Starr's post-earthquake activities is taken entirely from the diaries and letters contained in the Frederick Starr Collection, University of Chicago. The account of Reverend Eustace Strong's last days in Yokohama is drawn from articles in the *Japan Weekly Chronicle*, including "Burying the Dead: Last Rites over Yokohama Residents" from October 4, 1923, and "The Evacuation of Yokohama: System in the Midst of Chaos: Interview with the Rev. Eustace M. Strong," also from October 4. The *Japan Weekly Chronicle* devoted many articles and much analysis to the anti-immigration campaign in the United States in June and July 1924.

Details about the reconstruction of Tokyo came from "Goto and the Rebuilding of Tokyo" by Charles A. Beard in *Our World* magazine, April 1924; *The Reconstruction of Tokyo and Aesthetic Problems of Architecture* by Ino Dan, a booklet published by the Japan Council of the Institute of Pacific Relations in 1931; Busch's *Two Minutes to Noon;* Edwin Seidensticker's *Tokyo Rising: The City Since the Great Earthquake* (New York: Alfred A. Knopf, 1990); and articles in the *New York Times*. A February 28, 1924, *Japan Weekly Chronicle* article described the construction of sheds on top of Tokyo's ruins and the shrine on the grounds of the Army Clothing Depot. A January 10, 1924, *Japan Weekly Chronicle* article described the recovery of skeletons in the ruins of Yokohama. A February 14, 1924, article in the same newspaper reported on the construction of a tent city near the Grand Hotel.

The January 3, 1924, *Japan Weekly Chronicle* contained an article on the light sentences imposed on murderers of Koreans, including Morita Kichiemon. I gathered details about the Amakasu murder trial from the same newspaper. I found Thomas Ryan's September 18, 1923, thank-you note to Lyman Cotten in Cotten's papers at the University of North Carolina, as well as an article from the *Raleigh News & Observer* detailing the circumstances of Cotten's death. The *Chapel Hill Weekly* of October 9, 1942, contained an article entitled "U.S. Navy Destroyer to Be Named for Ambassador Lyman Cotten." Captain Cyrus Woods's obituary appeared in the *New York Times* on December 9, 1938. Captain Samuel Robinson's obituary appeared in the *Times* on September 7, 1958, and I obtained further information about him from *The Pacific Empresses*. The *Times* carried a lengthy report about Ellis Zacharias's life and death in a June 29, 1961, obituary under the headline "Admiral Ellis Zacharias Dies; Psychological Warfare Expert; Broadcast to Japan in 1945 Urging Surrender—Called Atom Bomb Use Unnecessary." I found the memorial tribute to Frederick Starr in an article by T. Oda, "Some Reminiscences of Dr. Frederick Starr," published in *Young East* magazine, a periodical of the International Buddhist Society, published in Tokyo in 1936. The reconciliation of Imamura and Omori and Omori's death were described in several Japanese newspaper articles and biographies of the seismologist, notably "The Self-Believer: Pioneer of Earthquake Prediction Imamura Akitsune," by Makoto Sakae, which appeared in the *Sankei* newspaper on April 19, 2004. For a critique of the "science" of earthquake prediction I relied primarily on interviews with Robert J. Geller of Tokyo University and Robb Eric S. Moss, a seismologist with Fugro West in Ventura, California; the article "The Relationship between Catfish and Earthquakes" published on the Tokai University Science Department's Web site; and "Earthquake Prediction: A Critical Review," by Robert J. Geller in the August 1997 issue of *Geophysical Journal International*, volume 131, pages 425–450. The portrait of the Yokohama Foreigners Cemetery was drawn from my two visits there in July 2004 and from *Gaijin Bochi: The Foreigners' Cemetery Yokohama, Japan* by Patricia McCabe) London: Bacsa Publishers, 1994).

239 *"It is awful"*: Letter from Frederick Starr to his mother, September 19, 1923, personal correspondence, Frederick Starr papers, University of Chicago.
240 *"Most . . . are poor"*: Ibid.
240 *"I hate to return"*: Ibid.
241 *"According to the Asahi"*: *Japan Weekly Chronicle*, October 4, 1923, p. 494.
241 *"Greater love hath"*: Quoted in "Burying the Dead: Last Rites over Yokohama Residents," *Japan Weekly Chronicle*, October 4, 1923.
242 *"[Babbit] is in"*: Letter from Secretary of Commerce Herbert Hoover to Ambassador Cyrus Woods, files of the American Embassy, Tokyo, volume 16.
242 *"And so in plots"*: "Burying the Dead," *Japan Weekly Chronicle*.
244 *"I found marine shells"*: R. Anderson, *Bulletin of the Seismological Society of America*, February 1924.

244 *"did enormous damage"*: "Anniversary of a Disaster," *Japan Weekly Chronicle*, September 4, 1924.

244 *"This catastrophe"*: Woods, files of the American Embassy, volume 17.

244 *"While most observers"*: J. B. Powell in *Chicago Tribune*, September 13, 1923, p. 1.

245 *"One naturally compares"*: "Anniversary of a Disaster," *Japan Weekly Chronicle*, September 4, 1924, p. 1.

245 *"Reported to Chief"*: Lyman A. Cotten, diary entry November 19, 1923, Lyman A. Cotten papers, University of North Carolina.

246 *"As soon as I learned"*: Lyman Cotten, "The Japanese Disaster," speech at the Algonquin Club, December 2, 1923, transcript in Lyman A. Cotten papers.

246 *"I have heard the idea"*: Ibid.

247 *"is always to Tokyo"*: Walter A. MacDougall, *Let the Sea Make Noise: A History of the North Pacific from Magellan to MacArthur* (New York: Basic Books, 1993).

247 *"a Jap is a Jap"*: Ibid.

247 *"It has been impossible"*: Frederick Starr in *Union Record* (Seattle), quoted in *Japan Weekly Chronicle*, July 3, 1924.

247 *"rising tide of color"*: James Phelan, quoted in *Japan Weekly Chronicle*, March 6, 1924.

248 *"the Prussia of the East"*: Quoted in MacDougall, *Let the Sea*.

248 *"New arrivals should"*: Quoted in ibid.

248 *"Japs, don't let"*: *Japan Weekly Chronicle*, March 6, 1924.

248 *"The bill tends"*: *Japan Weekly Chronicle*, February 28, 1924.

249 *"No greater ovation"*: "Friendly Japanese Bid Woods Goodbye," *New York Times*, June 6, 1924, p. 19.

249 *"has completely destroyed"*: *Osaki Asahi*, quoted in *Japan Weekly Chronicle*, July 3, 1924.

249 *"The nations of the world"*: Prime Minister Yamamoto's official proclamation, September 16, 1923, files of the American Embassy, Tokyo, volume 16.

250 *"In laying out the streets"*: Charles Beard, quoted in "Old and New to Vie in Rebuilding Tokio," *New York Times*, September 16, 1923, p. S6.

250 *"The main emphasis"*: Edwin Seidensticker, *Tokyo Rising: The City Since the Great Earthquake* (New York: Knopf, 1990), chapter 1.

250 *"Tokyo has become"*: *Japan Weekly Chronicle*, February 28, 1924.

251 *"In Yokohama little seems"*: Lyman Cotten, diary entry, September 23, 1923.

251 *"This is a great business"*: Letter from U.S. Consul Nelson T. Johnson to Ambassador Cyrus Woods, files of the American Embassy, Tokyo, September–October 1923, September 24, 1923, volume 17.

252 *"[It is] warmer"*: *Japan Weekly Chronicle*, February 14, 1924.

253 *"My [prediction] has stood"*: Imamura interview in *Mainichi Shimbun*, quoted in *Japan Weekly Chronicle*, September 20, 1923, p. 412.

253 *"Dr. Omori is now"*: *Japan Weekly Chronicle*, October 11, 1923, p. 496.

254 *"We were very much worried"*: Letter from Clarence Darrow to Frederick Starr, October 12, 1923, in Frederick Starr papers, University of Chicago.

254 *"You can imagine"*: Letter from H. S. Mallory, secretary, Correspondence-Study Department, University of Chicago, to Frederick Starr, October 24, 1923 Frederick Starr papers, University of Chicago.

254 *"grave consequences"*: Frederick Starr, in *Japan Weekly Chronicle*, July 17, 1924.

254   *"The only hope of China"*: Frederick Starr, quoted in *Japan Weekly Chronicle*, July 17, 1924.

255   *"This pile of stones"*: *American Contractor*, December 1923.

255   *"the emergence, unharmed"*: Louis H. Sullivan, *"Reflections on the Tokyo Disaster,"* *Architectural Record* 55, no. 2 (February 1924): 114.

256   *"the most striking example"*: *Japan Weekly Chronicle*, October 25, 1923, p. 559.

256   *"many in immediate need"*: U.S. Embassy citation for Thomas J. Ryan, Lyman A. Cotten papers, University of North Carolina.

256   *"One of the most gratifying"*: Robinson, "Official Report," p. 19.

257   *"A terrific gale"*: "U.S. Navy Destroyer to Be Named for Captain Lyman Cotten," *Chapel Hill Weekly*, October 9, 1942.

258   *"In the old days"*: Poole, *Death of Old Yokohama*, pp. 131–32.

258   *"The Yokohama I still see"*: Ibid., p. 132.

258   *"Yokohama will . . . never"*: Lyman Cotten, "The Japanese Disaster."

259   *"He goes scot free"*: *Japan Weekly Chronicle*, January 3, 1924.

261   *"made diplomatic history"*: *New York Times*, obituary, December 9, 1938.

261   *"Professor Starr was often"*: T. Oda, "Some Reminiscences of Dr. Frederick Starr," *Young East Magazine* (Tokyo: International Buddhist Society, 1936).

261   *"The adventurous scientist"*: "Dr. Starr Dies," *New York Times*, August 15, 1933, p. 17.

262   *"had earlier warned him"*: "Admiral Ellis Zacharias Dies; Psychological Warfare Expert," *New York Times*, June 29, 1961, p. 33.

263   *"I heard that there"*: Interview with Shigeo Tsuchiya, Yokohama Ward Office, July 15, 2004.

263   *"U.S. reporters who"*: "Made in Japan, U.S. Designed," *Time*, September 24, 1945.

264   *"hideous, inconvenient"*: "Down Comes the Landmark," *Time*, December 8, 1967.

264   *"a swan afloat"*: Ibid.

264   *"spiritual presence"*: Ibid.

264   *"preeminent hotelier"*: *Japan Times*.

264   *"the most admired"*: Note from anonymous acquaintance of the Cotten family in Japan, found in Box 36, volume 31, Lyman A. Cotten papers, University of North Carolina.

265   *"Captain Cotten spoke"*: Ibid.

266   *"All my years"*: Makoto Sakae, "The Self-Believer," *Sankei* newspaper, April 19, 2004.

266   *"Dr. Imamura had conducted"*: *New York Times*, obituary, January 3, 1948, p. 14.

267   *"Earthquake prediction"*: C. B. Raleigh, quoted in Robert J. Geller, "Earthquake Prediction: A Critical Review," *Geophysical Journal International*, no. 131, 1997, p. 434.

267   *"There may well have been"*: Carl Kisslinger, quoted in Geller, "Earthquake Prediction," p. 434.

267   *"Buoyed by their"*: Cover story, *Time*, September 1, 1975.

268   *"earthquake prediction research"*: Geller, "Earthquake Prediction," p. 425.

ACKNOWLEDGMENTS

D URING THE SUMMER that I spent in Japan in 2004, Taeko Kawamura served as my researcher, guide, and interpreter. She was invaluable on all fronts, tracking down hundreds of articles, diaries, and books; introducing me to Shinto priests, local historians, and Japanese seismologists; and sitting with me for long hours in Tokyo coffee shops, painstakingly translating materials. Hideko Takayama, Kay Itoi, and George Wehrfritz of *Newsweek International*; Hideko Kataoka of *Newsweek Japan;* and Peter Blakeley, a longtime friend and fellow globe-trotter, hosted me in Tokyo and turned what could have been a lonely stay into something of a lark. Bob Giles, the curator of the Nieman Foundation, made possible my year at Harvard in 2004–2005, during which I made great progress in researching the story at the university's astonishingly rich libraries. Mark Kramer, director of the narrative nonfiction workshop at the Nieman Foundation, with his fine ear and his graceful touch, helped me to jump-start the writing. Peter Beinart of *The New Republic* and Kim Campbell, formerly of the Kennedy School of Government at Harvard, supported my Nieman Fellowship application; Mark Whitaker, Jon Meacham, Fareed Zakaria, Jeffrey Bartholet, and Marcus Mabry of *Newsweek,* as always, were behind me all the way and gave me the time off to research and write. With infinite patience, Mitchell Cotter guided me through the thickets of radio wave technology and provided insights on everything from Japanese scientific strategy during the Taisho era to the possible reasons for Lyman Cotten's postearthquake failures. My mother, Nina Hammer, led me to Lyman Cotten's marvelous collection of papers and carried on research for me at the University of North Carolina's Wilson Library all through last year. I am also indebted to Phillip Hogan, Paul

Somerville, Robert A. Geller, and Robb Maas for sharing their seismological expertise; and to my father Richard Hammer, Arlene Hammer, Joanna Chen, Andrew Purvis, David Dobrin, and Susan Arnott for their feedback and moral support. Also to Matthew Olsen of the National Archives in Washington and the research staffs of the University of Chicago Library; the Wilson Library; Harvard University's Widener, Houghton, and Lamont Libraries; Harvard's Pusey Center Map Room; and the Boston Athenaeum Library for directing me to a wealth of primary source material. My editor at Free Press, Martin Beiser, was an enthusiast from the start, and his passion for the project and editorial insights inspired me and steered me through the rough patches. Martha Levin, publisher of Free Press, and my agent of many years, Flip Brophy of Sterling Lord Literistic, also cheered me onward. Andrew Paulson and Edith Lewis of Free Press steered the manuscript toward production with dedication and efficiency. Finally I want to express my love and gratitude to my family—my wife, Nadja, and my sons, Max and Nick—for bearing with me as we shuttled across three continents during the past three years, and for helping to keep me centered and sane. As the Japanese say, *Domo arigato gozaimasu.*

ILLUSTRATION CREDITS

I AM GRATEFUL to the following for permission to use photographs in their possession or in their copyright, and to have made photographs available to me:

Getty Images—121

Harvard University Lamont Library Map Collection—14–15

Library of Congress—9, 16, 18, 20, 39, 203, 223, 229

Naval Historical Archives—207, 218

The New York Times—189

Norway Heritage Project—51

University of North Carolina Southern Historical Collection (Lyman Cotten papers)—28, 34

University of Tokyo—63, 74

Yokohama Historical Archives—137

INDEX

About the Author

JOSHUA HAMMER is a veteran foreign and war correspondent for *Newsweek* who has covered conflicts on four continents, including the 1994 genocide and civil war in Rwanda, the civil war in Sierra Leone, the American intervention in Somalia from 1992 to 1994, the 1998–1999 war in Kosovo, the Colombian guerrilla war, the Palestinian al-Aqsa intifada, the 2003 U.S. invasion of Iraq, and the civil war in Kashmir. He has also been *Newsweek*'s TV critic and media business writer and has freelanced for numerous publications, including *The New Republic, Mother Jones, Men's Journal, Rolling Stone, The New York Times* and *Smithsonian*. He is the author of *Chosen by God* and *A Season in Bethlehem*. He currently lives in South Africa.